Our Labeled Children

*What Every Parent and Teacher
Needs to Know About Learning Disabilities*

Our Labeled Children

*What Every Parent and Teacher Needs to
Know About Learning Disabilities*

Robert J. Sternberg
Elena L. Grigorenko

PERSEUS PUBLISHING
Cambridge, Massachusetts

A Catalog Card Number is available from the Library of Congress

ISBN: 0-7382-0365-3

Perseus Publishing is a member of the Perseus Books Group

Text design by Rachel Hegarty
Set in 11-point Stone Serif

1 2 3 4 5 6 7 8 9 10—03 02 01 00
First paperback printing, August 2000

Perseus Publishing books are available at special discounts for bulk purchases in the U.S. by corporations, institutions, and other organizations. For more information, please contact the Special Markets Department at HarperCollins Publishers, 10 East 53rd Street, New York, NY 10022, or call 1-212-207-7528.

Find us on the World Wide Web at http://www.perseuspublishing.com

This book is dedicated to the people of the world with learning disabilities.

Contents

Preface   ix

Part I
What Are Learning Disabilities, Who Has Them,
and What Has Been Done About Them?   1

1   The LD Lottery: Who Wins, Who Loses?   11

2   What's at Stake? Abilities, Disabilities, and Lotteries   29

3   Picking the Lucky Tickets: Difficulties in Identifying
    People with Learning Disabilities   43

4   Pretend That No One Lost: Issues Regarding
    Accommodations and Special Services   75

Part II
The Science of Reading Disabilities   91

5   The Mind of the Child with LD: Cognitive Bases of
    Reading and Reading Disabilities   97

6   The Brain of the Child with LD: Biological Bases of
    Reading and Reading Disabilities   119

7   The Genes of the Child with LD: Genetic Bases of
    Reading and Reading Disabilities   155

Part III
Learning Disabilities in
the School, Courtroom, and Society   191

  8   Getting a Better Ticket: LD in the School   193

  9   There Are No Jackpots: LD in the Courtroom   223

Part IV
What Needs to be Done   243

  10   LD: The Lottery That Everyone Wins and Loses   245

Notes   261
Index   279

Preface

Some labels reflect biological realities. For example, the "male" and "female" labels reflect patterns of chromosomes (XY for males, XX for females) that are determined at conception. Other labels reflect social realities. Labels such as "American" or "Russian" reflect no biological reality at all, but are ways societies have developed of describing people. The argument of this book is that the label "learning disability" (LD) is neither purely biological nor purely social, but refers to an interaction between the two factors. Whether someone is labeled as having an LD depends not just on the person's biological makeup or social situation, but on what amounts to a lottery that throws a certain biological makeup into a certain social milieu. Whether a given individual will be labeled as having an LD varies with time and place. The labeling process varies not only across years or countries: It can vary from one school district to another within a single state or province! The LD label, therefore, reflects an interaction between a certain biological makeup and the environment. One is not limited to a single lottery ticket. A parent unhappy with the way his or her child is or is not labeled in one place potentially can change the label by moving to another location, or by seeking an alternative diagnosis in the same location.

The story of learning disabilities is a story not only about a set of learning disorders, but also about individuals, families, schools, and even courtrooms in distress. The effects and implications of learning disabilities have permeated almost every aspect of U.S. society.

While we were writing the book, a monumental court case was decided regarding identification and treatment of students with LD at the college level. Sternberg wrote what he thought was a fairly innocuous Op Ed piece for the *New York Times*, giving some figures regarding prevalence of and spending on children with LD. The article noted that current systems of identification are confusing and inconsistent and stated that accommodations for children with LD can be useful, but only to the extent that they support correction of weaknesses. The article further argued that the time has come to use current psychological theory and research as a basis for interventions.

Accompanying the article was a cartoon inserted by the newspaper. Sternberg had not seen the cartoon before it appeared along with the article, nor did he know that any cartoon would be included. He interpreted the cartoon as offensive to and belittling of individuals with attention-deficit hyperactivity disorder. He called the newspaper and asked that a statement be published to the effect that the cartoon was the newspaper's and was placed alongside the article without the author's knowledge. The newspaper refused. He asked if he could publish a letter to the editor denying responsibility for the cartoon. The newspaper refused to publish such a letter. The newspaper suggested that Sternberg ask someone else to write a letter indicating that the cartoon was the newspaper's idea and responsibility. Sternberg did ask someone else, who wrote and submitted the letter. The newspaper failed to publish it.

The article, with the cartoon as its context, set off something of a furor. Many letters were written in response, and a handful of them were published. In virtually no instances did the letters criticize anything that actually had been stated; rather, they criticized positions that the letter writer assumed were the author's (but that usually were not). Sternberg also received a flurry of e-mail.

Things got worse when Sternberg went to give a keynote address previously arranged by an LD organization. An introduction usually greets the speaker and mentions a few academic credentials. Instead, the introducer, a high official in the organization, used the podium largely to denounce the speaker, adding that the speaker was invited despite his views. Sternberg was described as a wolf among the sheep. Later the same day, in a roundtable discussion, leaders of the organization were unable to find any significant areas of disagreement with Sternberg. The discussion ended on a concordant note.

The lessons we learned from the Op Ed experience have not ended. LD is a highly politicized field in which people readily are branded as friends or enemies. This book is an attempt to reach out to all people interested in LD in the hope and belief that they can find a common ground.

This book is written for anyone with an interest in the field of learning disabilities—layperson, educator, researcher, or politician. We have tried to avoid highly technical jargon, but at the same time we have attempted to the best of our ability to strive for precision, especially in discussing scientific concepts. We believe that there is a need for books on LD that apply scientific findings to educational-policy issues and that represent what we really know about LDs, rather than fantasies of the political imagination.

This book goes a step beyond Spear-Swerling and Sternberg's earlier book, *Off Track*, and although the positions related here are generally consistent with the positions of that book, some of them diverge somewhat. *Off Track* emphasized social-environmental processes in the labeling of children with learning disabilities. This book emphasizes that the labeling process is the result of the *interaction* of the individual with the environment in which he or she lives.

This book concentrates on learning disabilities, especially reading disabilities, although it deals as well, in passing, with attention-deficit disorders. We view attention-deficit disorders as distinct from learning disabilities, involving at their base deficits in attention rather than in learning. But the two kinds of disorders often co-occur in individuals, and it is difficult to deal with one without taking the other into account. We focus in this book on reading disabilities not only because our own research is in this area, but also because reading disabilities are the most common learning disabilities and because they are highly detrimental to individuals' educational development and outcomes, motivation, self-esteem, occupational success, and other outcomes in life beyond school.[1]

The two of us have collaborated on a number of projects, but never in the area of learning disabilities, even though both of us have been doing work in this field. Sternberg was interested primarily in cognitive bases of learning disabilities—the mental representations and processes that distinguish individuals with learning disabilities from other individuals. He also was interested in the societal processes that lead people to be labeled as having learning disabilities. Grigorenko was interested primarily in genetic bases of learning disabilities (in particular, of specific reading disabilities)—the differences in genetic makeup between those who are identified as having learning disabilities and those who are not so identified and the manifestations of these differences in everyday performance. We decided to write this book as a collaborative effort that would meld our two approaches, both of which, ultimately, were concerned with figuring out the causes of learning disabilities, what could be done about identifying individuals with learning disabilities, and how disabled learning could be improved. For Sternberg, it was an opportunity to go beyond some of the ideas he had expressed in the earlier book written in collaboration with Louise Spear-Swerling, *Off Track*. For Grigorenko, it was an opportunity to go beyond the ideas expressed in articles written with a number of collaborators, especially David Pauls and Frank Wood. In working together, we have realized that each of us was dealing with only part of the story—that learning disabilities need to be understood not just as biological, or cognitive, or environmental, but as the interaction between individuals and environments.

We are grateful to Addison-Wesley for contracting the book; to Perseus (which bought the Addison-Wesley trade list) for publishing it; and especially to our editors, John Bell, Marnie Cochran, Hope Steele, Marco Pavia, and Jenifer Cooke, for their invaluable comments on the manuscript. Our special thank-you is extended to Dr. Rebecca Felton, who made extremely valuable improvements to Chapter 8 and provided us with cases discussed in that chapter. We are also thankful to Dr. Judy Adkins for her invaluable comments on selected chapters of this book and her contribution to the project ELATE.

We also thank all our collaborators in the field of learning disabilities for helping us form our ideas. The ideas expressed in this book, however, are our own, and almost certainly diverge in many respects from those of our other collaborators.

We are especially grateful to Louise Spear-Swerling for her collaborations and also her comments on the entire manuscript. Many of Sternberg's ideas are based on his collaborations with her, and sections of this book draw on ideas from their collaborative venture, *Off Track*.[2] However, she cannot be held accountable for any of the ideas expressed in this book, which represent only the views of the authors.

Preparation of this book was supported in part under grants under the Javits Act Program (Grant No. R206R50001, Grant No. R206A70001) as administered by the Office of Educational Research and Improvement, U.S. Department of Education. Grantees undertaking such projects are encouraged to express freely their professional judgment. This book, therefore, does not necessarily represent the position or policies of the Office of Educational Research and Improvement or the U.S. Department of Education, and no official endorsement should be inferred.

RJS
ELG

Part One

What Are Learning Disabilities, Who Has Them, and What Has Been Done About Them?

This book is about specific learning disabilities. Although specific learning disabilities can be and have been defined in a number of different ways, a consensus view has emerged that is based loosely on the point of view represented in the *Diagnostic and Statistical Manual* (4th ed., 1995) of the American Psychiatric Association. According to this consensus view, learning disabilities are marked impairments in the development of specific skills, such as reading skills, relative to the level of skills expected on the basis of an individual's education and intelligence. These impairments interfere with daily life and academic achievement. However, they are not due to physical deficits, such as visual or hearing deficits, or to acquired neurological conditions, such as those caused by brain trauma. Learning disabilities seldom can be diagnosed before the end of kindergarten or the beginning of first grade.

We view learning disabilities in a way that goes beyond this kind of standard definition. *The thesis of this book is that virtually everyone has a learning disability in something, but society chooses to recognize only some individuals with the* learning disability *label.* Whether someone is labeled as having a learning disability in many respects resembles the result of a lottery. Here's why.

All reputable theorists of abilities agree that abilities are multiple—there are many of them. Although theorists may disagree as to exactly what the abilities are or how they are structured, they agree that the abilities are distinguishable from one another. For example, the skills that constitute reading ability are different from the skills that constitute mathematical ability, which are in turn different from the skills that constitute musical ability. Thus, someone could be an able reader but a poor musician, or vice versa.

If one were to make a list of the many abilities people can have, one would find that virtually no one is proficient in all the skills constituting all these abilities, and virtually no one is hopelessly inept in all these skills. Rather, almost everyone is more proficient in some skills and less proficient in others. Some people may be proficient in more skills, or more proficient in particular skills, but virtually everyone shows a pattern of multiple strengths and multiple weaknesses.

Put another way, virtually everyone shows a complex pattern of abilities and disabilities. For example, even the straight-A student in school may be inept in certain aspects of interpersonal relations. Even the straight-F student in school may be able in many aspects of dealing with other people. This intuition is captured in modern theories of intelligence, which argue on the basis of plentiful and diverse data that interpersonal and practical skills actually are distinct from traditional academic skills. High levels of these different kinds of skills may or may not be found in the same persons.[1]

Given that everyone has a pattern of abilities and disabilities, how does it happen that some people are labeled as having learning disabilities whereas other people are not? *Labeling someone as having an ability or a learning disability is the result of an interaction between the individual and the society in which he or she lives.*[2] Learning abilities and disabilities reside neither totally in the individual nor totally in society. Rather, on the basis of many factors to be discussed, society selects some people to label as having learning disabilities and does not select others.

How does a society make this selection? It selects on the basis of the set of skills it values in school and on the job. If a society views a certain set of skills (such as reading skills) as essential and as constituting a specific rather than a general ability, then individuals with low levels of proficiency in these skills may be labeled as having a specific disability. One has a set of abilities and disabilities and metaphorically enters a lottery that determines whether the particular pattern will result in the person's being assigned the label of having a learning disability. We are not saying that the labeling process is arbitrary. Rather, we are saying that there are many different possible labeling processes, which can yield totally different results.

U.S. society currently defines seven areas of learning disabilities: (1) listening, (2) speaking, (3) basic reading skills, (4) reading comprehension skills, (5) written expression, (6) arithmetic calculation skills, and (7) mathematics reasoning skills.[3] These disabilities are viewed as specific. But in fact, there are no completely general abilities or disabilities. For example, IQ tests are sometimes seen as measuring general ability, yet a high score on an IQ test is no guarantee of a high level of creative ability, practical (commonsense) ability, athletic ability, musical ability, or any of a number of other abilities. So all abilities and disabilities are specific to a greater or lesser degree.

Where and when a child is born has a tremendous impact on whether that child will be labeled as having a learning disability. In a preliterate society, for example, no children are labeled as having a reading disability. One society might label someone with minimal musical skills as having a musical disability, whereas another society might not. In effect, each individual becomes a mandatory participant in a lottery that determines whether the particular pattern of abilities and disabilities he or she has will lead to the individual's being labeled as having a learning disability. But the lottery applies only to the labeling process. Everyone has a pattern of both abilities and disabilities. The lottery represents how society chooses to label that pattern.

Given that all individuals have both strengths and weaknesses, individuals labeled as having learning disabilities have many strengths to offer a society. But U.S. society often inadvertently positions these individuals to view themselves as potential victims rather than as potential victors. In this regard, we have three main contentions:

1. Individuals with specific learning disabilities often have considerable strengths in other abilities.
2. These individuals should be encouraged to see themselves as victors, who capitalize on strengths, rather than as victims of their disabilities, adopting the mind-set of people who are victimized.
3. Modifications of curriculum that excuse these individuals from learning important skills or from the normal experiences of schooling may be well-intentioned, but they often end up hurting these individuals more than helping them. A society labels people as having a learning disability in the first place when it views the ability the individuals are lacking as important for adaptive living in that society.

It is wrong to write off individuals identified as having learning disabilities. Ignoring these children or treating them as hopeless is unfair and not in the best interest of either the children or the society. These individuals are far from hopeless, as long as their hope is not stolen from them. We believe that individuals with learning disabilities should be helped to make the most of their potentials.

This book is about the problems arising from identifying and serving individuals with learning disabilities and about what we hope represent steps toward a solution. We believe that individuals with learning disabilities often have enormous strengths, which the current educational system frequently fails to tap or even draw out. Special services often do not help students with identified learning disabilities fully develop their strengths or encourage them to use their strengths to learn. Yet their learning disabilities may force children to develop strengths that children who are not identified as having learning disabilities may have no incentive to develop.

We challenge a system that, in meaning to do well, often is doing the opposite. We believe that society can do better, and that science can play a role. Right now, though, the effects of the educational and legal systems are often quite different from those that are intended. In this book, we discuss the system we now have, what's wrong with it, and how to improve it. We also discuss what we know scientifically about learning disabilities and how we can use this knowledge to create a better world for individuals with identified learning disabilities and perhaps for everyone else. We make the following points:

1. *The LD label can be and often is misunderstood.* Virtually everyone has a learning disability in some area or areas; what differs is whether society chooses to label lack of ability in a certain area as a recognized learning disability. For example, U.S. society labels certain poor readers as having a learning disability but does not label people who shoot poorly with a bow and arrow as having a learning disability. Another society might choose the opposite path, labeling only the poor archers (who are unable to feed themselves or their families) as having a learning disability.

2. *The LD label can be costly both to the individual and to society.* Once children are labeled as having an LD, a complex set of mechanisms is put into effect that renders it likely that the label will become a self-fulfilling prophecy, whether it originally was correct or not. A well-intentioned labeling procedure thus can become harmful to youngsters. In this book, we show how *LD* and other labels can become self-fulfilling prophecies, sometimes creating problems for children that the children did not originally have.

3. *Genuine LD is an interaction between the individual and the environment.* Certain biological predispositions can put an individual at risk for the development of specific kinds of learning disabilities. These biological predispositions do not determine whether the individual actually will have a learning disability. For example, as noted above, in a pre-

literate society, no one manifests reading disabilities. Even among literate societies, some orthographic (writing) systems impose challenges that others do not impose, challenges that affect the probability of individuals' manifesting reading disabilities. For instance, Spanish is pronounced almost exactly as it is written; English is not. Chinese uses a logographic (picture-based) writing system, whereas Indo-European languages, such as English, French, German, and Russian, use alphabetic writing systems. Whether a child will have a reading disability will be affected not only by that child's biological makeup, but also by where and when the child grows up.

4. *Biological does* not *imply immutable.* Even to the extent that the origins of learning disabilities are biological, these biological origins have nothing at all to do with whether the symptoms of learning disabilities are modifiable. Put another way, the partially biological origins of learning disabilities in no way preclude successful educational interventions. Contrary to a popular misconception, "biological" is in no way synonymous with "fixed."

The remedies used to improve performance of individuals with learning disabilities always should depend on the specific deficits individuals experience, not on how these individuals are labeled. Lumping together all labeled children into one global category, such as LD, and then giving them what usually amounts to a single form of remediation, systematically hurts a majority of the students and helps only a few.

5. *We know what to do; we do not do it.* Cognitive theory provides effective interventions, to be described, for many of the conditions today lumped together as LD. Schools make little and sometimes no use of any of this knowledge. Why?

A. *Financial interests of the schools.* Schools regrettably often have a financial interest (state and local funding, often deriving from federal funding) in overidentification. When they are paid by the head for identifying children as having a learning disability, they obviously are tempted to give that label to more children.

B. *Getting out of the pressure cooker.* Overlabeling children may take parental pressure off school administrators by soothing the feelings of those parents who were clamoring to have their children labeled as LD.

C. *Looking good on the tests.* Labeling children as having an LD can provide a way of coming closer to reaching the Holy Grail of improved test scores. By giving children more time on tests and providing other accommodations for test taking, such as special quiet rooms, administrators potentially can raise the test scores of children with LDs and thus raise the averages for their schools or districts. The schools or districts then look better and receive extra federal or state funds in the process.

D. *Labeling is not tantamount to understanding.* Unfortunately, people sometimes believe that they understand a phenomenon merely because they are able to assign a label to it. They then do not try to understand the phenomenon because they do not know that they do not understand it. A teacher or administrator may believe that the LD label is all that is needed to understand the child's deficiencies and perhaps even to remediate them.

E. *Communication gaps.* Much of the cognitive-psychology literature has been communicated in ways that are not fully comprehensible to educators involved in the schooling of children with learning disabilities. As a result, these educators could not make use of the findings of cognitive psychology even if they wanted to. There is a communication gap that will be closed only when researchers better understand the problems of educators and educators better understand the language of researchers.

F. *Teacher training.* Children with LDs once were taught primarily by teachers with advanced training in special education. Today, with the advent of full-inclusion models whereby most children with LDs are placed in regular classrooms, these children are taught much or all of the time by teachers who have received no specialized training in how to deal with these children effectively.

G. *What is changed.* Educational bureaucracies often function so that structural administrative changes that are irrelevant to improved learning outcomes are far easier to achieve than are educational changes that result in genuine changes in instruction and assessment.

In sum, the LD label produces many effects. But we need to remember that the label is only a label. Pretty much everyone has both learning abilities and learning disabilities. The label is not only about whether people have disabilities, but about whether the disabilities they have are ones the society chooses, for reasons of its own, to label as such. Whether an individual is labeled is the result of a lottery into which he or she is automatically entered, like it or not.

Chapter One

The LD Lottery
Who Wins, Who Loses?

In the recent past, more and more children have been labeled every year as having a learning disability. Although there are many motivations for giving children this label, it is important to remember that the LD label in the United States means different things to different populations. For children whose parents have a high socioeconomic status, the label can provide a means of ensuring that the children continue to receive the benefits of the society that their parents have enjoyed. For these parents, the thought that their children may be downwardly mobile, for whatever reason, may be distressing. These parents may view the LD label as their last hope that their children will maintain their socioeconomic status and prestige when they reach adulthood.[1] In essence, U.S. society has created a legal means to help ensure that children of well-to-do parents who can afford to have the children diagnosed will remain at the top of the heap.

For children of parents of low socioeconomic status, the LD label also may help ensure that the children stay where they are. Ironically, when these children are identified, they, too, may end up being assured a stable socioeconomic environment for the rest of their lives. They get special attention, but it often comes in the form of warehousing, whereby the children are given insipid and ineffective educational fare labeled as interventions. These interventions sometimes ensure only that the children will fall further and further behind.

We wish to make one thing clear at the outset: There are children who genuinely have specific reading, mathematics, or other difficulties, and who deserve special services to help them achieve mastery of the skills that are especially difficult for them. Our argument is not with providing special services to such children, but with a system that, however well-intentioned, sometimes may do more harm than good.

Why do some schools in essence conspire with parents to assign children these labels? There are a number of reasons. First, schools may get additional resources from state and sometimes local governments for every child who is labeled as having an LD or attention-deficit hyperactivity disorder (ADHD); they then may be able to hire more teaching staff, which they usually desperately need because of funding cutbacks. Second, schools may be able to give these labeled children tests with generous time limits or even without time limits, sometimes in special rooms, thereby increasing the average test scores that are so crucial to the evaluations of the schools (and often to the evaluations of the schools' administrators as well). Finally, some schools may view labels as providing a fallback excuse should the children not achieve to standards. Their low achievement cannot be blamed on the school—even though many kinds of deficits in performance can lead to a child's being labeled as having an LD.

Some Varieties of LD

Consider five hypothetical children: Tom, Dick, Harriet, Hato, and Josefina, all in upper primary grades. As it happens, all have WISC-III (Wechsler Intelligence Scale for Children, third edition) performance IQs of 100, meaning that on tasks that require them to work with pictures and forms, they are exactly average—in the 50th percentile. Their reading-comprehension scores are at the 10th percentile, which places them well below average. Thus all are labeled as having a reading disability because of the discrepancy between their performance IQs and their reading scores. But the similarities end with the label.

Tom reads a passage, and despite satisfactory reading instruction in school, has great difficulty understanding the words. Tom has trouble decoding phonemes, which are the basic sounds of the language. *Miser* comes out sounding like *missur,* and Tom has never heard any word that sounds like that. Nor does he know a word that sounds like *booreed* or like *gould.* Because Tom cannot sound out the words, his comprehension is poor. Tom is genuinely lacking in phonemic-decoding skills and is labeled sensibly as having a reading disability.

Dick reads the passage and is able to sound out almost all the words. But when he has finished reading, the passage doesn't mean much to him because he doesn't know what *miser, treasure,* or *thief* means. As a result, Dick misses the point of the passage, and his comprehension is poor. Although Dick actually has a verbal-comprehension deficit, he nevertheless is labeled as having a reading disability and is in the same remedial class as Tom, receiving the same instruction despite a different syndrome and etiology. This instruction is largely a watered-down version of the regular reading curriculum; the students get only a portion of the regular curriculum or a diluted version of it. This kind of curriculum is one major reason why about three-quarters of students who are unsuccessful readers in third grade still will be unsuccessful readers in ninth grade.[2]

Harriet reads the passage, too. She can sound out all the words, and she knows what every one of them means. But she cannot organize the information in working memory to put the ideas in the story together. As a result, despite her micro-understanding of the individual points in the passage, she lacks macro-understanding of what the passage is about. Harriet is placed in the same class as Tom and Dick.

Hato has just moved to the United States. Although quite intelligent, he has no experience at all with U.S. formal education, and especially with testing practices and procedures. He is
anxious and confused when taking the WISC-III, but the exam-
iner for this individual test is able to put him sufficiently at
ease and to describe what is required sufficiently well so that
Hato can make a decent showing. On the group reading test,
however, Hato is totally flustered. He is so nervous that he cannot concentrate on the reading passages, even though he
would have no trouble understanding them were he not experiencing the stress and anxiety linked to the testing situation.
Hato bombs the reading test and joins Tom, Dick, and Harriet
in their class for readers with disabilities.

Josefina also reads the passage. Josefina grew up in southwest
Texas speaking Spanish. She now is expected suddenly to
switch to English. As a result, she is not learning to read Spanish, and she could not read the passage in Spanish. Nor is she
making much sense of the passage in English, as she barely
speaks English. She rapidly is becoming a "subtractive" bilin-
gual and soon will have poor facility in both languages.[3] Josefina, with a societally imposed language deficit, shows no
cognitive characteristics of having a reading disability, but is so
labeled and is placed in the same class as Tom, Dick, Harriet,
and Hato, receiving the same watered-down instruction.

When we label poor readers, or poor math students, or poor
anyone else as having an LD, essentially we are treating them
as Tom, Dick, Harriet, Hato, and Josefina were treated—as
though they have the same problem. Initially, they don't.
Soon, they may.

The Role of Closed Systems

In order to understand how we have gotten to where we are,
one has to understand the role of closed systems. In the context of a society, a *closed system* is one that perpetuates itself by

providing resources to individuals in power, as well as to their progeny, and by failing to provide such resources to individuals who are outside the power structure. The U.S. system of education is, in large part, although certainly not entirely, such a closed system. In it, socioeconomic privilege tends to beget privilege.

Some theorists have suggested that because the United States has something approaching a true meritocracy, an invisible hand of nature has created a system whereby those who truly are deserving rise to the top and those who are not deserving sink to the bottom.[4] Thus, these theorists argue, we see the formation in U.S. society of a "cognitive elite."

This line of reasoning is fallacious. It is true that people with higher IQs tend to rise to the top of U.S. society socioeconomically and that people with lower IQs tend to fall to the bottom socioeconomically. But this phenomenon reflects in large part the extensive use of standardized tests as gating mechanisms in the United States. Students who do not do well on standardized tests—the SAT and SAT-2 for college admission, the LSAT (Law School Admission Test) for law-school admission, the MCAT (Medical College Admission Test) for medical-school admission, and the GRE (Graduate Record Examination) for graduate-school admission, among many other such tests—are blocked from the educational routes that would enable them to acquire the tickets to the best jobs. These tickets take the form of higher education in the most prestigious universities. Countries other than the United States often use other tests, but the results are largely the same.

There is no "invisible hand of nature" at work in this system of providing or blocking access routes to success. Societies, not nature, create such systems. Although U.S. society relies heavily on standardized tests for this purpose, it uses other criteria as well. For example, social class, race, religion, physical appearance, and other factors also play a part. At different times, different factors have weighed in.

For example, at one time, top universities such as Harvard and Yale had quotas that restricted admissions of people belonging to certain religious groups. Women as well as members of some racial groups also were barred. Now women and members of those same racial groups are encouraged to apply to many universities so that these universities can meet informal quotas. Thus the very attributes that at one time might have blocked admission at a future time might come to favor it. Once again we see how the way one is labeled and the opportunities one thereby receives largely depend on a sort of lottery. Where and when one is born obviously make a major difference in the opportunities available.

Societies across space and time have used a variety of criteria to provide or block access to their higher ranks. For example, during the Middle Ages, a person born a serf, died a serf, regardless of IQ. A person born a noble, died a noble. IQ had no effect on the social privilege one would attain. In many parts of the world today, caste, race, religion, and physical appearance still play a major role. Arguably, they do in U.S. society as well.

It is important to realize that *any* attribute or set of attributes can be used as a gating mechanism. Suppose, for example, we decided that we did not like standardized tests because they are not sufficiently precise and reliable. Moreover, it is possible to study to improve performance on them, and it is relatively easy to cheat on them. So we decide, as a society, to use a criterion that is more precise, more reliable, less easily modifiable, and harder to fake. Height is an example of such a criterion. (Lest this sound like a ridiculous criterion, remember that U.S. society currently uses height for job-irrelevant decisions: Taller presidential candidates almost always win; CEOs of major corporations tend to be taller than the people who work for them; and military officers tend to be taller than enlisted troops.) Height provides the kind of objectivity people in any system would long for!

So now, to get into Harvard College, you perhaps have to be seven feet tall, whereas to get into Squeedunk College, you need be merely four feet tall. To get into Harvard Law or Medical Schools, you have to be seven feet two inches tall, at the very least.

Twenty-five years after universities start using height as a principal criterion for admission, suppose the progeny of the authors of *The Bell Curve*, Richard Herrnstein and Charles Murray—or really anyone—decide to do a study of who is attaining success in the society. They note that people who are succeeding in the society tend to be tall and that people who are not succeeding tend to be short. They conclude, as did Herrnstein and Murray, that an invisible hand of nature is at work—but one favoring tall people. They are wrong.

Like Herrnstein, Murray, and many others, they have confused correlation with causation. In other words, the existence of a relationship between two variables is seen as having only one possible causal path, when in fact there are many possible causal paths. In our height-based meritocracy, the correlation between height and success was caused not by nature, but by the closed system the society put into place.

Once a closed system is in place, it tends to be self-perpetuating, regardless of the criteria on which it is based. This self-perpetuation occurs because the people who profit by the system typically are the people who hold power in the society, and they, of course, tend both to think the system is fair and to want to perpetuate the system that has brought them society's rewards.

More important for the argument of this book, the same system that has brought them rewards is likely to bring those rewards to their children as well. Thus, in a society that rewards certain castes or certain religions, one can be reasonably confident that children will be of the same caste or religion as their parents. In a society that rewards social class, children generally will be of the same social class as their parents. Even height will perpetuate the rule of the winners, because height is highly heritable and thus tends to favor the progeny of tall people in successive generations.

Scores on IQ-like tests, like height, are heritable in some degree; that is, variability in IQ scores is due in some degree to variability in genes.[5] One could argue about the degree of heritability of IQ, but few serious behavioral scientists still question whether there is some degree of heritability of IQ. However, it is important to realize that because IQ measures only a part of intelligence, the heritability of IQ tells us nothing about the heritabilities of other aspects of intelligence, which scarcely have been studied.

The passage of societal privileges from one generation to the next is enhanced by the correlation between genes and environment. People with advantageous genes for IQ tend to give their children advantageous environments for promoting the children's IQs. Even parents with no such advantageous genes for higher IQ can give their children advantageous environments for promoting performance on IQ-like tests, thereby potentially enhancing the children's future upward mobility. Virtually all serious behavioral scientists also believe that scores on IQ-like tests are affected by environment, independent of any genetic effects of IQ passed on from one generation to the next.[6]

Sometimes parents who have advantageous genes for higher IQ and who have provided an advantageous environment for promoting IQ-like skills do not get the results they anticipated. In some cases, they get terrible results. It may be that the genes the children inherited for specific abilities, such as reading or mathematical abilities, are less favorable than those they inherited for IQ; or the environment may contain unfavorable aspects over which parents have little or no control. The result is sorrow, frustration, and, often, humiliation. All the parents' efforts to provide for their children the same benefits the parents have enjoyed seem to be going for naught. Worse, the parents recognize that the poorer educational achievement of their children eventually will block the children from gaining the full measure of benefits from their society. The children are at substantial risk for downward socioeconomic mobility.

In some cases, parents may be able to pass on to their children sufficient money to allow the children to maintain a comfortable lifestyle. Yet the children then may be branded with the stigma of having gotten what they have only by virtue of their parents' largesse; that stigma is likely to remain in the minds of the parents as well. The children's poor performance not only makes the children look bad, but it also may make the parents look bad. There is always the risk that some contingent of neighbors, teachers, friends, or whoever will silently think that if the child is such a loser in the IQ sweepstakes, it is likely that the parents are losers, too, however well they may be disguising it.

Enter the LD diagnosis. The LD diagnosis gives some parents a chance to do something about those children who render imperfect the correlation between socioeconomic class and achievement. The LD diagnosis as it now exists has provided some children who seem to be underachieving, based on their socioeconomic status (SES), a way out.

How did we get to this point? Let's consider first some of the formal definitions of learning disabilities and then some of the history of the study of learning disabilities.

Defining the Concept of Learning Disabilities

What are learning disabilities? There is no complete consensus. Let us consider two widely accepted definitions. First:

> *Learning disabilities* is a generic term that refers to a heterogeneous group of disorders manifested by significant difficulties in the acquisition and use of listening, speaking, reading, writing, reasoning, or mathematical abilities. These disorders are intrinsic to the individual, presumed to be due to central nervous system dysfunction, and may occur across the life span. Problems in self-regulatory behaviors, social perception, and social

interaction may exist with learning disabilities but do not by themselves constitute a learning disability. Although learning disabilities may occur concomitantly with other handicapping conditions (for example, sensory impairment, mental retardation, serious emotional disturbance) or with extrinsic influences (such as cultural differences, insufficient or inappropriate instruction), they are not the result of those conditions or influences.[7]

We do not accept this definition in its entirety because it views learning disabilities as intrinsic. We believe that learning disabilities represent an interaction between the individual and the environment. Hence a definition viewing learning disabilities as arising wholly in the individual misses out on the environmental component.

The U.S. government's definition is somewhat different, although related. The first part of the definition is as follows:

"Specific learning disability" means a disorder in one or more of the basic psychological processes involved in understanding or in using language, spoken or written, which may manifest itself in an imperfect ability to listen, think, speak, read, write, spell, or to do mathematical calculations. The term includes such conditions as perceptual handicaps, brain injury, minimal brain dysfunction, dyslexia, and developmental aphasia. The term does not include children who have learning problems which are purely the result of visual, hearing, or motor handicaps, of mental retardation, of emotional disturbance, or of environmental, cultural, or economic disadvantage.[8]

The second part of the definition requires that children identified as having learning disabilities have a "severe discrepancy between achievement and intellectual ability" (p. 65,083) in at least one of seven specified areas: basic reading skill (i.e., word recognition), reading comprehension, listening comprehension, oral expression, written expression, mathematics calculation, or mathematics reasoning.

In summary, the U.S. government's definition of learning disabilities includes three key elements. First is the idea of some intrinsic disorder in basic psychological processing. Second is the idea of a discrepancy between achievement and underlying potential. Third is the idea that the discrepancy should be with respect to one or more of seven particular areas of psychological functioning.

We consider this definition inadequate, as it, too, emphasizes intrinsic deficits. Moreover, it does not specify what constitutes a severe discrepancy, and as we shall see later, the concept of a difference score poses problems, whatever discrepancy is used. Furthermore, the federal definition does not specify how intellectual ability is to be measured, which also proves problematic. These areas are fuzzy enough, however, to allow the emergence of many kinds of disabilities, such as foreign-language disability.

In practice, the federal definition holds sway. Learning disabilities typically are defined as a discrepancy of a certain magnitude between general intelligence and performance in a specific area of endeavor, such as reading or mathematics.[9]

History of the LD Concept

One might think that the concept of LD originated in some laboratory. But the origin of the concept, like its present form, is far from any scientific laboratory.

In 1963, a group of parents met in a hotel in Chicago.[10] These parents had in common a similar problem: They each had at least one child who was not succeeding in learning to read. Many of the parents had tried bringing their children to a variety of specialists—medical doctors, psychologists, learning specialists—with disappointing results. Often the problems of the children were diagnosed in difficult-to-understand terms. Whatever labels may have been used, the labels were not helpful in uncovering the source of the problems the children were having. In those days, terms such as *brain-injured* or *minimal brain dysfunction* were common, but the specialists knew little, if any, more than the parents about what these terms actually meant. The parents were frustrated not only with these specialists, but with the services their children were receiving in school. Many of the children were receiving no special services at all; others were receiving services that were patently inappropriate. The children did not fit into any category that immediately suggested a placement. They did not have mental retardation or any sort of physical disability, nor was it even obvious what was wrong with them. For the most part, the schools either ignored them or treated them as incompetent.

At the meeting was a psychologist named Samuel Kirk.[11] Recognizing that the terms specialists had used gave little insight about why the children were having difficulty, Kirk suggested in his keynote address to the organization that the children be viewed as having *learning disabilities*. The idea was to pinpoint the problem in a way that would make some sense of what was wrong with the children's performance. The parents adopted the term and formed an organization called the Association of Children with Learning Disabilities (ACLD). A major goal of the organization was to gain recognition by the government and by schools of the problems faced by these children. In this respect, the organization and others like it were highly successful.

Curiously, then, the origins of the LD field as we know it today stem not from any conference of professionals or from some major scientific discovery, but from a meeting of laypersons who were frustrated with the education their children were receiving. There is certainly nothing wrong with such a meeting. But the social-advocacy agenda that dominated this meeting has continued to dominate the field as it applies to education.

Identification of LD Cases Takes Off

This meeting was pivotal in the development of learning disabilities as a field of study. In the 1960s, involvement by schools and educators in the field of LD took off.[12] At the same time, more and more children started to be identified as having LDs. For example, in 1976–1977, just under 800,000 children were identified as having one or more LDs. In 1989–1990, the number exceeded 2 million. The number continues to increase and now exceeds 2.25 million.[13]

Perhaps the numbers would not have risen so rapidly were it not for legislation that was to play a pivotal role in U.S. society. The year 1975 brought the passage of the Education for All Handicapped Children Act (P.L. 94-142), which since has been amended as the Individuals with Disabilities Education Act of 1990 (P.L. 101-476). The original P.L. 94-142 was a federal mandate that states provide a free and appropriate public education to all children, including those with learning disabilities and any other special needs. More important, federal reimbursement to the states, contingent on the states' meeting the conditions of the act, became mandatory. These laws had important implications for the way schooling was done.

First, public schools could no longer view the education of children with learning disabilities as someone else's problem. It was now their problem. The schools could continue, in cases of severe problems, to send children to special schools outside the public-education system. But the public schools had to pay the costs of such special schools, making the special schools much less attractive.

Second, P.L. 94-142 required that special-education services be provided in the "least restrictive environment" possible. Put another way, children no longer could be weeded out of the regular classroom just because they had a disability. If it was possible to accommodate children with disabilities in the regular classroom, then they had to be so accommodated. But the law did not clearly state what would define the least restrictive environment. Thus, it was possible for children with severe physical, emotional, or learning disabilities to find their way into regular classrooms and literally to consume most of the time of their teachers, at the expense of the other students.

There were several ironies in this approach. First, the hypothetical gain to one student could mean a real loss to twenty-nine others in a classroom of thirty children. The other children in an average class of thirty, who may or may not have been receiving the attention they needed before, now almost certainly were not.

Second, a child with a severe disability who was placed in the regular classroom actually might have been better served elsewhere. The other children, for the most part, would treat this child as other than normal. The teacher would be treating the child as other than normal. And the child would be expected to compete with children with whom he or she might be unable equally to compete, through no fault of his or her own.

Third, many teachers were and continue to be inadequately prepared to serve some of the children who have ended up in their classes. Few teachers have adequate training in dealing with children with severe disabilities, and some teachers may not be able to deal adequately with children who have only mild disabilities. Although children with disabilities might receive services from a specially trained professional on an occasional basis, for the most part the burden fell on a teacher who had little idea how to serve these children or how to divide attention among all the children in the classroom.

The LD field has continued to be driven, in large part, by social-advocacy groups.[14] The children identified in many cases truly have needed special services. The fact that so many of them have been from the middle class and that their parents thus have had the economic, social, and political clout to advance their cause has helped propel that cause forward.[15]

Perhaps the number of children identified as having LDs and the money spent on these children would not have grown so rapidly had very clear and consistent criteria been drawn up for identifying such children. No such criteria exist. A risk arising from the absence of such criteria is that the children who most need services will not receive them and that other children who need them less will receive them, simply because the latter children have received the label that was denied to the former.

Although the modern history of LD has its roots in a meeting of parents, there is an earlier history that has its roots in medicine. To be informed about the origins of the LD concept, it is important to understand this earlier history as well. We will consider here both so-called intrinsic and extrinsic approaches.

Two Types of Approaches to Understanding LD

Intrinsic Approaches

Intrinsic approaches, represented by most definitions, view LD as initiating inside the individual. These approaches have a long history. In 1836, Marc Dax, a country doctor in France, presented a little-noticed paper to a medical society meeting.[16] Dax had treated more than forty patients suffering from loss of speech as a result of brain damage. This condition, *aphasia* ("no speech"), had been reported even in ancient Greece. Dax noticed a relationship between the loss of speech and the side of the brain in which damage had occurred. In studying his patients' brains after their deaths, Dax found that in every case there had been damage to the left hemisphere of the brain. He was not able to find even one case of speech loss resulting from damage to the right hemisphere only. Despite this provocative finding, the paper aroused no scientific interest.

The next major figure to produce a similar finding was Paul Broca, also a Frenchman. At a meeting of the French Society of Anthropology in 1861, Broca claimed that a stroke patient of his who was suffering from aphasia had been shown in an autopsy to have a lesion in the left cerebral hemisphere of the brain. Despite an initially cool response, Broca soon became a central figure in the heated controversy over whether functions, such as speech, are indeed localized in particular areas of the brain, rather than generalized over the entire brain. By 1864, Broca was convinced that the left hemisphere of the brain was critical in speech, a view that has held up over time. In fact, the specific area Broca identified as contributing to speech is referred to today as Broca's area. Another important early researcher, German neurologist Carl Wernicke, studied language-deficient patients who could speak, but whose speech made no sense. He also traced language ability to the left hemisphere, although to a different precise location, now known as Wernicke's area of the brain.

This early work came long before the days of identified learning disabilities, but the recognition that functions of the brain were specialized and could be pinpointed, rather than being diffuse and generalized, had important implications for this later work. The conceptual underpinning of the LD concept is that someone can have a specialized dysfunction that leaves other functioning intact. Dax, Broca, and Wernicke showed at the levels of both behavior and brain functioning that such a hypothesis is indeed supported by the scientific data.

It is important to note that many less reputable types made similar claims, but without the scientific data to back up those claims. Franz Josef Gall became a leader in a movement whose origins go way back in time, phrenology. The idea of phrenology was that one could diagnose many aspects of a person's functioning simply by feeling patterns of bumps and ridges on the person's head. Although there was no scientific support for this claim, it found its way into popular psychology, even as late as the early 1900s in the United States. Some people still believe in phrenology. The question, of course, is whether the modern field of LD is better traced to the spirit of Dax, Broca, and Wernicke, or to that of Gall. We believe that there is some influence from both camps.

Fast-forwarding to the early twentieth century, a large group of researchers sought to understand specific dysfunctions.[17] Most of these researchers were physicians with a special interest in medical bases of such dysfunctions. Among these researchers were W. P. Morgan, James Hinshelwood, Alfred Strauss, Grace Fernald, and Samuel Orton. Probably the most influential proved to be Orton.

Orton introduced the concept of *strephosymbolia*, which literally means "twisted symbols." He believed that reading disability is characterized by individuals' frequent reversals of letters or inversions of words. Thus, a child with strephosymbolia might read *d* as *b* or the word *was* as *saw*.[18] These ideas, introduced in the 1920s and 1930s, are still believed by many educators and parents, *even though they are wrong*. Orton also believed that children with this syndrome tended to have trouble establishing handedness. Some of Orton's colleagues, including Morgan and Hinshelwood, who were ophthalmologists, believed that these errors were caused by problems in vision. This view, also held by many people today, is also dead wrong.

Orton further thought that children with strephosymbolia could be helped if they were taught reading by an approach that placed heavy emphasis on phonetics and on multisensory activities (such as reading a letter, saying the letter, writing the letter, hearing the letter read, and so forth). These ideas, unlike some of Orton's other ideas, have been shown to be largely correct.

Ironically, many reading educators, believers in the exclusive use of a whole-language approach, eschew any form of phonetic training. Thus, many educators accept what was wrong in Orton's ideas while rejecting what was right, a disheartening state of affairs.

Not all investigators have taken an intrinsic approach to learning disabilities, the view represented by Orton and his associates. Some have taken an extrinsic view, seeing the origins of LDs as societal in nature.

Extrinsic Approaches

People who take an extrinsic approach to understanding LD view the phenomenon as rooted in the environment rather than in the child. Of course, these theorists recognize that some cases are intrinsic, that is, they acknowledge that intrinsic factors may matter. But these theorists tend to ignore or downplay such factors, much as intrinsic theorists ignore or downplay extrinsic factors.

One such theorist, Carol Christensen, has pointed out that the LD label enables the educational system to deflect attention from problems in school and instruction as the source of reading failure and instead to localize the blame within the child.[19] In essence, schools use labeling to exculpate themselves. Another extrinsic theorist, Thomas Skrtic, points out that the very existence of special education serves as a legitimizing device for institutions that are failing to teach reading adequately.[20] Essentially, they can say they are doing all they can, justifying children's failure from the start by the need of these children to be placed in "special education."

We are as reluctant to place all the blame on the system of schooling as we are to place it all on the individual. Like Gerald Coles, we believe that intrinsic characteristics interact with extrinsic ones to produce children with learning disabilities.[21] In the next chapter, we explain what some of these intrinsic and extrinsic factors are.

Chapter Two

What's at Stake? Abilities, Disabilities, and Lotteries

In order to understand fully *disabilities*, you need first to understand *abilities*. So let's start there. To make things easier, we will use the metaphor of investment. Like all metaphors, ours is imprecise, yet it may help make things clearer.

Abilities Start as Nature's Investment

Imagine that nature gives you, as your lot in life, an amount of money. You get from nature a certain amount, whereas someone else gets from nature another amount, which may be more or less than your amount. You may be lucky; you may not be. But you start off with a certain sum.

There is a complication. Some of what nature has given you is invested in land, some in stocks, some in bonds, some in cash. You thus start life with diverse assets.

So it is with abilities. Nature, expressing itself through the genes you inherit from your parents, gives you a certain potential allocation of different kinds of abilities. For any given ability, you may get more or less than someone else gets. Basically, it's the luck of the draw in the lottery of life—or, to be more precise, the luck of who happens to be your parents and what you get from them when you are born.

Many discussions of learning disabilities use technical concepts, such as *heritability, IQ,* and *mental age.* These concepts are often not well understood and are frequently misused. In order to understand properly the crucial issues involving learning disabilities, you need to understand some of these technical concepts.

Effects of nature are often quantified through a coefficient of heritability, or h^2. Heritability is the ratio of genetic variation to total variation of a trait within a population. In other words, it tells, in theory, the proportion of variation among individuals in a trait due to the effects of genes. Thus, one could measure the extent to which learning disabilities or intelligence or any other trait is inherited.

Observable variation in a trait, as it is expressed in a population, is referred to as *phenotypic,* whereas genetic variation in a population is referred to as *genotypic.*

Heritability typically is expressed on a 0-to-1 scale, with a value of 0 indicating no heritability whatsoever and a value of 1 indicating complete heritability. Heritability, and its complement, environmentality, sum to unity. Heritability tells us the proportion of variation among people in a population in a given trait that is heritable within the population. Thus, if, say, a biological predisposition to intelligence were to have a heritability of .50 within a certain population and environmental context, then, in theory, 50 percent of the variation in scores on the trait within that population would be due to genetic differences.

This statement is completely different from the statement that 50 percent of the trait is heritable. The difference is important, because we have no way of knowing what percentage of a trait is heritable, nor is it even clear what it means to talk about a percentage of a trait. Consider an example.

IQ is often used as a comparative basis for determining whether someone has a learning disability. The concept of IQ will pop up again and again in this book, but what, exactly, is IQ?

IQ originally was defined as the ratio of a person's mental age to that person's chronological (physical) age, times 100, with mental age defined as the average level of IQ-test performance for a person of a given age. Thus, someone with a mental age of 12 would be performing at a level on a test that is average for 12-year-olds. So if a person had a mental age of 12, but a chronological age of just 10, the person's IQ would be (12/10) x 100, or 120.

Today the concept of mental age is not widely used, as it has proved to be problematic for several reasons. For example, after a chronological age of roughly 16, increases in people's scores on IQ tests start to slow down. Then, in later adulthood, scores on some tests actually tend to decrease. Today IQ-test scores are determined by a different procedure, whereby the IQ is a function of a person's standing among people of his or her own age cohort. For example, a score of 100 represents the average score; a score of just 85 is better than that achieved by about 16 percent of the general population, whereas a score of 115 is better than that achieved by about 84 percent of the population.

IQ scores are obtained from IQ tests, which measure skills that are very important for success in school and somewhat important for success in life. But the skills measured by IQ tests are not the only skills that, in combination, constitute intelligence.[1] In our own preferred theory, for example, we distinguish among analytical intelligence (which the tests measure), creative intelligence (which the tests do not measure), and practical intelligence (which the tests also do not measure). IQ tests thus measure a part of intelligence, not all of it.

IQ is expressed on an interval scale, meaning that arithmetical differences are meaningful: In theory, the difference between an IQ of 80 and an IQ of 90 is the same as the difference between an IQ of 110 and an IQ of 120. Multiplicative differences are not meaningful, however: An IQ of 120 does not indicate twice as much intelligence as an IQ of 60. Multiplicative differences cannot be meaningful, because there is no known meaningful 0 point for intelligence, the underlying trait for IQ. We don't know what zero intelligence would be. An IQ of 0 certainly does not mean "absence of intelligence."

As an analogy, the Celsius temperature scale is an interval scale (as is the Fahrenheit scale): 0 degrees Celsius does not mean "absence of temperature"; it refers to the temperature at which water freezes and becomes ice. In contrast, the Kelvin temperature scale is a ratio scale: 0 degrees Kelvin truly means no temperature. There is literally no heat at 0 degrees Kelvin, which is sometimes called absolute zero.

IQ is like the Celsius scale (or the Fahrenheit scale), not like the Kelvin scale. The analogy to temperature breaks down, however, because whereas we know what 0 would mean in terms of temperature, we do not know what 0 would mean in terms of intelligence. An extraterrestrial alien, a dolphin, an ape, or an infant, for that matter, might score 0 on an adult test of intelligence, but such a score would not indicate a total lack of intelligence. We thus have to be careful in the conclusions we draw about differences in intelligence or in any other ability.

Heritability is *not* tantamount to genetic influence. An attribute could be highly genetically influenced and have little or no heritability. Heritability depends on the existence of individual differences. If there are no individual differences, there is no heritability (because there is a 0 in the denominator of the ratio of genetic to total trait variation in a given population).

For example, being born with two eyes is 100 percent under genetic control. Except for people with extremely rare genetic disorders, which we will disregard here for the sake of simplicity, a human being will have two eyes, regardless of the environment into which he or she is born. But it is not meaningful to speak of the heritability of having two eyes, because there are (virtually) no individual differences. If we lived in a world that also had significant numbers of Cyclops types, there would be meaningful individual differences in numbers of eyes. But we do not live in such a world.

Nature is not the only source of individual differences. Environment matters, too.

Environmental Effects on Intelligence

Nature's deposit on your conception in your intellectual bank account is only the beginning. The intellectual assets with which you are born can be invested wisely, or they can be squandered. If your mother used drugs or drank significant amounts of alcohol while you were in utero, she began to squander your biological makeup before you were born. On the other hand, if your mother received excellent prenatal care, watched her diet, and refrained from taking drugs, she already had begun to invest your intellectual stakes wisely.

The investments continue after birth. If you are born into an environment that contains a lot of support or scaffolding for your intellectual development (the luck of the draw in yet another lottery), then you quickly will begin to reap the interest and dividends in terms of enhanced intellectual abilities. If, however, there is little support and stimulation of your intellectual development, the investments nature has made in you already are beginning to be frittered away.

Whatever the investment nature has made, possibilities for environmental intervention remain legion. One of the most pernicious misunderstandings afoot is that if something is largely heritable, it is fixed. According to this view, if learning disabilities are largely or even partially biological, children who show the symptoms of LD—poor reading, poor math, or whatever—are doomed to stay that way, and the best society can do is just hope they can scrape by.

Numerous examples show that this argument is false. Consider height. Heights in much of the world have been rising steadily over generations, largely because of better nutrition, even though height is highly heritable (about .90 to .95 on a 0-to-1 scale, where 1 indicates maximal heritability). An even more powerful example is phenylketonuria.

Phenylketonuria, a genetic disease, has a heritability of 1, meaning that if you inherit the gene for it, you are certain to get it. In the past, being born with this disease meant a life of mental retardation. No longer. It was discovered that phenylketonuria is caused by the inability of the body to metabolize the amino acid phenylalanine. Buildup of this amino acid in the body results in mental retardation. The plausible inference was that if children were fed a diet free of phenylalanine, they would not have mental retardation. This inference has proved basically correct. It is thus now possible largely to prevent the mental retardation that in the past always accompanied the disease. Note that the disease itself does not disappear, but its most baleful symptom typically does.

The implication for learning disability is straightforward: Having genes that predispose an individual toward a learning disability does not entail that the individual will have a learning disability. Later we will present evidence that it is possible for an individual to have such genes and to become a normal learner.

Some theorists of abilities have argued for years that because abilities are partially heritable, there is not much we can do to improve them. This reasoning is just as specious as is the argument that the heritability of phenylketonuria implies that we can do nothing to improve the lives of those born with phenylketonuria. For one thing, several programs have been shown to have positive effects on measured abilities, including reading abilities.[2]

The importance of environment has been shown in a number of ways for intellectual abilities as measured by IQ. We know that IQs have been rising steadily since the 1960s or earlier. This phenomenon is known as the Flynn effect, after the man who discovered it.[3]

The effect is powerful, showing an increase in IQ of about 18 points per generation for tests of so-called fluid abstract-thinking abilities. Moreover, the effect now has been shown for all twenty nations for which full data are available, as well as for some other nations for which partial data are available. Fluid tests include tests such as the Raven Progressive Matrices, which measure a person's ability to cope effectively with relatively novel stimuli and the relations among them. The Raven test measures a person's ability to extrapolate patterns from sequences of geometric forms. The mean effect has been inexplicably greater for tests of fluid abilities than for tests of crystallized, or knowledge-based abilities, which show an increase only about half as large. But if linearly extrapolated, the difference would suggest that a person at the 90th percentile on the Raven test in 1892 (i.e., someone who scored higher than 90 percent of the others who have taken the test) would score at the 5th percentile in 1992 (i.e., higher than only 5 percent of the others who have taken the test).

The Flynn effect must be environmental because a successive stream of genetic changes of such dramatic magnitude could not have occurred and exerted a strong influence in such a short period of time. Psychometric tests of intelligence indicate that environment must be exerting a powerful effect on intelligence and other cognitive abilities, including reading abilities, perhaps in interaction with genes.

One might ask, How could IQs be rising, when the mean is always 100? The answer is that every so often, IQ tests are renormed so as to set the mean at 100. But what would qualify for a score of 100 today is quite a bit more impressive than what would have qualified for a score of 100 in the past.

The Flynn effect has serious implications for our understanding of the concept of learning disabilities, because this effect suggests that who will be identified as having an LD varies greatly over time. Reading scores have not been going up in the same way as IQs, so in absolute terms, many more people might appear to have reading disability today than might have appeared to have it in the past. One reason for the increase in reading-disability diagnoses may be that the standard for making the diagnosis has changed such that today people are more likely to appear to have a reading disability relative to their general ability. Thus, to identify people with disabilities, it is extremely important to use tests that were standardized at roughly the same time.

In the United States, reading levels as measured by conventional tests actually have decreased in many cases.[4] Given the increases in IQ, this decrease cannot be due to decreases in conventional intelligence, as some doomsayers might have us believe. The causes of declining verbal skills are complex, but in large part they have to do not with our children, but with the kinds of reading materials we give them.[5]

A number of researchers have pointed to startling declines in reading levels of textbooks over time.[6] What now passes for a fifth-grade textbook, for example, is roughly at a level that would have passed as a third-grade textbook only a couple of generations ago.[7] It is hard to believe that a nation would systematically dumb down its textbooks in a way that almost guarantees decreasing literacy on the part of its children, yet that is exactly what the United States is doing. What the United States is doing in its schools is educationally perverse, yet it is being done glibly and often with the best of intentions.[8]

Several factors contribute to publishers' dumbing down of textbooks.

First, the process of revising reading materials becomes a downward spiral. Every time the publishers dumb down the texts, reading levels go down. Then the next new books have lower reading levels, resulting in decreased reading skills, resulting in still lower reading levels of books, then still further decreased reading skills, and so on.

A second factor is the way in which textbooks are adopted. Schools talk about keeping standards high much as individuals talk about keeping weight low: Neither schools nor individuals are very successful in transforming thought into action. Teachers may find the books they are using too hard for their students, so they may pressure textbook-adoption committees to choose easier books. So, again, levels can keep declining. Although committees may talk about higher standards, publishers quickly see that the easier books more often are adopted, and they react accordingly. Schools may talk the talk of higher standards, but they do not always walk the walk.

To the extent that there is pressure on authors of textbooks, it almost always is to lower, not to raise, the reading levels of books. Schools may require elementary and secondary textbooks to score at certain levels on readability formulas, which typically measure quantities such as number of syllables per word and number of words per sentence. The textbook editors therefore may substitute shorter but less specific words for longer words and shorten sentences. As a result, texts may be less readable to students, but more acceptable according to readability formulas. Schools end up with books that are dull, incoherent, and often not very meaningful to the students who have to read them. Whatever initial investment nature has made in these students is being squandered by educational practices.

The Interaction of Nature and Nurture

Nature does not just make an initial investment, however. Things are quite a bit more complicated. Only some of the investment shows up initially. Different genes turn on and turn off at different stages of the life span. Moreover, the effects of the environment can increase or decrease throughout the life span. Thus, as genes and environment interact throughout your life span, the investments in your intellectual account can be increasing or decreasing, usually without your even being aware of the deposits and withdrawals. Abilities and disabilities are not fixed: They can change at a phenotypic level.

Examples of the interaction of nature and nurture can be seen in two studies conducted in orphanages. One researcher found that children placed in Iranian orphanages had low IQs. Probably because they were reared in institutions of different quality, girls had a mean IQ of about 50, whereas boys had a mean IQ of about 80.[9]

Children adopted out of an Iranian orphanage by the age of two had IQs that averaged 100 during later childhood; they were able to overcome the effects of early deprivation. Children adopted after the age of two showed normal intellectual development from that point, but never overcame the effects of early deprivation; they continued to display mental retardation. These results suggest that interventions to foster cognitive development need to start as early as possible. They also suggest that, after a certain point in development, poor environment more adversely affects the modifiability of the individual, so that the person is less susceptible to change after that point than he or she was before.

In a similar study conducted in a Romanian orphanage, researchers found that orphans who went to the United Kingdom before six months of age had mean increases in IQ from 60 to 109.[10] These children showed complete recovery from early mental retardation. Infants who went to the United Kingdom after six months of age showed, on average, continuing deficits. This finding again suggests the need for early intervention and indicates that something in the individual shuts down after a certain point, rendering a compensatory environment less able to have an effect after a certain age.

The ongoing contributions of nature and nurture are not necessarily in equal balance. You might think that, with age, the contribution of nurture would increase and the contribution of nature decrease. Research suggests exactly the opposite, however.[11] The relative contribution of nature seems to increase with age. In other words, environment matters more in earlier years than in later years, perhaps because infants and children are typically more helpless in the face of the environment than are older people. Older people have more means at their disposal to shape their lives as they wish, despite the vagaries of the environment.

Abilities Are Differentiated

When nature makes its initial deposit in your investment account, it's not just a single, undifferentiated deposit. Rather, as noted earlier, nature invests in different amounts of different kinds of abilities, much as you might invest in a variety of mutual funds, say, some containing stocks, some containing bonds, and some containing cash.

Again, psychologists have somewhat different views as to just what the different abilities are. Almost all psychologists would agree that there are distinctive verbal and spatial-visualization abilities (with the latter the kinds of abilities used to fit your car into a parallel-parking space or to fit your suitcases into the trunk of your car). Most psychologists would distinguish mathematical abilities from the other two. Other kinds of abilities that traditionally have been viewed as important include memory abilities and perceptual abilities.[12] Some psychologists also have proposed separate musical, bodily-kinesthetic, interpersonal, and intrapersonal abilities.[13]

Every viable theory or measure of intelligence specifies that multiple abilities contribute to people's adaptations to their environment. The only disagreement among theorists is with regard to the form these multiple abilities take. This point is so important that we will go into it in a bit of detail.

All contemporary major intelligence tests or tests of related abilities produce multiple scores. The most widely used intelligence test for children, the Wechsler Intelligence Scale for Children (WISC),[14] yields an overall score but also provides specific scores for verbal and performance sections. The verbal section includes tasks such as defining vocabulary words and recalling general information. The performance section comprises tasks such as putting pictures in order to form a story or arranging blocks in order to form a certain design. Other scores can be derived as well. Children with learning disabilities can show distinctive profiles on the Wechsler, but they do not always do so. For example, children with a verbal deficit may do worse on the verbal subtests. Clearly, then, the use of difference scores with the Wechsler is problematic, because the test has verbal content, yet is supposed to be a measure independent of the disability.

The other major intelligence test, the Stanford-Binet Intelligence Scale[15] (4th edition), yields an overall score as well as scores for various skills. This scale is based on a three-level hierarchical model consisting of "g" (a general reasoning factor) and three second-order factors (Crystallized Abilities, such as Verbal Reasoning and Quantitative Reasoning, Abstract-Visual Reasoning, and Short-Term Memory). This test measures skills such as vocabulary, arithmetical problem solving, and reasoning about geometric forms.

Another recent test, the Cognitive Assessment System,[16] yields an overall score plus scores for attention, planning, simultaneous processing (as when you solve a difficult reasoning item), and successive processing (as when you recall a string of digits). This test seems to show more systematic patterns for children with disabilities than do some other tests. For example, children with attention-deficit hyperactivity disorder should show a distinct deficit of performance on the attention scale and also may show a deficit on the planning scale.

The multiple nature of abilities also is recognized in theories of abilities. Some contemporary theorists believe that one can conceive of some kind of general ability,[17] but this ability is at the top of a hierarchy of abilities. Other theorists, such as

Howard Gardner,[18] believe that there are multiple intelligences that are relatively independent of one another, with no general intelligence interrelating all of them. Robert Sternberg[19] has suggested that, to the extent that a general ability exists, it is applicable only to the relatively narrow range of abilities that are rewarded in traditional schools.

As soon as we go outside the school setting, the generality of this so-called general ability disappears. For example, the abilities that lead to success as an auto mechanic and those that lead to success as a novelist are quite distinct, and the people who would make good auto mechanics typically would not make good novelists, and vice versa.

When psychologists move to a notion of multiple abilities or multiple intelligences, especially ones that are relatively independent of one another, the notion of learning disability as traditionally defined becomes problematic. For one thing, there is no general-intelligence score, or IQ, to which a specific ability score can be compared in order to identify a child as having a learning disability. Indeed, the probability of individuals' being labeled as weak in some specific area skyrockets, because by the law of normal distributions, some people will be weak in some areas, others in other areas.

Consider an example. Suppose we accept Gardner's theory of multiple intelligences. We have a student who is weak in linguistic intelligence relative to other intelligences. So perhaps we label the student as having a linguistic disability, or perhaps as having a reading disability, if the primary weakness is in reading. But now what do we do with the student who is relatively weak in bodily-kinesthetic intelligence? Do we label this individual as having a kinesthetic disability? If so, what kinds of special services do we provide?

Suppose that the physical education instructor arranges a running race. Should the child with a kinesthetic disability be required to run a shorter distance? Or should the individual be given a "handicap," so that he or she starts halfway down the

track? Perhaps we should do the analogue of what we are starting to do at the college level—drive the child in a car to the fin-
ish line to spare him or her the seeming embarrassment of not
being able to compete. These suggestions may sound silly. But
they are the path that U.S. society has chosen to follow in
other domains, and so why should physical education be any
different? Something is wrong with the way in which we identify and educate children with learning disabilities. We discuss
what is wrong in the next chapter.

Chapter Three

Picking the
Lucky Tickets

Difficulties in Identifying People
with Learning Disabilities

The multifarious nature of abilities is crucial to our argument because it logically implies something very important: *The conventional way in which learning disabilities are defined and recognized—in terms of differences between IQ and reading skill—is, and must be, wrong.*

Problems with Discrepancy Scores

Learning disabilities often are defined in terms of discrepancies between IQ and a specific kind of learning ability. For example, a child who scores much lower on standardized tests of reading ability than on standardized tests of intelligence might be viewed as showing a reading disability. On the surface, this judgment seems to make sense: The child is intelligent, but a poor reader. What is wrong with such a sensible procedure for recognizing the existence of learning disabilities? Plenty.

We will make seven points as to why this procedure is not really sensible at all. First, the assumption that IQ tests measure all there is to intelligence is extremely questionable. Second, even if one accepts IQs at face value, they are problematic because they are confounded with verbal and reading skills. Third, use of nonverbal IQ tests does not solve the problem of inadequate identification. Fourth, difference scores do not mean the same thing at different points along the IQ spectrum. Fifth, difference scores are extremely unreliable. Sixth, identification of LDs is plagued by statistical regression (a phenomenon that we will explain). Seventh, identification processes, particularly with regard to how test scores are used, differ across states and even across districts within states, rendering highly subjective the labeling of children as LD.

There Is More to Intelligence Than IQ

The assumption that IQ tests measure all there is to intelligence is extremely questionable. Many modern theorists dispute this assumption. For example, Howard Gardner, whose theory was mentioned in the Chapter 2, suggests that there are eight distinct multiple intelligences rather than just one intelligence:

- Linguistic intelligence, which is involved in reading this book, writing an essay, talking to someone, or listening to someone tell you why you should buy Crunchy Flakes. Someone with a reading disability would have a deficit in the reading aspect of linguistic intelligence.
- Logical-mathematical intelligence, which is involved in solving mathematics problems, such as "What percentage of 40 is 400?" or in making logical deductions, such as "If Donk is a wegan and some wegans are human, can you be sure that Donk is a human?" Someone with a mathematical disability would have a deficit in this intelligence.
- Spatial intelligence, which is involved in visualizing, for example, figuring out how to get suitcases in the trunk of

your car or whether you can fit into a tight parallel-parking space. Many people have some kind of spatial disability and find it hard to make judgments about spatial relations.

- Musical intelligence, which is involved in listening appreciatively to music, playing a musical instrument, singing a song, or writing a sonata. Many people lack musical skills, but it is usually difficult to know whether this is from lack of ability or lack of training.
- Bodily-kinesthetic intelligence, which is involved in dancing, playing football, or running as fast as you can. We might refer to the many people who lack bodily-kinesthetic skills as having a kinesthetic disability.
- Naturalist intelligence, which is involved in recognizing patterns in nature, such as how different kinds of plants or animals might be related to each other. Someone with a disability in this area would be unable to detect such natural patterns.
- Interpersonal intelligence, which is involved in understanding others, such as deciding what you safely can say to your boss or what you should tell your new significant other about your past. Someone who has little sense of what to say to other people when might be viewed as having a disability with respect to this intelligence.
- Intrapersonal intelligence, which is involved in understanding yourself, such as whether you are ready for a permanent commitment or whether you are someone who is suitable for being a parent. Someone who is notably un-self-aware might be viewed as having a disability with respect to this intelligence.

If one accepts Gardner's view of multiple intelligences,[1] then a conventional intelligence test can tell only a small part of the story of intellectual abilities. Looking at the difference between reading ability and IQ would be an empty exercise. At best, IQ tests measure linguistic and logical-mathematical abilities and perhaps a bit of spatial abilities as well. They do not measure the other intelligences. Moreover, reading ability itself would be a part of an intelligence, and reading disability would manifest itself through a depressed level of linguistic intelligence. So in, say, subtracting a reading score from an overall intelligence score, one would be partly subtracting a thing from itself.

Consider the hypothetical case of Jocelyn, a high school student. Jocelyn is a brilliant musician and a wonderful dancer. She gets along well with other people, in part because she understands herself and knows how to play to her strengths in her relations with others. Jocelyn's academic record is only average, however, because her linguistic and logical-mathematical abilities are undistinguished. She is not overly concerned, because she plans a career in dancing and has already begun to attract attention in the world of ballet. Professional dance companies have shown interest in hiring Jocelyn and anticipate a brilliant future for her.

From the standpoint of Gardner's theory of multiple intelligences, Jocelyn excels in at least four intelligences: musical, bodily-kinesthetic, interpersonal, and intrapersonal. But her IQ comes out only around average, because the limited set of abilities measured by an IQ test does not do justice to her strengths. What sense does it make to use her IQ as an overall measure of her intellectual abilities? If one believes in Gardner's theory, it makes no sense at all. And what sense does it make to use IQ as a comparative basis for assessing learning disabilities? Again, it makes no sense at all.

Other contemporary views of intelligence lead to the same conclusion. For example, according to Sternberg's theory of successful intelligence, mentioned in Chapter 2, intelligence comprises three parts: analytical, used in analyzing, judging, evaluating, and comparing; creative, used in creating, inventing, discovering, and imagining; and practical, used in putting into practice, applying, using, and implementing. IQ tests measure only a portion of the analytical abilities; they typically measure creative and practical abilities either minimally or not at all. So, according to this theory, too, using an IQ test as a basis for evaluating someone's intelligence will provide only a highly incomplete measurement at best. And, as with Gardner's theory, to the extent that reading involves analytical (or other) abilities, one is in part subtracting a thing from itself to obtain this measurement.

Consider the hypothetical case of Barry. Barry lives in a rural environment in Vermont. The nearest candy store is far from his home and the homes of most of his friends in school. But kids always want candy. So every week, Barry rides his bike three miles to the candy store and stocks up on candy. He is only ten years old, but already he is running a little business selling candy to his classmates who don't want to bother to trek the three miles to the candy store. Barry wants someday to have the bank balance of Bill Gates. He may or may not, but he clearly has high practical-intellectual skills. His academic skills, though, are nothing special. The result is that with Barry, as with Jocelyn, academic test scores do not reflect well what the child is able to do. Taking an IQ as *the* measure of intelligence really is not justified.

In a number of studies, we and our colleagues have explored the practical aspects of intelligence.[2] For example, we have devised tests of practical intelligence for business managers, salespeople, college teachers, military leaders, and students. In study after study, we have found that scores on tests of practical intelligence predict real-world performance as well as or better than do IQ tests, but that these tests of practical intelligence are not correlated with conventional IQ tests. In other words, one cannot predict a person's practical intelligence from his or her score on an IQ test, and vice versa. If we had available only a person's modest IQ score, we might conclude that the person was not very intelligent; yet that individual might be high in practical intelligence and thus have the ability to excel in the everyday world. Or the person high in IQ might have low practical intelligence. Should we refer to such an individual as practically disabled? Once we expand our conception of intelligence, the notion of disability becomes problematic.

In the United States, we and our colleagues typically have found little or no relation between IQ and practical, everyday intelligence. We found an even more surprising result in a study we did in Kenya.[3] Children who live near the village of Kisumu, Kenya, are ill much of the time. They continually are being assaulted by various kinds of parasitic infections that are not found or at least are found much less frequently in the developed world. Remaining well is therefore an essential aspect of practical intelligence.

Part of the indigenous education of these children is learning about natural herbal medicines that the Kenyan villagers believe fight parasitic infections. Village children may know the identities of many such medicines. Children in the developed world, of course, would not know the name of even one of these medications.

We constructed a test of the practical intelligence of the village children in which the children had to identify these medicines, as well as when and how to use them. This test thus measured implicit knowledge that is considered important in the Kenyan village. We correlated scores on our test of indigenous practical intelligence with scores on two tests of vocabulary and with scores on a test of abstract-reasoning ability that consisted entirely of geometric figures. The two vocabulary tests were in different languages: One was in English, the language of the school; the other was in Dholuo, the language of the Luo residents of the village. The critical finding was that scores on the test of indigenous practical intelligence were significantly *negatively* correlated with scores on the test of vocabulary for the language used in the school—English. In other words, the children who did better on the indigenous test actually did worse on the Western types of tests. Scores on the indigenous intelligence test were also negatively correlated with scores on the vocabulary test in the Dholuo language and with scores on the test of abstract-reasoning ability, although these latter correlations did not reach statistical significance.

Given this information, just how seriously can we take the scores on the IQ tests, not only for certain Kenyan village children, but for children from any subculture in the Western world that perhaps takes the kinds of skills measured by IQ tests less seriously than does the mainstream U.S. culture? In the rural villages of Kenya, many of the children are failing in school, and the parents often show little or no concern. They simply do not much value the types of skills valued by Western education, and many of them plan to separate their children from these schools as soon as they legally are able to. They value the skills that matter in the community, and they perceive the training their children receive in school as largely irrelevant.

The Kenya study also has implications for our understanding of verbal disabilities. Do we judge such disabilities from the standpoint of *academic vocabulary* and its use or from the standpoint of *everyday vocabulary* and its use? The children in the Kenya study generally did not score well on conventional academic verbal tests, even in their home language of Dholuo. But they scored fine on such tests when the words were used to ask them about indigenous medicines. The same issues can apply anywhere. A person may be able to read and understand the material he or she confronts in everyday life, but may be unable to read the more difficult passages typically found on reading tests.

Variation in conceptions of intelligence is found not only outside the United States, but within it as well: Different groups have different notions of what constitutes intelligence. For example, one study investigated the language development of children in three communities in North Carolina, referred to by the investigator as Trackton, Roadville, and Gateway. Trackton was a lower-socioeconomic-class African American community; Roadville was a lower-socioeconomic-class white community; and Gateway was a middle-socioeconomic-class white community.[4]

Shirley Heath, the investigator, found that parents in the Trackton community emphasized nonverbal communication much more than they did verbal communication.[5] Almost from the day the children were born, they were being taught—directly and indirectly—skills of nonverbal communication, including how to use gestures, posture, tone of voice, facial expressions, and similar kinds of nonverbal cues. In contrast, children in Roadville and Gateway were receiving much more intensive instruction in verbal skills and relatively little instruction in nonverbal skills.

The kinds of instruction the children in the two communities were getting made sense. They were learning what they needed to adapt to their own community environment. But teachers in the schools also had ideas about what was worth learning, and, unsurprisingly, their ideas corresponded more closely to the ideas of parents in Roadville and Gateway, the communities in which the teachers were more likely to have been raised. The teachers naturally valued the kinds of skills their own communities valued and did not particularly value the kinds of skills valued in Trackton. As a result, to the teachers, the children from Trackton did not appear very bright.

In general, teachers tend to value more highly and to give higher grades to children who think the way they do,[6] so it is no surprise that the teachers in this study valued the Roadville and Gateway children over the children of Trackton. Moreover, most IQ tests and reading tests place a premium on the kinds of skills emphasized in Roadville and Gateway, rather than on those emphasized in Trackton. Children from Trackton will tend to do more poorly both on conventional intelligence tests and on reading tests, so that when difference scores are used for identification, few of the children will be identified as having a reading disability. They are more likely to be labeled as having mental retardation because they do poorly on all the conventional tests, even though they may have valuable skills not measured by such tests. Children from Gateway tend to do fairly well, on average, on conventional intelligence tests, so if they do poorly on a reading test, they will have a greater probability of being identified as having a reading disability if a discrepancy score is used.

Notice an ironic implication of this fact. Children from Trackton are likely to score lower on IQ tests than do children from Roadville and Gateway because the content of such tests favors the skills that are valued in the latter two communities. Children from Trackton are also likely to score lower on reading tests, because these tests require very similar skills. Trackton children, because they perform worse on both IQ and reading tests, are less likely to be labeled as having a learning disability and therefore are less likely to get the special services that come with these labels. In effect, they are disadvantaged twice—first, when they take the tests, and second, when it comes to receiving special services based on these tests. The Trackton children are more likely to be labeled as having mental retardation, and many children with this label are apt to be viewed by the educational system as beyond salvage.

One could argue, of course, that the skills valued in Roadville and Gateway really *are* more valuable. But in our everyday lives, nonverbal skills are extremely important. Consider some examples.

Nonverbal communication skills are crucial to discerning people's true intentions or true beliefs when they are talking.[7] During a job interview, nonverbal cues may communicate to the person conducting the interview whether what an interviewee is saying can be trusted; or, they might communicate to the person being interviewed a sense of what the interviewer really wants to hear. Interviewers rarely communicate verbally to the people whom they interview their true assessments of those people, but they may, without intending to, reveal such information nonverbally. Job candidates who are strong in nonverbal skills may be able to pick up valuable information that the interviewer would prefer to keep secret. And, they can use this information to their advantage, adjusting their responses (verbal and nonverbal) so that they are more likely to land the job for which they are interviewing.

Nonverbal skills also are valuable in discerning when people feel upset or depressed, even when they say otherwise. For example, a significant other may be unhappy with one's behavior but be reluctant to say anything. How much better off we all would be if we could determine when our partner was unhappy with us. Often a relationship has gone downhill substantially by the time a partner is ready to communicate verbally a feeling of what is wrong. A person who is sensitive to nonverbal communication, however, may pick up through nonverbal channels information that another is reluctant to disclose.

These nonverbal skills are crucial to everyday intelligence, even though they have little or no relation to what is measured by IQ tests, or by any other conventional academic tests for that matter.[8] As is often the case, what the academic tests measure matters more in school than outside school or after schooling is over. The nonverbal skills so critical to life success are not measured much in school. And because schools generally do not emphasize or even value these skills, we do not refer to someone who is low in these skills as having a learning disability. U.S. society, at least, is more likely to label as disabilities the absence of skills valued in school than the absence of skills valued in life beyond the school, even though the latter may be more important to real-world adaptation.

Confounded Conclusions

Even if one accepts IQs at face value, they are problematic because they are confounded with verbal and reading skills. The large majority of IQ tests involve reading material, or at least verbal material that may be presented orally. The comprehension skills needed to understand the material on the IQ test overlap with the comprehension skills measured by reading tests. Thus, subtracting reading scores from IQ scores yields an invalid result because what is being subtracted (verbal-comprehension skills) is a part of the thing it is being subtracted from.

What types of items actually appear on IQ tests, and how are they verbal?

A frequently found type of item is the vocabulary item. Individuals are asked to name the meanings of words. At the lower levels, for younger test takers the words are presented via pictures. Later, they are presented orally or in writing. For example, one might be asked what *pretentious* means. Vocabulary testing is done for individuals at all age levels. Vocabulary questions appear on many tests of intelligence and related constructs, such as scholastic aptitude tests. Obviously, these questions require verbal skills and often reading skills.

A second kind of item is the comprehension item. The individual has to show an understanding of social and cultural norms, by explaining, for instance, why people borrow money or why people vote. How does one learn these things? Often through reading, or at the very least, oral verbal comprehension. Thus verbal skills enter in again. But there is a further problem.

Why do people really borrow money? Ostensibly, they borrow because they need funds to buy something they cannot afford to pay for in full at the time they make the purchase. Although this is one reason people borrow money, it is not the only reason. Sometimes, as when buying a house, people may borrow money to get a tax break. Sometimes people want luxuries—cars, boats, or mansions—that they cannot afford and probably should not buy. Sometimes people borrow to get extra cash that they have no intention of paying back. Sometimes people borrow money to buy controlled substances, which ultimately will kill them. Sometimes, of course, people borrow money for the reasons given in the answer key. A person could generate a practically intelligent answer to this question but be marked wrong. No answer key could do justice to all the reasons people borrow money, or to all the reasons people do practically anything else.

Why do people vote? In a country where 99.6 percent of the people vote for the incumbent dictator (the most recent and not so amazing victory margin of Saddam Hussein), it's presumably because they have to vote for the government-approved candidate, or else. Sometimes people vote because they want to show their dissatisfaction with all the offered candidates, as when a U.S. citizen writes in a preferred candidate. Sometimes people vote because they have been paid to vote. Of course, sometimes people vote freely to express their political sentiments, as a test would require examinees to say. But in many cases, this question has no meaning at all, because people in much of the world do not vote and never will.

A test of comprehension is, in large part, a test not of what people know to be true but of what they know a test scorer wants to hear. To the extent that you aim to measure people's understanding of the testing game, such a test is an appropriate measure. It well may correlate with people's understanding of the same game in school. But it is no measure of intelligence for those who were not brought up to understand these games.

Another test item has to do with verbal relations. Here the individual has to say what the first three words in a set have in common that a fourth word does not. For example, what do an apple, a banana, and an orange have in common that a cup does not have? Sounds pretty easy, but it helps if you come from an environment where all these fruits are available, so you know what they are. Do you know what a guayaba is? In some countries in the world even very young children would know without hesitation. Often tests that are supposed to measure verbal reasoning end up measuring vocabulary, and once again, it is difficult to separate what a reading test is supposed to measure (because it heavily involves vocabulary) from what an IQ test is supposed to measure (because it also heavily involves vocabulary). So how can the difference score between the IQ test and the reading test be meaningful?

Consider an analogy. You have $10,000 invested in all your different kinds of investments, including a variety of mutual funds plus individual stocks. You have $6,000 invested in the individual stocks. You want to know how much of your investment is not in stocks, so you subtract the $6,000 from the $10,000, yielding a difference of $4,000. You conclude that you have $4,000 invested in things other than stocks. You are wrong.

The reason you are wrong is that some of the mutual funds in which you have invested themselves are invested in stocks. Both the $10,000 and the $6,000 contained stock investments, so the subtraction was invalid in yielding a "pure" amount that is invested in investment vehicles other than stocks. The same problem plagues the subtraction of reading scores from IQ scores.

Because both reading scores and IQ scores involve verbal components, the subtraction cannot give you a pure measure of verbal or reading skill, separated from everything else. The truth is, the subtraction tells you little because you do not know how much of the IQ score was dependent on verbal ability any more than you know from the information given in the investment example how much of the money invested in mutual funds was invested in stock funds.

A hypothetical student, Letitia, receives a standard score of 85 on a reading test and a standard score of 100 on an IQ test. A subtraction yields a difference between the two scores of 15 points. But what does the 15 mean? Does it really indicate the extent to which Letitia's reading ability is below her general intelligence? On the IQ test, Letitia was asked on one subtest explicitly to define the meanings of a number of words. Other subtests also required her to know the meanings of challenging words, although she was not explicitly asked their meanings on these other subtests. The reading test also required Letitia to define the meanings of words, and then to recognize the meanings of difficult words in the context of her reading. So what does a difference score mean when both the IQ test and the reading test require recognition of difficult vocabulary? Not much; perhaps, nothing.

Nonverbal Tests Are No Answer

Use of nonverbal IQ tests does not solve the problem. In an effort to get around this problem, some psychologists use nonverbal IQ tests, that is, IQ tests that contain no words. These tests might contain geometric figures on the basis of which one is supposed to reason. For example, one might be asked to say which one of five geometric figures does not belong with the other four.

The good news is that the test appears to contain no words. The bad news is that things are not quite as they appear. The directions are verbal (whether oral, written, or both), and some children do not understand the directions they are given for tests. Solution of the problems is also often verbal, as children talk out answers to themselves. But the greatest problem is that now the IQ test represents an even smaller portion of the full range of intellectual abilities, so that to the extent that it is supposed to measure all of intelligence, it is being used to do something it cannot possibly do.

Reasoning with abstract geometric forms is a far cry from the kind of intelligence we need to adapt in our everyday lives, and a test that contains nothing more than such sterile problems cannot possibly give a complete representation of a person's intelligence. Such a test should not serve as the basis for a score from which to subtract a reading score.

Difference Scores Change Meanings

Difference scores do not mean the same thing at different points along the IQ spectrum. Imagine someone who is a near genius in abilities overall, but who is only above average in reading abilities. If one views reading disability as defined in terms of the difference between IQ and reading ability, the near genius actually might be classified as having a reading disability. This person's reading ability is way below his or her overall abilities, but so what? Society would not want to invest resources to bring this individual's reading up to the level of his or her other abilities.

Min is a hypothetical honor student in his high school and one of the school's best mathematicians. He has won the school's top math award every year he has been there. He is also outstanding in the sciences and in many other subjects. Having grown up in South Korea, it is scarcely surprising that his verbal skills in English do not match his quantitative skills. Even if he had not grown up in South Korea, however, the story would probably have been the same, because in South Korea, as in the United States, his strength was in mathematics. He is not a bad reader, but reading is not his strength. Yet he is so superior in quantitative and symbolic skills that, by conventional definitions of reading disability, he is officially eligible for the label.

In a case such as Min's, the label is worse than meaningless, because it misleads people into believing that, somehow, there is something wrong with Min. In fact, there is something wrong with a system that would label him as having a reading disability.

The same problem that can arise near the top of the abilities spectrum can also arise, with more serious consequences, near the bottom of the abilities spectrum. Suppose an individual is slightly below average in general abilities but way below average in reading. However, the difference between the IQ score and the reading score does not quite reach the threshold for classifying the person as having a learning disability. In this case, someone who really could profit from special services to improve his or her reading does not get them.

Carmen, a hypothetical student with an IQ of 95, is slightly below average in IQ. Her reading score is at the third-grade level, but she is in fifth grade. She could truly benefit from special services. The bizarre thing is that she is not entitled to any special services at all. Why? Her school requires a discrepancy between IQ and reading level just slightly greater than the discrepancy Carmen shows. Had her score on the IQ test been three points higher or her score on the reading test three points lower (differences well within the errors of measurement of the tests), she would have qualified for special services. So, oddly, Carmen, who needs special remedial services, does not qualify, whereas Min, who does qualify, does not need any special remedial services at all.

The irony in Carmen's case is even greater than it might appear. Carmen's native language is Spanish, and she did not learn to read English until third grade. Her reading of Spanish is not so good, either, so had she continued to be taught in Spanish, she would have needed special help. The IQ test Carmen received was, in part, a verbal test, requiring her to know the meanings of words in English that she just did not know. Her IQ score was thus artificially deflated. Had she been given a nonverbal IQ test, her score would have been higher, which would have resulted in her being entitled to special services because the difference between her IQ and reading score would have been greater. Here we have a somewhat bizarre situation in which a higher IQ would result in a special level of service because of a lack of ability!

Carmen's case points out one of the horrors of using strict cutoffs for determining eligibility for any kind of special service, whether for LD, giftedness, mental retardation, or anything else. No psychological test yields exactly the same score again and again. Rather, people score somewhat differently each time they take the test. So, for example, Carmen might score 97 one day, 101 the next, 95 some other day, and so on. These fluctuations are not limited to IQ tests. They occur for all tests. People who take the SAT (Scholastic Assessment Test) or the ACT (American College Test) for admission to U.S. colleges routinely find their scores unsystematically varying from one administration to the next, sometimes by 100 points or even more. These unsystematic fluctuations are a matter of what is sometimes called the *reliability* of a test. The more stable the pattern of test scores, the more reliable the test. No psychological test, of course, is perfectly reliable.

The difference between what Carmen would have needed to qualify for special services and the scores she received was well within what is called the error of measurement of the test. In other words, it is quite likely that on another day Carmen's scores would have been sufficiently different that she would have qualified for the special services. Thus, a decision affecting her school career and possibly her life was made on the basis of scores on tests that, taken another day, might well have led to a totally different result.

Difference Scores Are Unreliable

Difference scores are extremely unreliable. Indeed, difference scores are much more unreliable than simple IQ or reading scores.[9] What does this mean?

Imagine a group of individuals taking a test, such as an IQ test or another ability test, twice. To what extent are their rank orders the second time the same as the first time? In other words, do the people who do relatively well (or poorly) the first time also do relatively well (or poorly) the second time? Recall that reliability measures the extent to which people do about the same relative to others when they are retested.

The more closely related the constructs being measured, the more unreliable the difference scores (for technical reasons that go beyond the scope of this book). Reading ability and intelligence, or math ability and intelligence, are obviously related. The relation is far from perfect, but it exists. As a result, difference scores involving IQ and either reading or math scores can be expected to be quite unreliable. Schools are thus making high-stakes decisions on the basis of difference scores that have been proven to be unreliable bases for making any kind of decision whatsoever.

Many psychologists and other diagnosticians, of course, understand this situation, yet feel compelled to use a system that they recognize as problematic. Those who do not recognize the problems may end up contributing to them. But those who do recognize the problems are caught in an awful bind. They may be reluctant to report a set of scores that they know will deprive a child of special services that the child needs. Such a decision is extremely unpleasant to make, especially for those devoted to their work. These professionals may also administer further tests to the child (such as an additional reading test or IQ test) to see whether some other combination of test scores will produce the desired diagnosis.

Statistical Regression

Identification of LDs is plagued by statistical regression. What is statistical regression? We will explain this concept first in everyday terms and then explain its relevance to issues of reading disabilities.

People sometimes are lucky enough to find a restaurant whose food is just wonderful. They go out to dinner and experience one of the great culinary events of their lives. The steak could not be better, or perhaps the fish could not be fresher. In such situations people often feel fortunate that, after visiting their share of mediocre restaurants, they finally have found at least one that is truly distinguished in its culinary offerings.

As often as not, though, repeated visits to the restaurant turn out to be disappointing. Often the disappointment sets in on the second visit. Sometimes it is on the third visit. But the restaurant seems to be going downhill. The whole thing turns into a depressing experience. Perhaps the restaurant owners got cocky and kept the food around just a bit longer than they should have. Or maybe they started buying cheaper cuts of meat. Or maybe the chef spent just a little bit less time in preparation. Whatever the reason, the restaurant seems not to merit a return visit, and often such restaurants actually go out of business.

The disappointing decline in quality is not limited to restaurants. It occurs with sports rookies as well.[10] The rookie of the year in any sport virtually never has a second year that is as distinguished as the first. People often conclude that the rookie had beginner's luck, or took his or her skills for granted and did not work as hard the second year, or simply lost his or her touch.

These cases illustrate instances in which our initial expectations are high, but we are later disappointed. Things equally often go the other way. Restaurants that seem really bad, if people ever visit them again, often turn out to seem better on the second trip. Athletes who have a really bum year often find the next year is a much better one.

The same effect applies to parents and their children. Take two parents of very high IQ, say, an average of 131, which puts them roughly in the top 2 percent of the population. Is their child likely to have an IQ of about 131, or an IQ that is higher, or an IQ that is lower? The answer is *lower*. Chances are very high that the child's IQ will not reach the average of the parents' IQs.

Now take the inverse of this situation. Two parents have an average IQ of 69, which is as far below average as the IQ of 131 is above average. Are the chances greatest of these parents having a child whose IQ is below, roughly equal to, or above 69? Chances are that the child will have an IQ greater than 69.

These situations all illustrate *statistical regression*: When prediction is less than perfect, predicted outcomes are likely to regress (move) toward the mean, which is the average. Statistical regression is not a psychological effect; it is a statistical effect that arises as an outcome of imperfections of prediction.

In other words, when current data lead one to predict that a restaurant or an athlete will continue to perform at an above-average level, the performance of the restaurant or athlete usually will get worse over time, all other things being equal. And children of really smart parents tend not to reach their parents' averaged level of smarts. At the same time, when current data lead one to predict that a restaurant or an athlete will continue to perform at a below-average level, the performance of the restaurant or athlete usually will get better over time, all other things being equal. And children of parents of very modest abilities tend to excel beyond their parents' averaged level of smarts. The greater the departure of the observations from the mean (average) of the measurements being made, the greater the amount of statistical regression, that is, the more the predicted observations tend to regress toward the mean. Thus, really good restaurants show more statistical regression than do merely pretty good ones, and the same holds for really bad restaurants versus so-so ones.

The reasons for statistical regression are complex and beyond the scope of this book, but the implications of statistical regression are very relevant for this book. When there is statistical regression, the test scores of individuals tend, on retesting, to be closer on average to the mean. Suppose, for example, that someone does really poorly on a reading test. Chances are better than 50–50 that if the person is retested, the score on the retest will be closer to the mean than was the first score. Similarly, if someone does really well, chances are that the next score will be closer to the mean.

Because diagnoses of reading disabilities are based on very low reading scores, these diagnoses are susceptible to error because of problems of statistical regression. Statistical regression can lead to overdiagnosis because it takes people who just happened to score very poorly on a reading test one day (relative to an IQ score) and labels them. If their reading score is much lower than their IQ score, and their IQ score is closer to the mean IQ score than their reading score is to the mean reading score, chances are their reading score will regress toward the mean if the reading test is taken again. Of course, such misdiagnoses can be reduced if repeated testing rather than just a single testing is used. In addition, statistical corrections can be applied to help correct for regression effects.

Variability in Identification Procedures

Identification processes, particularly with regard to how test scores are used, differ across states and even across school districts within states, rendering the labeling of children as LD highly subjective. Different states (and even different local school districts) may have different degrees of discrepancy in what they accept as indicative of a learning disability, or they may use different criteria of identification altogether. Thus, the easiest way for parents to gain an LD diagnosis for a child is often to move their residence or to place their child in a different school district. Even if one district does not identify the child as having an LD, another well might. Consider some examples from one state, Connecticut.

The state of Connecticut recently published prevalence rates by district for students with disabilities in grades kindergarten through twelve.[11] It is interesting to compare some of these figures. Hartford is a district serving a relatively poor population, with a diagnosed prevalence rate of 17.4 percent, quite high by statewide standards. New Haven is roughly comparable socioeconomically, but the prevalence rate is only 12.9 percent, or roughly three-quarters of that in Hartford. But then, Greenwich, one of the wealthiest towns in the state, has a prevalence rate of 16.2 percent, near the top. Another comparable district, New Canaan, has a prevalence rate of only 9.5 percent, and Hebron, another generally well-off district, is down at 7.2 percent.

At the top is Canaan, largely white and working class, at a whopping 23.8 percent. Clearly, standards for identification must differ across districts. A parent who is dissatisfied with results in one district may do better moving to another.

Another option is waiting. In each school year since 1991–1992, the prevalence rates in special education have increased. A child who is not identified as having an LD one year may be identified in a future year, not because the child has changed, but because the standards of labeling have changed.

In sum, the use of difference scores in diagnosing reading disabilities is analogous to the building of a house of cards. Millions of high-stakes decisions are being made on the basis of a procedure that is flawed and greatly in need of modification.

Difference scores are not the only basis on which LD diagnoses can be made, but they are probably the most common basis used today, despite their glaring inadequacies. It is time to change.

How Much Can Tests Tell Us?

We believe, on the basis of these various arguments, that IQ has no place at all in the diagnosis of learning disabilities. For all the reasons cited here, diagnoses involving IQ are badly flawed, yet decisions are being made every day, and children are either receiving or not receiving special services, on the basis of IQ. Furthermore, decisions that should be based on sound psychological and educational criteria are being made on the basis of social or even political criteria.

Although our greatest concern is with the use of IQ tests, it is worth pointing out that all tests are nothing more than indicators of performance at a given time in a given place. Administration of any test can lead to erroneous judgments, so test scores, whatever they may be, need to be interpreted carefully.

When Adam was in first grade, he moved from one school to another. In the first school, he was in the top reading group. In the second school, he was placed in the bottom reading group. How could he suddenly have gone from being an excellent reader to being a poor reader? Of course, he didn't.

When he arrived in the new school, the school felt a need to give Adam a reading test to place him in the appropriate reading group. There is nothing wrong with giving a child a reading test, but it is a poor idea to give a test to a child on the child's first day in a new school. The child is confronted with a new physical setting, a new teacher, new classmates, probably a new home, and as much instability as he or she is likely to have encountered at any time. The youngster may not be at his or her best on this first day in a new school (any more than immigrants were at their best when, newly arrived in the United States, they once were required to take IQ tests and risk being sent back to their home countries if their scores were unsatisfactory).

Although the first day in a new school is scarcely a day for testing, that is exactly when many schools give tests. Elementary and secondary schools are not alone: Some universities give placement tests as soon as students arrive!

So, to return to Adam, he took the test, flubbed it, and ended up in the bottom reading group. The way the test was used is highly problematic.

Any test should be only one of a number of indicators used to determine a placement. It should never be the sole basis for deciding a placement. It is actually illegal under federal law to use a single test alone to determine placements for special education. But Adam's placement was not a special-education one, so the use of a single test for placing him in a reading group was perfectly legal. Other information was readily available, however.

For example, a simple call to Adam's old school would have revealed that Adam had been in the top reading group in that school. That information should have been more valuable in making a placement decision than a score on a short test given at an inopportune time.

So there Adam was in the bottom reading group, receiving reading instruction that was watered down and totally inappropriate for him, not to mention the other children receiving it! Fortunately, the reading teacher was alert enough to notice within a relatively short period of time that Adam was reading at a level beyond that of other children in the group. One might think that the reading teacher or other professionals would realize, quite simply, that they had erred in Adam's reading placement. After all, his reading was better than the test score had predicted.

Instead, school personnel decided to give him the reading test again. This decision was, in some ways, quite extraordinary when one considers its implications. The goal of a test is to serve as a predictor of some criterion. Thus, a reading test serves to predict actual reading performance. The test has no value other than its predictive value. So, if the test is mispredicting, it has no value. The test Adam took had mispredicted. But, rather than make this admission, the school decided to use the reading test again. In other words, the predictor—the reading test—had become more important than the criterion it was supposed to predict—reading performance. This situation would be comparable to treating an earthquake as irrelevant if it happened that our seismological tests did not accurately predict its occurrence! Again, we would be saying that it is the predictor that counts!

Fortunately, when Adam took the reading test again, it was no longer his first day in school, so he was in a better position to do well on it. He did do better this time, and he was placed in the middle reading group. After a while, the reading teacher noticed once again that Adam was reading better than the other children in his reading group—this time, the middle reading group. As you can no doubt guess, it was back to the reading test. Once again, the test score was viewed as more important than what it was supposed to predict.

This time, Adam scored at the level of the children in the top reading group. His parents therefore expected him to be placed in the top reading group. He wasn't, which seemed strange. So his parents made an appointment for a conference with some of the school's heavyweights—the principal, the reading teacher, and a school psychologist. This panel of trained professionals explained, in all sincerity and correctly, that Adam was now one full basal book behind the children in the top reading group. They were reluctant to put Adam in the top group because they feared he would miss all the skills contained in that book.

This situation clearly illustrates the self-fulfilling prophecies that can result from test scores. Once a child is labeled, the child is treated in such a way as to make the label come true, almost without regard to what the label is. In this case, though, the parents thought they had an ace in the hole. They explained that they were willing to work with Adam to make up for lost time. Adam's mother was a specialist in school curricula. With a doctoral degree and many years of high-level experience working with school curricula, she was in an excellent position to work with Adam. Adam's father had done extensive research in the area of reading. So who better to help Adam? All Adam had to do was bring the reading book home, and his parents could help him catch up.

Of course, there was a catch. Isn't there always? The school officials explained that school policy forbade students from taking their reading books home. (This policy is not unique to that district: Adam's father's elementary school had had an identical policy in the 1950s.) Thus, it would not be possible for Adam's parents to help him catch up with this book. And here is the greater irony: Not only may educational institutions create self-fulfilling prophecies, they also inadvertently may take steps to make sure these prophecies come true!

Of course, the parents could argue. After all, their credentials in the field of reading were at least as good as, and perhaps better than, those of the school personnel with whom they were conferring. But it was by no means clear that an argument was the best course of action. The parents were afraid of winning the battle and losing the war. In other words, the school officials would place Adam in the top reading section, but then consciously or subconsciously might fail to support him, or might even undermine him, to show that they were correct in the first place. Adam's parents decided to leave things alone. Fortunately, institutions do not always have good memories, and the next year, Adam was placed in the top reading group.

Adam's experience shows why researchers in the field have been concerned with what sometimes are called Matthew effects, a reference to the Book of Matthew in the Bible, in which Matthew avers that the rich get richer and the poor lose what little they have. Students who are given enriched instruction are likely to benefit from it and to excel even more as a result of it. Students given watered-down, remedial instruction or dumbed-down textbooks are likely to fall further and further behind and eventually to lose their competitiveness in even weak academic competition. For this reason, some educators have argued that students who have fallen behind need not remediation, but enrichment.[12]

Matthew Effects and Self-Fulfilling Prophecies

Matthew effects are prevalent in reading instruction because later skills build so heavily on earlier skills. If students are not given a solid foundation in basic skills, they are not in a position to acquire more advanced skills. They are like the building with a weak foundation that starts to crumble even as higher floors are placed on top of lower ones. For example, without sound word-recognition skills, higher-order comprehension is impossible. It is in part for this reason that many children who are poor readers show poor phonological-decoding skills in the early grades and poor higher-order comprehension in the later grades. They cannot understand meaning when they cannot decode the words on which the meaning is based.

Matthew effects are pernicious, and they occur throughout the U.S. system of education. Once they start, there may be no end to them. Consider, for example, what happens to poor readers. Because of the importance of reading both in the world of school and in the world of work, schools should do everything they can to enrich students' reading experiences to the greatest extent possible. In many schools, however, poor readers are likely to get a watered-down program for improving their reading skills. In an attempt to give poor readers "appropriate" reading material for their skill levels, schools give them material that actually may lead them to fall behind. For example, giving fifth-grade readers who read on the third-grade level a third-grade reading textbook is a counterproductive strategy. Why? Because the content of the stories is no longer age appropriate and is likely to be boring or even demeaning to fifth graders, who then are not likely to be motivated to read the material. Moreover, fifth-grade students are more sophisticated than are third-grade students in terms of life experience and learning strategies, and they need a pedagogical approach that reflects their level of sophistication.

Soon, children who are getting the watered-down reading program do start to fall further and further behind in reading. Teachers label them as slow or incompetent and then start to expect incompetent work, which is exactly what they get.

As the years go by, these children are placed in lower tracks or else receive diminished opportunities in standard tracks. Reading performance continues to slide. Eventually, the students may wish to go to college, and, in the United States, to take tests such as the Scholastic Assessment Test (SAT) or the American College Test (ACT). Performance on these tests, of course, is heavily dependent on reading. Even the quantitative sections require students to read the words in the mathematics problems. So poor readers are likely to do poorly, which may make it more difficult for them to get into a competitive college, or perhaps into any college at all.

Eventually, these students may find that they are employable only in menial jobs or in jobs that require little or no specialized academic training. A reading deficiency thus may affect an individual's whole life, not only his or her performance in school.

Enter the doomsayers, such as Richard Herrnstein and Charles Murray, authors of *The Bell Curve*.[13] They have pointed out that scores on a variety of verbal as well as nonverbal tests of intellectual skills predict what kinds of jobs people will get and their ability to perform on those jobs. Of course they do, at least in the United States. U.S. society has become a test-dependent society, in which poor scores on tests that require reading predict later success in part because the society uses these tests to control access to the educational routes that will allow later success. In effect, U.S. society created a system that produced a certain result, and then "discovered" that this result had occurred. Rather than recognizing the extent to which society itself caused the result, society attributes it elsewhere.

For example, Herrnstein and Murray have attributed the social mobility resulting from intellectual skills, or, to be more exact, from scores on tests that measure a narrow band of intellectual skills, to the operation of an invisible hand of nature. There well may be an invisible hand, but, as mentioned earlier, it is not a hand of nature, but of society. The United States has created this system, starting with the very first reading-readiness tests given to pre-first graders, which are supposed to measure a child's level of preparedness for initiating reading. A society should not give credit to nature for a system it has created.

Reading skills are certainly of great importance in U.S. society and in many other societies. These societies could have chosen to emphasize other things. For example, in times past in the United States, and still today in many parts of the world, social class, religion, or caste determine much of what a child in the society will be able to achieve in his or her future. Arguably, these variables continue to matter in the United States as well. Other variables may be made to matter, too. At times, the law of primogeniture ensured that the firstborn son would receive all the holdings of the parents. In essence, being the firstborn and male was substituted for scores on educational tests as a basis for deciding who should get richer and who should not.

People in the United States may view their system, which emphasizes the use of supposedly objective tests, as fair, while viewing systems that emphasize social class, religion, caste, or sex as unfair. The important thing to remember is that the people in power in any society most likely think that their system is fair. When career opportunities in the United States were determined by social class, those in the upper social classes often viewed themselves as the ones who were worthy of the opportunities made available to them. They still often do. Today in the United States, people who get high test scores may view themselves as worthy of the opportunities they get. Some things change, but one doesn't: Those who hold power tend to believe that they are entitled to it, by whatever means they may have gotten it. Social Darwinism lives on.

Social Darwinism holds that survival of the fittest applies in the social as well as in the biological domain. Just as the most adaptable organisms survive and their progeny continue on, so, according to this theory, do the socially most adaptable reach the heights of the societal game of survival. As a scientific theory, social Darwinism has been thoroughly discredited. But as a social ideology, social Darwinism endures, albeit hidden behind a variety of disguises.

Some parents, recognizing how the system works, compete and even claw for the educational opportunities they believe their children deserve, such as extra learning time with specialists or special arrangements for homework assignments or tests. If their child is underperforming, they may view special services as the answer, and frequently the only way to get such special services is for their children to be labeled.

The worst of it is that the special services often are given only if children receive the LD label. This method for allocating resources creates a perverse situation in which parents, and even the children themselves, actually may want the children to be labeled as LD—as having a disability—so that the children will qualify for special services. Many people find it difficult to believe that parents would want their children to be labeled as having something wrong with them so that they could qualify for special services. But from their standpoint, the parents are acting in a rational way: They have found what they may believe is the only route to the special services they desire for their children.

We know that poor achievement tends to be associated with lower socioeconomic status (SES), so we might well expect that diagnosed incidents of learning disabilities would be high in low-SES towns and low in high-SES towns. But we would be wrong. In the state of Connecticut, as mentioned earlier, some of the towns with the *highest* levels of diagnosed reading disabilities are among the wealthiest towns in the state. On statewide mastery tests, children from these towns typically score at or near the top in terms of levels of academic achievement. How, then, could these towns have high reported incidences of reading disabilities?

The answer, unfortunately, is that the educational system has driven these diagnoses. Schools may be conservative in labeling children as having disabilities, but parents do not have to be. Parents who are wealthy enough can afford to have a private diagnostician test their children and, potentially, assign them a label. Professionals who are being paid to label may be reluctant not to assign the label, because if they, like the schools, are conservative, they may find that their client base will be diminished. What parents want to spend as much as several thousand dollars only to be told that their child is fine and not in need of special services?

So the pressure may be on the diagnostician to give the child the diagnosis the parents want. Such a scenario can be played out only in a town where the parents are wealthy enough to afford one or more private diagnoses. And the parents, indeed, may have to shop around to find a diagnostician willing to make the diagnosis they seek. This system is warped, and it works against special services going to those children who may need them most.

It seems odd that parents have been driven to seek a diagnosis that something is wrong with their children. In the past, such a diagnosis was probably the last thing most parents would have wanted for their children.

Schools can question the private diagnoses they are handed, of course. But in U.S. society today, when almost anyone seems willing to sue almost anyone else for almost anything, schools are chary of litigation. They do not want to get involved in multiple, expensive lawsuits which they have a fairly substantial likelihood of losing. Moreover, if a school loses, it has to pay the parents' legal fees, whereas if the parents lose, they do not have to pay the school's legal fees. There is little doubt that, in today's social and legal climate, the system favors those who are willing to pay for diagnoses. There is also a tremendous incentive for schools to avoid litigation by giving in to parental demands. These demands for special services and accommodations are considered in the next chapter.

Chapter Four

Pretend That
No One Lost

*Issues Regarding Accommodations
and Special Services*

When we say that children with LDs receive a variety of special services, what exactly do we mean by special services? That question is not easily answered. Just as the law is vague as to exactly what measurements constitute a basis for an adequate diagnosis of learning disabilities, so is it vague as to what services should be provided to children diagnosed as having learning disabilities. Moreover, the exact accommodations vary with the learning disability.

Pros and Cons Regarding Accommodations

Accommodations can serve a valuable purpose when they help a child correct a deficiency. Thus, if a child has difficulty processing the sounds of words, it makes sense for someone to help the child learn how to process these sounds. If a child has trouble in mathematics, it makes sense to provide extra help in mathematics to enable the child to achieve parity with other students. But some of the time, accommodations lead the child to worse, not better, achievement.

Sometimes children who cannot do something well—read or do mathematics—are given watered-down instruction that not only fails to help them correct their weakness, but actually leaves them even weaker relative to their peers. Their self-esteem may increase because they learn better in the classroom and their grades may go up as their performance improves, but the diluted instruction impairs the development of their reading and leaves them even less able to compete in the real world than they were before. When they leave school, employers may be reluctant to hire them because they may lack the basic literacy skills expected of employees in most semiskilled and skilled jobs.

Alva, a hypothetical student, is not doing well in his fourth-grade reading program. Although he is in the lowest reading group, he is failing to keep up with the other children in that group. Alva is mainstreamed, so it is his teacher's responsibility to provide him with the services he supposedly needs. The teacher "solves" Alva's reading problem by finding him a textbook that is two years below his grade level, and from a program that is different from the one used in the school. Alva is able successfully to handle the material in this basal and starts to feel better about his reading skills. His parents are happy to see that he is gaining more confidence in himself. But when Alva takes the statewide mastery test, he receives a score lower than that he received the preceding year, reflecting the diluted program of instruction that he received.

Diluted instruction is a poor option, because even if it improves self-esteem, the improvement is at the expense of better performance. The student thinks more and more of him- or herself for accomplishing less and less. Besides, not all students respond to such instruction with higher self-esteem. They may realize that they are receiving a watered-down program and as a result actually feel worse about themselves.

Another way accommodations are made, more often at the college level than at the elementary and secondary levels, is simply to excuse students from subjects in which they have difficulty. So, for instance, students who have trouble in mathematics are excused from taking mathematics. This approach represents an educationally bankrupt policy and is extremely detrimental, for several reasons.

First, the assumption seems to be that if students find a subject difficult, they should not have to study that subject. The more general message may be that as soon as students encounter something difficult, they should look for a way out. Most important, they may learn that society advocates copping out as soon as a task becomes truly challenging.

Second, this option assumes that these children are unable to learn the subject or subjects with which they have difficulty. This assumption is also false. Anyone who does not have profound or severe mental retardation can learn basic reading and mathematics skills. Schools may make things easier on themselves when they spare the bother and expense of having to teach children who find subjects very challenging, but in the long run, they do not make things easier on the children.

Teaching to Strengths

Often, the problem is not what is being taught but how it is being taught. Consider an example from the experience of a teacher who for years taught a difficult statistics course. He discovered that some students simply seemed to get it, whereas other students simply did not. Some students seemed to be smart in the mathematics of the course, others not, and there did not appear to be much he could do to change things. Perhaps the students who were doing poorly had a math disability; those students may well have thought so.

One day the teacher picked up a book on how to teach this particular statistics course. The book showed how topics that

he was teaching algebraically—through formulas and equa-
tions—also could be taught geometrically—through diagrams
and pictorial representations. The day after he finished the
book, he decided to try out a sample lesson. Instead of teaching
the lesson algebraically, as he always had in the past, he taught
the lesson geometrically, using diagrams and pictures.

The results were astonishing. Students who previously had
seemed to understand practically nothing in the course understood the lecture very well. Other students, who had been class
stars when the class was taught algebraically, now found the material difficult to understand. The teacher realized that the problem had not been with the students all those years, but with
him. He had taught in a way that did not well suit their multiple
ways of learning. When he changed the way he taught, students
who might have seemed to be have a disability in math proved
to be anything but. Students who seemed to be mathematically
talented no longer seemed quite so adept. The point is that all
students will learn better if they are taught at least some of the
time in a way that matches their strengths.

The problem is that teachers typically teach to their own
strengths, rather than to those of their students.[1] In other
words, they teach in a manner with which they are comfortable. The statistics teacher in our example taught his course algebraically because that is how he processed the material.
Moreover, he was uncomfortable teaching the course geometrically because that was not his preferred way of thinking. Unfortunately, teachers are susceptible to thinking that the way they
best process the material is the "right" way to process the material, with the result that students who process the material in
another way may be viewed as stupid or as having a disability.

The problem applies elsewhere. A newly popular learning disability is foreign-language disability. Students seek this label
primarily to get out of foreign-language requirements. We believe this disability is a fiction. It does not make sense. Virtually
all children, including almost all children who seek and even

those who are given the diagnosis of having a foreign-language disability, learn to speak a native language. Now ask yourself, How does nature know which language is a foreign language? If a child learned a first language, why would he or she somehow have a disability in learning another one? A child may have trouble learning, say, Spanish, as a second language, but millions of children around the world learned it as a first language, and this child would have learned it as a first language had he or she been born in a Spanish-speaking culture.

There probably is no specific foreign-language disability, but there is a lot of inadequate teaching of foreign languages. People in the United States should be suspicious. Why is it that Flemish children in Belgium routinely learn three, four, or more languages? Do they have a foreign-language hyperability? Why do many children in the Netherlands and in Switzerland routinely learn several languages? Yet children in the United States are much less likely successfully to learn languages other than English. The problem is not in any so-called language-learning disability, it is in attitudes toward learning foreign languages and in the manner in which they are taught.

Students in Flemish-speaking Belgium or in the Netherlands quickly learn that they will not be able to thrive knowing only their native tongue; to succeed as adults, they will need to learn other languages. And they do. But children in other countries, such as France, French-speaking Belgium, and the United States, grow up among people who believe, for the most part, that others should learn their language, that is, French or English. Children in these countries thus are much less likely to learn languages other than their own. They suffer not from a foreign-language disability, but from a lack of motivation to learn foreign languages.

The way in which foreign languages are taught often does not help matters along. Some teachers themselves barely speak the languages they are supposed to be teaching. Or they may speak them, but not know how to teach them in a way that accommodates the variety of thinking and learning styles of their students.[2]

For example, when Jeffrey was in secondary school, he studied German. He was not particularly motivated to learn German, seeing it primarily as a requirement for college admission rather than as a skill that might prove useful to him later in life. He was taught German largely through what is sometimes called the mimic-and-memorize method: The teacher says a phrase; the students repeat the phrase; then the teacher says a variant of the phrase, and the students repeat that variant. Eventually, the students learn how to build up many variants of the phrase. This audiolingual method certainly works well for some students, but it does not work well for others. Some students may prefer or even feel that they need visual presentation of the words; some students may learn better if they are presented with the grammar first; and so on.

Jeffrey's performance in these courses was not very good and was well below his performance in other courses. If one were to subtract his IQ from some kind of mimic-and-memorize aptitude score, he might well appear to have a foreign-language disability. One of his German teachers thought so. She commented that she could tell from the way he performed that, to the extent he was succeeding at all, it was because of his general intellectual ability. She could tell from the kinds of errors he was making that he had little foreign-language ability. He was inclined to believe her, because his foreign-language performance was not so good. He placed out of foreign language in college and never took a foreign-language course again. He did not want to risk the low grades and low self-esteem that would be the inevitable results of taking such a course.

Many years later, when Jeffrey was an adult, he was called on to work in France. Jeffrey used the general ability on which his teacher had complimented him to figure out that he had better learn some French. So he hired a student as a tutor and started taking French lessons.

To his amazement, he learned French quite rapidly and with no great pain. Within a few years of once-a-week lessons he was speaking and reading, and today he is fluent enough to carry on conversations and to do his work in French. How was this possible? It was really quite simple. He was taught French by a method different from the one that had been used to teach him German. He learned French by the direct method, or the method of learning from context, which teaches a language in the natural context in which it is spoken. In addition, Jeffrey was highly motivated to learn French because he needed it to work in France.

The point of this story is that what appeared to be some kind of foreign-language disability was no such thing. It was the result of teaching that was a poor match to Jeffrey's style of learning. There was nothing wrong with the method of teaching per se; it just didn't fit him. Too often, we excuse teaching that is inappropriate for a student by claiming that the student has some kind of disability. It is so easy to place on the student the blame that correctly belongs on our inadequate methods of instruction.

We hasten to add that children with various kinds of disabilities may have extra difficulty in aspects of foreign-language learning. For example, the student who has a disability in reading English can expect to have difficulty in learning to read German or French. But this difficulty is not the result of a special foreign-language disability, it is the result of the original reading disability.

The same general ideas we discussed with respect to learning a foreign language apply to learning to read. In recent years, the whole-language method has dominated the teaching of reading. In this approach, students read stories and other literature and are supposed to acquire reading skills in their whole, natural contexts rather than through phonics or drills. The use of this method without any phonics training is a good example of the dissociation of practice from research. Research does not support a pure phonics approach either (i.e., an approach that emphasizes sound-symbol relationships exclusively), which can be boring, unmotivating, and unnatural to many students. In general, research supports a blending of whole language with phonics training that helps children learn the correspondences between visual patterns and various sound combinations.[3]

Teaching many students who have reading disabilities exclusively by the whole-language method is like prescribing running exercises to help an individual who is temporarily confined to a wheelchair. The individual in the wheelchair is no more ready for running exercises than is the student with a reading disability for the exclusive use of the whole-language method. As a complement to this method, the student also needs the phonics training that will enable him or her to decode the words.

We wish to repeat that we are not opposed to the whole-language method, but rather support a skillful blending of whole language with phonics. Almost no one wants to go back to the sterile Dick, Jane, and Sally basal readers of some of our childhoods. But by itself, whole language is not teaching many children to read any more than mimic and memorize teaches all children foreign language. Children need to be taught in a style that fits them. Pure whole language is not for many children, and it certainly is not for the large majority of children with reading disabilities.

There are always some who will say that empirical research conducted by university researchers represents performance under unrealistic conditions. If you do not trust such research, you can conduct your own simple test by comparing the textbooks of today with the textbooks of twenty, forty, or sixty years ago. As noted earlier, the more recent texts at a given grade level, in each case, represent a lower level of difficulty.[4] The difference is large. If you go way back, to the McGuffey readers, you will be stunned that young children were ever expected to read such difficult material. There is no better way to see that instruction in U.S. schools is not succeeding for many students than to look at this evidence of decreasing levels of literacy. Students need to learn to read, not to be given accommodations in the demands made on their reading.

Accommodations have been applied not only to instruction but to assessment, and for many parents, accommodations in assessment can be the primary motivation for seeking an LD diagnosis. The prize accommodation is in the administration of tests without time limits.

Almost all children in the United States have to take standardized tests in school. These may be statewide mastery tests or they may be nationally administered standardized tests. Examples of the latter include the Iowa Tests of Basic Skills (ITBS), the Metropolitan Achievement Tests (MAT), the California Achievement Test (CAT), and especially college-admissions tests such as the Scholastic Assessment Test (SAT) and the American College Test (ACT).

The option for a child to take such tests without time limits can be very attractive to parents. The points garnered by answering problems that otherwise would have gone unanswered could be the points that get the child into a higher track, a better private school, or a better college.

The preoccupation with the question of whether LD children should be given untimed or generously timed tests, and thus be given what many see as an unfair advantage, has obscured a more important issue: Why are standardized tests so strictly timed in the first place? Why should any child have to take such tests?

The reasons are complex. One is practicality: Schools generally want standardized tests that can be administered in the minimum time possible. Schools have many items on their agendas and do not want to divert too much time to testing. A second reason is that if tests were untimed, it would be difficult to say when the people taking the test would have to leave.

They might want double time. Or they might want to stay overnight, just in case the solution to a particularly intractable problem occurred to them. But the main reason tests are strictly timed probably relates to implicit theories (preconscious conceptions) of intelligence on the part of those who create the tests.

Some years ago, Sternberg and a group of colleagues decided to initiate a study of people's conceptions of intelligence. Just what do people mean when they speak of someone as being intelligent?[5] We tested several people in diverse settings, such as a supermarket, a train station, and a library. The study revealed a number of things, among them that people viewed intelligent individuals as fast—as thinking fast, reading fast, speaking fast, and so on. Speed was an important ingredient in people's recipes for what makes a person smart.

When we presented the results of our study to the granting agency that was funding the research, the officials of the agency were skeptical. We had done our study using laypeople as participants, and the granting agency wondered why we would ask laypeople what they thought constituted intelligence. What would such people know about intelligence? We should have studied experts in the field, they told us.

Not wanting to see our funding disappear, and believing that their suggestion was a reasonable one, we decided to study experts in the field of intelligence as well. So we conducted essentially the same study, but this time we used experts from the United States and Canada—people with Ph.D.s in psychology who had published extensively on intelligence. We found that the experts, when asked the same question, said that the intelligent person is someone who thinks quickly, reads quickly, speaks quickly, and so on. In other words, the experts said essentially what the laypeople had said, although in a more complex way, with respect to speed of processing.

We were not surprised. For one thing, the experts and the laypeople were part of the same culture. For another thing, many of the experts were among those responsible for the strictly timed tests. Of course they believed speed was important to intelligence!

The problem is that the notion that speed is essential to intelligence is a culturally bound notion. Many and probably most cultures of the world do not closely associate speed with intelligence.[6] Instead, they may associate intelligence with profundity, care in problem solving and decisionmaking, and careful consideration of all options when making a judgment. This notion is not limited to non-Western cultures. An American famous for his work on conventional intelligence tests at one point defined intelligence as the ability to withhold an instinctive response.[7] An Australian theorist of the evolution of intelligence came to exactly the same conclusion, starting from a totally different theoretical standpoint.[8] In other words, even those theorists whose roots are in Western culture realize that there may be more to intelligence than just responding quickly to test items.

If one thinks about intelligence in an everyday sense, one almost certainly will come to the same conclusion. When we are trying to decide whether to take a particular job or whether to marry a particular person or whether to have children or whether to buy a certain house, we are scarcely in a position to want to rush to judgment. People will not be impressed if we tell them that we made important decisions such as these in the thirty seconds to a minute or two that we typically spend on individual intelligence-test problems. In other words, in real-world judgment and decisionmaking tasks, people generally do not rush to judgment.

Of course, in some situations rapid decisionmaking can be important. An air-traffic controller constantly needs to be making rapid decisions, for instance. And the driver of an automobile scarcely has time to reflect deeply on the situation if another automobile is bearing down from the other direction, but in the same lane. In the large majority of everyday situations that people confront, however, quick judgment is neither common nor desirable.

A more useful view of the relation between speed and intelligence is that intelligence involves the ability to be fast (or slow) in judgment and decisionmaking, but, more importantly, it involves knowing when to be which. In other words, the most important decision may be one of time allocation: How much of one's time is a particular problem worth?

From this point of view, the question of whether children with learning disabilities should receive a special accommodation with respect to time limits is moot, because the time limits are themselves largely inappropriate. Instead of measuring how fast children can solve problems and make judgments, we should be measuring whether the children know how much time various problems are worth. This assessment should be made for all students, not just for those with learning disabilities or for those without them.

Inventing special accommodations for tests represents at least as much a sociopolitical agenda as it does a psychological or educational one. In some respects doing so creates a two-tier society, encompassing one group that is held to one standard and another group that is held to a different standard. The result, which already has started to permeate U.S. society, is that those who do not receive the accommodation—or who do not see their children receive it—may feel that those who do receive it are benefiting from an unfair advantage—that those children are "jumping the queue."[9] In essence, they may view the accommodations as a double standard that enables some children who are less able—or who have disabilities—to exploit the system in a way that benefits them to the disadvantage of others.

Are they right? There is no one answer to this question, but the question gets to the heart of what we mean by an equitable society. Suppose we are using test scores in high school to predict performance in college. The accommodations will make sense if the children who receive the accommodations in instructions and testing in high school receive the same accommodations in college. After all, then the same special conditions are applied to both predictor and criterion. Now suppose we are using test scores to predict job performance. Again, should there be accommodations? It depends on whether the same accommodations will be made on the job. This is where we enter a particularly difficult situation.

Suppose someone wants to hire a lawyer. The individual reasonably may expect the lawyer to read about as many principles of law and as many potentially relevant cases as possible. But what if the lawyer cannot read or can read only haltingly? Can the individual expect the same level of service from such a lawyer as from any other? Or do we foresee a society in which tax money someday will go toward providing accommodations to professionals, such that lawyers certified as having a reading disability will be provided with readers who do their reading for them? To have such a society, we must be willing to pay for it, or for a society in which accountants with math disabilities hire others to do their math for them, or whatever. There may exist law firms today that have the financial wherewithal to provide these accommodations, but we suspect that law firms that willingly would provide such accommodations, especially at their own expense, are few and far between.

The kind of society being described here poses certain problems. For one thing, tax rates would be exorbitant. More important, the society would be encouraging people to capitalize on weaknesses rather than on strengths. This is the road down which accommodations as they now are conceived ultimately may lead U.S. society. It could become a society of people who sue when they cannot become lawyers or be accepted to law school because they cannot read, or who sue when they cannot become accountants or be accepted to accounting school because they cannot do basic mathematics.

U.S. society is moving down this road. Almost all individuals have notable strengths. A person may have a reading disability but be very creative, or have a math disability but be very good in practical decisionmaking. Yet, sadly, whatever strengths the individual has are sometimes ignored in favor of attention to the person's weaknesses.

Some would like to create a society based on a Jacksonian kind of democracy, with an underlying philosophy that anyone should be allowed to do and must be capable of doing almost anything.[10] A better model might be one in which people's strengths are nurtured. In such a society, people who received the best instruction in reading but still were not optimal readers would find a job that did not put a premium on reading. These people might have creative skills, for example, that could lead to success in hundreds of occupations, including many highly skilled occupations, such as sculpture, painting, conducting, composing, photography, playing a musical instrument, and computer programming.

The Wrong Path

How could we have started down the path of encouraging people to capitalize on weaknesses rather than on strengths? As is often the case, the goal was noble—to ensure that students with learning disabilities received the kind of education to which they were entitled. Too often in the past, teachers gave up on these students rather than allowing them to make full use of their gifts.

Along the way, though, some things began to go wrong. In typical American fashion, what began as a quest for justice became perceived by some people as an entitlement. Some children and their parents began to see accommodations as a right. Powerful organizations wielded their political and economic clout to ensure that the system would continue to develop in the way it had been going. Now there are so many individuals with a vested interest in the developing system that it will be difficult to change it.

Who are these people? One group comprises some of those diagnosed as having learning disabilities. A second group comprises some of their parents. A third group includes some of the people who earn a living making diagnoses. If parents did not find it worthwhile to seek private diagnoses that would benefit their children, a whole cadre of diagnosticians would quickly be out of jobs. Finally, all those engaged in formulating and providing the special-service accommodations would be at risk of finding themselves without anything to do.

One should not criticize these individuals for having vested interests: Everyone does. But in this case, the vested interests may not be in the ultimate best interest of either children with learning disabilities or the society in which they live.

Those individuals who do not receive special accommodations may not want to appear to begrudge those who do receive them. So, for the most part, the unaccommodated are likely to say nothing. The result is that an imbalance is created whereby increasingly large proportions of school budgets are allocated to increasingly small proportions of schoolchildren.

We believe that children with LDs should receive special services. But we believe that the fairest way for them to do so is not at the expense of other children, but in addition to full services for other children. Because education budgets often are fixed and less than generous, this does not usually happen. As a result, other groups may receive proportionately less of the school-budget dollar.

The irony is that U.S. society may be hurting rather than helping children with LDs. The society may be giving these children false expectations, when in fact it does not continue to provide after the school years the crutches that it provides during these years.

A society can decide to provide the same support throughout an individual's career that it provided to the individual in school. There could be tax-supported professional note takers for prosecutors or judges, or perhaps for doctors attending conferences. Such a possibility perhaps needs to be considered seriously. From one point of view, such assistance represents an attempt to achieve equity for all members of a society.

There are three potential problems with this proposal. The first problem is paying for it. As the number of individuals identified as having a learning disability approaches 20 percent of the general population, can society afford this kind of canopy of protective services? The second problem is finding appropriate jobs for these individuals. Does the state want a prosecutor who cannot understand fully what the judge is saying because of a language disorder? Do individuals want lawyers who understand only a fraction of what goes on in a courtroom because of an attention disorder? The third problem is another point of view on equity. Does the society believe that professionals in jobs that typically require reading, who do not read for themselves, are truly comparable to those without such difficulties? The answers to these questions are not straightforward. A society has to make hard decisions about how to educate children and what best to educate them for.

Clearly there are many problems with the way in which U.S. society is educating children who have learning disabilities. Might society have a better handle on educating these children if its members better understood the science behind their disabilities? We consider the science of learning disabilities in the next part of the book, concentrating on disabilities in reading.

Part Two

The Science of
Reading Disabilities

At the beginning of the book, we stated as our main thesis that learning disabilities are labeled as such through the interaction of an individual with the environment. Virtually all individuals have disabilities of one kind or another, but society chooses to label only some of these as learning disabilities.

In the first part of the book, we emphasized how the interaction between the individual and the environment plays a crucial role in determining who is labeled: Society decides it particularly values certain specific abilities, and people who show lower levels of those specific abilities are said to have specific disabilities. Moreover, certain environments tend to nurture some skills, whereas other environments nurture other skills. A child will ultimately be identified as having a learning disability or not depending on the kind of environmental support that child received in the home for the development of certain skills. Every child enters a lottery of sorts when he or she is born. But the lottery is not biological; a child is not born with a disability. Rather, it is the environment in which the child happens to live that determines whether that child will be labeled as having a learning disability.

We believe we have made a strong case that disabilities are not solely or even primarily a function of the individual. In emphasizing the role of the environment, we set ourselves apart from investigators who are sometimes called intrinsic theorists, meaning that they view learning disabilities as a function solely or primarily of the individual.[1]

The environment is only part of the story, however. Learning disabilities are identified through the interaction of the individual with the environment. In this second part of the book, we concentrate on the internal workings of the individual. We argue that there are important cognitive and biological bases of learning disabilities. In so arguing, we set ourselves apart from investigators who theorize that learning disabilities are exclusively or primarily a societal phenomenon with no significant biological component at all.[2]

Let's start over then, concentrating on the cognitive and biological processes of the individual. As we have pointed out, and as Joseph Torgesen and others have stated as well, what schools and society do in labeling children as having a learning disability has little or nothing to do with the science of LD.[3] Labeling decisions often are largely politically and ideologically driven. This state of affairs may seem odd. After all, why would there be a science of LD, if not to help identify and teach children with LDs? But there are several reasons why societal practices are largely independent of the science of LD, which has progressed rather far. Three of these reasons are:

1. *The technical prose and jargon of science.* Scientists have a language of their own, not because they want to be obscure, but because they want to be precise. A typical scientific article is written in a scientific jargon with which few laypeople are familiar; thus it is easy for laypeople to misunderstand. Whereas scientific jargon improves communication among scientific professionals, it impedes or can even destroy communication between scientific professionals and laypeople, or even educators trained in the LD field. The inaccessibility of the prose results in its being largely ignored by the educational, legal, and other communities with a stake in the issues.

2. *Different opinions as to what constitute the burning issues.* For parents, a burning issue is whether their child with a learning disability is going to get the services they believe that child needs. For school superintendents, a burning issue might be where to find the funds for special-education efforts to meet legal requirements. For scientists, a

burning issue might be to determine what chromosome or chromosomes carry the gene or genes that contribute to the development of a particular type of learning disability. Another burning issue for scientists might be understanding the kinds of errors children with reading disabilities make when they read nonwords (letter strings that sound like words but are not words). Nonscientists, including educators of children with learning disabilities, might have different views on what the hot problems are. Because the hot issues for scientists are often not the hot issues for those who have to deal on a day-to-day basis with children with LDs, the work of the scientists may seem largely irrelevant to everyday concerns.

3. *Inaccessibility of published information.* Scientists often tend to publish their work in what are, for the public, obscure and difficult-to-obtain scientific journals. These journals cannot be found in bookstores and even in most town or city libraries. Moreover, the subscription prices tend to be so high that no one other than a scientist or a librarian would be likely to obtain a subscription. Thus, even if laypeople wanted to read these journals, they probably would have great difficulty obtaining them.

Why do scientists often publish in such obscure places? For better or worse, they seek out these publications because they know where the academic credit is to be found. They get credit within their field for publishing in these journals, much as students get credit for their performance on tests. Often, the more rigorous and technical the journal, the greater the amount of scientific credit to be had. So, ironically, the more inaccessible the scientific article is to the general public, the more the scientist is likely to be rewarded in the field for his or her work. To the extent that scientists care about their fame and fortune within their field, as well as their ability to get grants that enable them to do their work, they have to care about the academic system.

Books such as the one you are reading now, in contrast, typically earn their authors little or no scientific credit, or may even earn the authors penalty points. Some scientists consider it lowbrow, unscientific, and even a waste of time to write for a popular audience. The result, of course, is that the diffusion of even useful scientific results into the world at large is slow.

A corollary result is that books on LD for lay audiences sometimes are written by people who know the least about the science of the field. Of course there are exceptions. But the more people know of this science, the less incentive they may have to write an easy-to-read book!

We believe that schools could do much better if they took the science of learning disabilities into account. For this reason, in this part of the book we present the science in a form that we hope will be both comprehensible and useful.

Chapter Five

The Mind of the Child with LD
Cognitive Bases of Reading and Reading Disabilities

In this chapter, we concentrate on the cognitive bases of reading and reading disabilities. Virtually all tests assessing learning disabilities are cognitive tests. To understand how and why these tests are used to identify individuals with learning disabilities, it is important to understand the cognitive processes underlying learning disabilities. Interventions are also at the cognitive level, so understanding these interventions requires an understanding of basic cognitive theory as well.

There are many different paths to learning to think and learning to read. In this chapter we discuss some of the most common paths. Many steps are common to all children. What differs is how well the children complete the steps and how quickly they complete them, or, in some cases, whether they complete them at all. Our account meets with consensus among many, though certainly not all, investigators of reading.

Figure 5.1, adapted from *Off Track*, shows how the stages in the development of reading can lead either to proficient reading or to reading disability. Ultimately, proficiency of accomplished

98

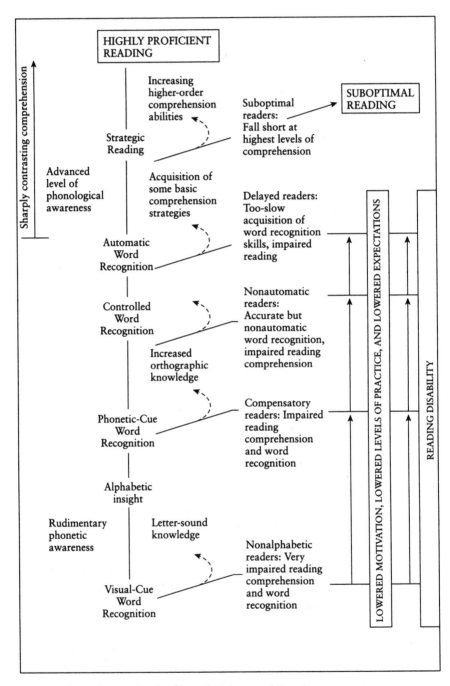

Figure 5.1   Stages in the Development of Reading

reading is a function of two factors—comprehension (accuracy) and fluency (speed). Accuracy and speed evolve as the individual passes through five stages of development of reading skills: visual-cue word recognition, phonetic-cue word recognition, controlled word recognition, automatic word recognition, and proficient adult reading. These stages are described next.

Visual-Cue Word Recognition

Children may start along the road to reading by recognizing visual cues to words.[1] In this phase of reading acquisition, children use visual shapes to aid them in recognizing words. Some of what they are learning is actual reading, for example, the distinctive visual appearance of the word *I* or the equally distinctive appearance of the word *a*.

Other cues may be quite different in kind. For example, prereaders may recognize golden arches as the symbol for McDonald's. They may use both the shape and the color of the arches to achieve this recognition. Indeed, advertisers try to choose logos that will be easy to recognize, and advertisers who want to appeal to children know that their logos have to be colorful and visually distinctive.

Relatively few children with reading or other disabilities have difficulty in this phase of learning to read. Those who do have difficulty at this stage develop severe disabilities. They become nonalphabetic readers who are extremely impaired in their ability to recognize words. Contrary to earlier beliefs about visual deficits,[2] problems in visual recognition are actually quite rare. When they occur, they most likely can be remedied with that most basic of all aids—glasses. Most preschoolers and kindergartners achieve this phase of reading (or, one might properly say, "prereading") with little or no difficulty between the ages of two and five years.

Advocates of a pure whole-language approach to reading—in which children learn to read by recognizing whole words in natural contexts—often exaggerate the importance of visual cues to word recognition. Such cues are important, but there are probably virtually no children who learn English who rely exclusively on visual cues.

Phonetic-Cue Word Recognition

The second phase in the acquisition of reading skills might be referred to as phonetic-cue word recognition. In this phase, children learn how to use some phonetic cues to aid in word recognition. Typically, this phase occurs between five and six years of age, in kindergarten or first grade. Children will be helped through this phase if they receive at least some instruction in phonics. Some children begin to show signs of having reading disabilities at this time.

Many component skills go into phonetic-cue word recognition. What are some of these main skills?

A first skill is *phonemic awareness,* also called phonological awareness, phonological sensitivity, and phonemic segmentation.[3] We know quite a bit about this skill because it has been probably the most widely studied of the skills involved in the acquisition of reading.

Strictly speaking, phonemic awareness pertains to spoken rather than to written language. It develops as children begin to decode the spoken structure of a language. One can learn quite a bit about a language just by becoming phonemically aware. For example, people who are illiterate may have no idea how sounds correspond to written symbols, but they may be able to speak and understand spoken language perfectly.

Several exercises can help children develop phonemic awareness. Becoming aware of and recognizing rhymes sensitizes children to word endings. As children learn that the words *me, see, tea,* and *key* rhyme, they learn that the words have in common the long *e* sound, regardless of how they are spelled and what they mean. Alliteration sensitizes children to word beginnings. For example, as they hear that Little Lorie lit the lamp, children begin to be aware of the common *l* sound at the start of each word.

Failure in phonetic-cue recognition can result in reading disability, but it is not the most common cause. When children fail in this phase, they show many of the same signs evinced by children who fail in the visual phase. They become essentially compensatory readers, trying to devise compensatory strategies to increase their understanding. They use visual cues to recognize words, but this recognition is highly incomplete. Their reading comprehension will be extremely poor, in large part because of their inability to recognize the words they are supposed to comprehend. They will have difficulty developing comprehension strategies simply because the input needed for good comprehension is never fully received and adequately processed by the brain.

How do reading specialists actually measure children's ability to process phonemes? A number of different tasks are used, both in the laboratory and in other situations in which it is necessary to make a diagnosis concerning reading disability. These tasks can be used with children from roughly the first-grade level (about six or seven years of age) through adulthood, as adults who are deficient in phonemic-awareness skills have difficulty with these tasks as well.

One such task is called *phoneme deletion:* Children are asked to say a word with a phoneme deleted. So, for example, they might be asked to say the word *make* with the /k/ sound deleted, producing the sounds of *may.* For children without phonemic awareness this seemingly simple task can be quite difficult.

Another task, which measures a slightly more advanced level of skill, is the *pseudoword reading* task. In this task, the individual might be asked to say what the word spelled b-l-e-t-s would sound like. Because individuals have no meaning cues on which to draw, they must rely exclusively on the correspondence between the letters and the sounds that these letters produce.

Educators also may be interested in developing a second skill, phonological coding in working memory. Normal readers find it easier to memorize rhyming than nonrhyming material because they use the rhyme as a clue for encoding the material they are learning and later for retrieving the material they have memorized. Readers who have difficulties in utilizing phonological coding recognize rhymes, but are less able than normal readers to use rhyme as a clue for encoding material into working memory and later retrieving it as needed. An exercise that helps develop phonological coding in working memory is to have children memorize poetry and then retrieve the poetry as much as possible. The instructor repeatedly points out to the children how the rhyme can help them encode and later retrieve the poetry.

Assessors, too, may be interested in assessing children's skill in phonological coding in working memory. In a *phonological coding in working memory* task, children may be asked to memorize two lists of words, one that contains phonetically confusable words and another that does not. For example: (1) dog, (2) set, (3) tab, (4) pit, (5) flu, (6) eat; and (1) man, (2) fan, (3) ban, (4) tan, (5) can, (6) pan. The question of interest is how much worse the person will do memorizing the second list. A normal reader will be confused by the phonetic similarity of the words in the second list, and thus will do worse remembering these words than remembering the words in the first list. An individual with a reading disability who has a difficulty with phonetics, however, will experience less interference as a result of the phonetic similarity of the words.

Controlled Word Recognition

In controlled word recognition, children make full use of phonetic (sound) and orthographic (spelling) cues in single-word reading. This level of word recognition usually develops around six to seven years of age, typically when, in the United

States, children are at about the second-grade level. For early readers at this level, the accuracy of single-word reading predicts about 80 percent of the individual-differences variability across children in their reading comprehension.

Children who begin to manifest a reading disability at the phase of controlled word recognition become deficient single-word readers. They show impaired word recognition as well as impaired reading comprehension. They are likely to attempt to read by developing strategies that enable them to make greater sense of what they are reading. For example, because they fail to recognize words, they may rely on the context in which a word occurs to figure out what the word is.[4] Note that the kinds of compensations these children make are different from those made by compensatory readers, who cannot even recognize phonetic cues, much less whole words.

At first blush, the use of context would appear to be a *good* reading strategy. After all, this strategy involves using higher-level decoding skills in reading, and what is wrong with that? The problem is not that children are using such strategies, but that they are using them for a nonoptimal purpose. For one thing, context cues are not reliable means of decoding single words. For another thing, these children are using the context cues *instead of* developing single-word recognition skills, and thus are likely to fail to develop fluent reading.

One way to determine whether children are using context cues to assist them in single-word reading is to present them with single words in different contexts that are more or less helpful in figuring out the words' meanings. Good single-word readers will show the same level of performance in reading the single words regardless of the relevance of the context, whereas poor single-word readers will show variable performance, depending on the helpfulness of the context.

Children who are good readers typically use decontextualization strategies, not to sound out words, but to seek understanding of words whose meanings they do not know. Deficient single-word readers, in contrast, use decontextualization strategies to figure out what the words are.[5]

Consider the sentence, "The *saccharin* had a sickly-sweet taste, perhaps because it was an artificial rather than a natural sweetener." A deficient single-word reader might use the context to figure out what word might plausibly go where the italicized word is. If the reader is familiar with the word *saccharin,* but is unable to recognize it as the letter string presented, he or she can match the sound of the word *saccharin* stored in memory to the letter string appearing in the sentence. The able single-word reader, on the other hand, would not use context in this way, because he or she would recognize that the letter string spelled *saccharin.* Rather, the able reader would use the context to figure out what the italicized word might mean, if he or she did not know.

As deficient single-word readers put more effort and attention into such compensatory strategies, they have fewer resources left over to help them get through difficult material. Even modestly difficult material may overwhelm them. They thus fall further and further behind in the development both of their reading skills and of their knowledge base.

Deficient single-word readers have a great advantage over nonalphabetic readers, however, because they at least understand the principles underlying the alphabet. They also have an advantage over compensatory readers, because they can sound out words—they don't just recognize the words as wholes. Thus, they may have a reading disability, but they can achieve limited degrees of reading proficiency.

Several tasks are used to measure controlled word recognition.

In one frequently used task, the *lexical-decision* task, real words or pseudowords (letter strings that look like words but have no meaning) are shown in random order for a very brief period of time, typically on a computer. The participant is asked to decide whether each word is a real word or a pseudoword. The primary measure of performance is the number of decisions correctly made.

A second task frequently used to measure controlled reading is the *single-word reading* task. In this task, words of different lengths and complexities are shown out of any context. The participant is asked to read these words aloud. The person's score on the task depends on the accuracy of his or her reading.

Automatic Word Recognition

In automatic word recognition, children learn to recognize words quickly, accurately, and with little conscious effort. This stage reveals individual differences primarily in speed rather than in accuracy of reading. Readers thus move beyond controlled word recognition not in their ability to recognize words, but in the speed and efficiency with which they recognize them.

Controlled versus automatic processing is on a continuum, and as a result, children can differ in the degree to which they automatize their recognition of words. Automatic word recognition is an important key to competent reading.[6]

In general, automatization is an important part of intelligence, broadly defined,[7] and plays a major role in many kinds of skilled performances. For example, when we learn to drive, we initially drive in a controlled and often halting fashion. Every movement—of our hands on the steering wheel, of our foot on the gas pedal or brake, even of our eyes as we scan the road—is likely to require a deliberate and conscious effort. One reason that novice drivers are so susceptible to accidents is simply that they have not automatized driving. When a situation arises that requires them to shift their processing resources, they are unable to shift because they still need to attend to the basics. Thus, a skilled driver, recognizing a situation that could lead to an accident, can basically ignore the fundamental elements of driving, which he or she has automatized, and therefore can devote full attention to the dangerous situation. A novice driver needs to keep attending to the fundamental elements of driving (such as where to put his or her foot to reach the gas pedal or brake) and thus cannot fully attend to the danger on the road.

Reading disability appears fairly frequently to result from automatization failure in reading.[8] The children who do not automatize tend to be nonautomatic readers, acquiring basic reading skills, but more slowly than and often not as completely as their counterparts. Moreover, the need of these children to devote a great deal of conscious effort to word recognition typically ends up impairing their comprehension skills. Often, children who start off with difficulties in automatization end up with difficulties in strategic reading, discussed next, because they just do not have the mental resources left to develop strategic-reading skills.

Skill in automatic word recognition can be measured by *naming* tasks. Participants are asked to name as quickly as possible relatively simple words that are shown to them. The measure of performance is the speed of word naming. Speed in naming pictures also proves to be an excellent predictor of automatic-reading skills, even though the task does not involve words.

Strategic Reading

The phase of strategic reading is the first explicitly to move beyond individual-word recognition.[9] In this phase, children develop specific strategies that help them understand what they are reading at the sentence and paragraph level.

Strategies in reading, or in anything else, sometimes are called *metacognitive strategies*, an expression that refers to one's understanding and control of one's own cognitive processes. In other words, in developing reading strategies, children understand what kinds of cognitive processes to apply when and in what measure.

What are some examples of such strategies? One strategy is adjusting one's reading to the difficulty of the material.[10] Children come to recognize that difficult material needs to be read more slowly and usually with more attention than does simple material.[11] Children who do not learn this strategy may find that they are reading difficult mathematical material in the same way in which they read novels, with potentially disastrous consequences.[12] Indeed, even many college students have not learned to adjust their reading speed to the nature of the material they are reading.

Another strategy is adjusting one's reading to the purpose for which one is reading.[13] For instance, one does not read the same way when preparing for a picky multiple-choice test on the material as when expecting a general essay question. And one reads differently still if there will be no test of comprehension at all.

In one study, college students were told to read sets of passages presented on a computer for the gist, for the main idea, for the nitty-gritty details, or for inference making. The students were given as much time to read as they wanted and could read passages for different purposes in any order they wished. A computer measured the amounts of time they spent on reading passages for the various purposes.[14]

The study showed that even average readers often read all the passages the same way, regardless of the purpose for which they were reading. As a result, they tended to be relatively ineffective readers when they had to understand nitty-gritty details or make inferences. Good readers, in contrast, varied the way they read material so as to spend more time and devote more effort to passages on which the test they received would be more challenging. Thus only the good readers were fully strategic.

Yet another important strategy involves utilization of knowledge. Good strategic readers recognize that they can and should use past knowledge to help them figure out the meaning of what they are reading. The more knowledge they can bring to bear on what they read, the better they are likely to understand it. Curiously, schools often teach knowledge in ways that render it inert. The student has the knowledge, but is unable to use it when he or she needs it. The result of such teaching is that students may not be able to make use of their knowledge when they are reading new and sometimes difficult material.

In this phase, it makes good sense for readers to use context to infer meanings of words. Note that strategic readers do not need such strategies to sound out the words, but to recognize what the words mean. A variety of cues help readers recognize the meanings of words.

Consider a very simple sentence that contains some of the kinds of cues readers might use to figure out word meanings: "It was early in the morning, and the *blen* shone brightly on the horizon."

A strategic reader would have little difficulty in figuring out that *blen* means sun. But how does the strategic reader do it? What does he or she do that is different from what the less strategic or even nonstrategic reader does?

The strategic reader uses three mental processes that are common to all strategic readers and to effective thinkers in general.[15] The first is called *selective encoding*. Selective encoding involves finding the cues in the sentence. The second process, *selective combination*, puts these cues together into a single package. The third process, related to the preceding discussion, is *selective comparison*, which brings past knowledge to bear on the present situation. "Early in the morning" is a temporal, or time-based, cue, which tells the strategic reader when the scene is taking place. "Shone" is a functional cue, which tells the reader what the *blen* does. "Brightly" is a descriptive cue, which tells how the *blen* shone. And "on the horizon" is a spatial cue, which tells where the *blen* shone. Other kinds of cues can be found in reading as well.

Children who manifest a reading disability at this phase fail to develop some or all of these strategies, or develop them so incompletely that they are unable to use them effectively. Part of our research has involved developing programs for teaching strategic reading to children in elementary school.[16]

The ELATE Reading Program

In our ELATE (Expert Learning for All through Teacher Education) program, developed through support from the U.S. Office on Educational Research and Improvement, children of roughly ten to eleven years of age learn to read strategically by applying analytical, creative, and practical skills to their understanding of what they read. This program, based on Sternberg's theory of successful intelligence,[17] is designed to help students read better in three related ways. First, it enables them to capitalize on their strength or strengths—analytical, creative, or practical—rather than to rely only on memory skills, in which many students do not excel. Second, it enables them to encode the material they read in three different ways rather than simply trying to memorize it. Third, it motivates students by increasing their interest in their learning. Students in the program have told us that they especially enjoy doing creative assignments because they rarely get an opportunity to express themselves so freely in school settings. Moreover, they are excited about reading when they see how they can use what they read in a practical way in their everyday lives.

The materials used in the ELATE program are more diverse and, from many students' points of view, more interesting and motivating than are the materials found in conventional basal (textbook) reading programs. In the following sections we give examples of both instructional and assessment materials. The instructional materials include both in-class assignments and homework assignments.

Examples of Instructional Materials

The instructional materials help students develop analytical, creative, and practical thinking skills that they can apply directly to their reading. We have chosen examples from the material we designed for the actual textbook the children were using, *Light Up the Sky*.[18]

Although activities are classified loosely as analytical, creative, or practical, these classifications represent emphases rather than fully discrete categories. Ultimately, we want children to learn to combine these skills rather than to use them separately.

In-Class Instructional Material
These materials are used in class to develop analytical, creative, and practical thinking skills to apply to reading.

Analytical
Analytical exercises develop analysis, judgment, and comparison skills. The following exercise also helps students learn to develop these skills in collaboration with other students. Each group is assigned a character from the textbook. Following is a set of instructions to teachers:

> ... Divide the students up into small groups and give each group a big piece of posterboard and assorted colored pens, pencils, etc. ... Tell the students that they are to spend time with their groups making a "portrait" of their assigned character. Emphasize that they should use their own understanding of a character based on the details in the story itself. Try to stress they should focus on what the words in the story tell them about the characters. ... Tell the students that when they present their character, they will also be expected to re-tell the events their character experienced in the story. . .

Creative
The goal in the creative items is not for students to generate "correct" answers, but for them to fantasize and invent imagi-

---

Words of Wisdom

By (Write your royal title here) _____

Why are there rainbows after a storm? How do rainbows get to be so many different colors? How can you get the pot of gold at the end of a rainbow?

Why do cows say "Moo" all the time? Why does this one word play such a big part in cow language? What are the cows saying?

---

native answers. In this exercise, students are asked to provide their own "words of wisdom" on challenging problems to which they are unlikely to know "correct" answers. In many cases, there are no correct answers.

Practical
The goal with these exercises is to encourage students to think of practical angles on what they read. The exercise here helps develop route-planning skills.

> Remind the students that, as they learned in the story, many slaves ran away from their masters and fled to the north, often with the assistance of the Underground Railroad. Tell the students that today they are going to do another small-group exercise to think more about what it must have actually been like to run away from slavery. . . . Each group is to imagine that they are coming up with a plan for a slave to travel from slavery in North Carolina to Canada [using a map, a set of tools, and a set of survival rules].

Homework Instructional Materials

These materials are used as homework instructional materials to help children develop analytical, creative, and practical thinking skills on their own.

Analytical

In the following exercise, students need to reminisce on an experience, and then describe, analyze, and communicate it so that another individual can understand it.

> Suppose you have just spent a special holiday with your relatives and friends. Your favorite cousin could not be there because he is in the Army and is stationed far away. Write your cousin a letter fully describing and analyzing the big day so that he will feel almost as if he had been there.

Creative

The children have read a story about the Bell family that refers to some good times and bad times. But these events are not fully described. The students are asked to take off from the text and invent descriptions of these events.

> The story is, in part, about the Bells' family history—the "good times" and "bad times" they have experienced living for generations along the National Road. Think of at least one "good time" and one "bad time" referred to in the story. As fully as you can, describe what these events may have been like and explain their importance to the Bell family.

Practical

An important part of everyday life is preparing for major events. In the story the children have read, the Bells are preparing for a major event. Children are asked to place themselves in the role of the Bells and describe what they would do to prepare for a big family gathering that is about to take place.

> In the story, the Bells have a large family gathering, full of food and different activities. It takes a lot of planning to put on such a big event. Pretend you are Jason's parents, and you are hosting the event. Describe some things you would do to prepare.

Examples of Assessment Materials

Here are some examples of actual materials we use to assess readers' analytical, creative, and practical vocabulary and comprehension skills. The first set of items measures vocabulary skills. Targeted vocabulary words are shown in italics. The second set of items measures comprehension skills.

Vocabulary-Skill Test Items
Analytical
In everyday reading, children never need to recognize vocabulary words out of context, as they sometimes do on vocabulary achievement tests. Words always occur in a context. We thus assess children's vocabulary skills in reading contexts, as shown.

> Scott played in the school marching band. On St. Patrick's Day the band was going to march in the town _____ . Scott was excited. He liked music, floats, and crowds of people.
>
> Which is the best choice to fill in the blank above?
> A. parade
> B. meeting
> C. hall
> D. movie

Creative

It is important for children not only to be able to recognize the meaning of a word, but also to be able to use the word in a sentence. Sometimes children are able to recognize the meaning of a word on a multiple-choice test, but are not able actually to use the word. We thus measure their ability to create a sentence that appropriately uses the word.

Use the word *imagination* in a sentence.

_____

Practical

If a student truly understands the meaning of a word, he or she should be able to use the word in context to understand what it signifies practically. We measure this skill with the following type of task.

After singing with the church choir three times on Christmas, Jodi found that her voice had become *hoarse*. To solve her problem, she should

    A. quit the choir.
    B. do some sit-ups before going to bed.
    C. learn more about horses.
    D. drink some tea and try not to talk.

Comprehension-Skill Test Items
Analytical
An important analytical skill is sequencing. We measure this skill through a time-line task.

Here is a "time line" of major events in the story in the order in which they happened.

Belva went to school → Miss Englehardt became dizzy → Belva taught the class → _____ → Belva used the lever to move the rock.

Which of the following events belongs in the blank above?

A. Miss Englehardt went home.
B. E.Z. went fishing.
C. E.Z. tried to move the rock.
D. Lewis Bennett moved the rock out of the cornfield.

Creative
In the next task, children are asked to create a description of a stage, given the context in which the stage occurs in the passage that they have been reading.

A theater company is putting on a play about Belva's life. The theater company has hired you to make the stage look like the inside of the schoolhouse where Belva went to school. Describe the stage.

Practical

An important practical skill is giving advice based on one's understanding of a situation. The task here measures this skill.

> Early in the story, Belva's mother says that the family has "a rock the size of hog" in the middle of their cornfield. What advice could Belva give her parents to help them solve this problem?

Early Data on the Program

The ELATE program has been implemented on an experimental basis in several inner-city middle schools, where improving reading levels was a top district priority. The first data-collection phase took place in the spring semester of 1998. Although the data are still being analyzed, some early data regarding teachers' and students' reactions to the program are available.

What we know so far is that teachers felt very positive about the program. For example, on a 7-point scale, with 1 low and 7 high, teachers rated the interestingness of the program to them at 6.4 and the interestingness of the program to the students at 6.0. They rated the level at which it motivated them at 6.2 and the level at which it motivated their students at 6.1. These numbers are very high in view of the overall dissatisfaction of the teachers with much of what they had been doing before.

When students were asked how they liked the program, 35 percent of the children indicated they liked the program very much, 51 percent liked it, 10 percent did not feel one way or another, and only 4 percent disliked it. Again, these figures need to be considered in the context of a student group that generally was not enamored of reading or the activities they were doing before.

We also found that the program had a substantial effect on teachers' classroom behavior. We made behavioral observations of teaching strategies both before and after teachers started implementing the program. The number of different memory and analytical activities the teachers presented to the students was about the same before and after the initiation of the program. But there was a whopping increase in the number of different creative and practical activities they used before and after introduction of the program. For a single lesson taught by nine different teachers, the average number of memory and analytical activities was eighteen both before and during the program. In contrast, the nine teachers had no creatively oriented activities before the program but fourteen during it. Similarly, they had only four practical activities before the program but eighteen during it. Thus, at the very minimum, the program has resulted in a major change in the way the teachers teach. Most important, we also found that the activities significantly improved many aspects of reading achievement,[19] although the data for this particular implementation of our ELATE program are not yet fully analyzed.

The main point we wish to make in describing our new intervention is that theory-based reading instruction is not a fantasy, but a reality. We can take existing cognitive theories, such as our own, and apply them to helping students to read better.

Basal readers are not theory based: They are designed largely to appeal to those who make decisions to buy textbooks. Such designs can and often do create useful material, but the material is likely to be less useful than material specifically designed to enhance theory-based targeted cognitive functions. Our own work on improvement of children's reading takes this latter approach. We design material to enhance targeted cognitive functions that have been shown to be important to reading and to thinking and learning in general.

Proficient Adult Reading

The last stage in the development of reading is proficient adult reading. In proficient adult reading, the individual has mastered higher-order comprehension skills. This phase can begin in later high school or in college, during the years of later adolescence, but many adults never reach this phase.

Individuals who are proficient adult readers go beyond both word-recognition skills and basic comprehension skills. They can analyze and evaluate arguments, pointing out strengths and weaknesses. They can recognize emotional appeals for what they are and not be swayed by them. They recognize fallacies in logic, both formal and informal. They can apply what they know to what they are reading, and conversely, transfer what they learn from what they read to other situations.

Many individuals never become proficient adult readers. They may grasp the gist of what they read, but not be able to analyze or evaluate it fully. Or they may not be able to infer the implications of what they read. Even a college education provides no guarantee that these skills will develop. On the one hand, individuals without these skills probably can get through their lives in an adaptive way and perform well at most jobs. On the other hand, they are likely to be highly susceptible to emotional appeals and informal logical fallacies. Thus, their comprehension tends to be more at the surface level of what they read rather than at the level of the deep structure underlying what they read.

What might be going on biologically while the cognitive processes of adult proficient reading are in action? This topic is considered in the next chapter.

Chapter Six

The Brain of the Child with LD

Biological Bases of Reading and Reading Disabilities

In Chapter 5, we discussed the cognitive bases of reading and reading disabilities pursuant to our argument that the individual as well as the environment is important in understanding reading disabilities. Cognitive functions all originate in the brain. In this chapter we will discuss what science has taught us about the biological bases of the cognitive functions involved in reading and reading disabilities.

There is one fundamental difference between cognitively and biologically oriented scientific work on the individual origins of reading disabilities. Whereas we believe and have attempted to show that cognitive work can be translated into better practices in school, we do not believe that biological work is yet at this point. So why even bother with it? The reason is that every day we come a little bit closer to understanding the linkage between biological functions and cognitive functions.

In the field of psychotherapy, biological understandings have contributed enormously to the development of a wide range of drug therapies. Today many individuals with symptoms of anxiety, depression, or other disorders can be helped more by a combination of drugs and psychotherapy than by either treatment alone. We believe that a day may come in the treatment of learning disabilities when drugs may be combined with cognitive interventions to yield more effective treatments than are now available through the cognitive interventions alone. But we are the first to say that we do not believe that day has come. We are still at the early stages even of mapping the mind.

In previous chapters we used the term *reading disability*. In this part of the book, along with this term, we will use the term *dyslexia,* because most genetic and biological studies use this term. Note that we use these terms interchangeably. When we refer to *dyslexia*, as when we refer to reading disability, we refer to a susceptibility that is expressed as an interaction between the individual and the environment, not just to a susceptibility within the individual or within the environment.

Mapping the Mind

Is there a difference between knowing something and merely believing that one knows something? Most people would argue that, even though there is an obvious factual difference between these two states (one either knows or does not know), confidence in one's knowledge and a willingness to articulate and promote it can have a significant impact on the field, whether the information is true or false.

For example, Herodotus, the Greek traveler, presumably thought he knew the world and how to get around in it pretty well. He bravely toured the Mediterranean, but mostly he collected stories about traveling from other people. Herodotus invested a lot of time and effort in synthesizing everything he and others observed in their journeys. He concluded, specifically, that Europe appeared to be as long as Africa and Asia put together and so wide that comparison with Africa and Asia was out of the question.

In general, Herodotus placed continents and islands in roughly accurate relative locations (i.e., Africa was to the left of Europe and Asia was to the right), but his estimates of relative sizes and distances were way off. He just had no idea of what the true comparative sizes were.

Herodotus strongly believed that he knew the world (and its map) very well, and his confidence was so convincing that his vision of the world served as the basis of knowledge for many cartographers. For two thousand years maps were made exclusively à la Greek—that is, based on Herodotus' recipe. Those maps indicated not only the location of particular features in the world, but also the state of knowledge about the world. For example, well-traveled bits of landscape loomed much larger than their actual size warranted. Eventually, the invention of compasses and mechanical clocks ushered in something of a cartographic revolution, which supplanted Herodotus' authority.

The irony is that although modern maps made Herodotus look somewhat foolish, the very existence of those maps was made possible by Herodotus and his feeling of knowing. Herodotus' belief in his own knowledge, even though the knowledge itself was mistaken, motivated the exploration of the world for two centuries and spawned a much more accurate understanding of geography.

Modern neuroscience, like the geography of many centuries ago, is primarily about maps.[1] Only, in neuroscience, experts map mental functions rather than continents or oceans. As in the case of geography, progress in mapping mental functions had to await the development of technology.

Medical doctors and philosophers always suspected that the brain had something to do with people's thinking and feeling. However, the first experimental breakthrough occurred only in the middle of the nineteenth century, when Paul Broca, a French physician, operated on the brain of a patient who suffered from aphasia, a specific speech disorder, and who could only say one word *(tan)*. Broca found a large cyst that produced a lesion in the left cerebral hemisphere. Similarly, eight other aphasic brains dissected by Broca also had left-hemisphere lesions. Broca correctly inferred that nine cases were way too many to be attributed to chance alone. He thus concluded that "the faculty for articulate language" is located in the left hemisphere.

Mountains of detail about the brain have been accumulated since Broca and other pioneers of brain mapping discovered that many mental functions are hardwired in the brain. This detail about the brain consists of added observations, however, not of new theoretical models. The huge advance in neuroscience in the last decades of the twentieth century has not been theoretical, but technological. Methodological developments, such as PET (positron-emission tomography) and MRI (magnetic resonance imaging), are not bases of theoretical ideas; they are tools.

Neuroscientists today are primarily cartographers, and the core of neuroscience is not scientific theory testing, but precise and accurate measurement. Nevertheless, this is not how the mass media and the public perceive neuroscience. The media, especially, all too often give a simplistic explanation of a complex phenomenon that, through simplification, loses the crux of that phenomenon. In popular belief, the brain has a location for everything, from speech to homosexuality. As is often the case in science, however, for better or for worse, reality is a lot more complicated than we usually believe it to be. As George Johnson, a *New York Times* writer, put it,

This is the next-to-last year of the much-vaunted *Decade of the Brain* and what is there to show for it? All kinds of data on which parts of the head light up when a person balances a checkbook or listens to classical rock, but very little about how all the chemicals sloshing around in the head combine to produce the neuronal buzz called thinking.[2]

Indeed, new brain sciences very well may reveal that everything we now believe to be true is way off. Yet the only way to arrive at a new point of knowledge is to believe, at some level, in our current knowledge, however inaccurate it may be, and to follow where it leads us.

The scientific enthusiasm for mapping the location of every mental function somewhere in the brain has not bypassed reading. The localization of both normal and deficient reading processes in the brain is being pursued with great passion and rigor. Before zeroing in on the brain processes of reading, however, we offer a brief overview of the stages in the development of the brain, which will help clarify our discussion.

The Developing Brain: What Can Go Wrong

The brain starts forming at the earliest stages of prenatal development. Driven by orders from genes, rapidly dividing cells of the gastrula (a hollow ball of cells from which the embryo arises) develop an indentation. The indented cells continue to extend into the interior of the gastrula, creating a two-walled ball. These inner cells form the foundation of the neural tube, which will develop into the brain and spinal cord and which generally is formed by the sixth week of fetal gestation.

Initially, the surface of the developing brain is smooth, with no fissures (also known as *sulci*) or folds (also called *gyri*). However, at about fourteen weeks of gestation, the process of brain division starts. The first fissure divides the brain into two halves *(hemispheres)*. The so-called *Sylvian fissure* separates the *parietal* (top, rear) and *frontal* (top, forward) parts *(lobes)* of the brain from the *temporal* (lower, side) lobe. By sixteen weeks, the division between the parietal and occipital (lower, rear) lobes is visible. The *central sulcus,* separating the frontal and parietal lobes, becomes apparent by the end of the twentieth week of gestation.[3]

Between the twenty-fourth and twenty-sixth weeks, the brain undergoes a dramatic change in weight. Because it is constrained by the bones of the skull, the brain folds itself (weeks 26 through 28), forming gyri. The process of the formation of gyri is called *gyrification*. This process reflects the formation of cortical neuronal connections, which is triggered by the migration of neurons to the *cortex* (the outer part of the brain). All neurons are produced in one brain "factory," called the *germinal matrix*, located deep down inside the brain. Once produced, neurons get assigned to their future work sites at the cortex of the brain. However, no transportation is provided, and neurons are expected to find their way to these locations themselves. This process is called *neuronal migration*. To grasp the magnitude of this endeavor, recall that the human brain has between 1 and 10 trillion neurons. This migration thus represents quite an exodus!

Neuronal migration happens in waves. The neurons leave the germinal matrix in patches and form brain layers, starting with the deepest layer and finishing with the most superficial layer. Neurons from every subsequent patch move through the neurons from the previous patch, forming columns. Once the migration is completed and columns are formed, neurons introduce themselves to their neighbors and form communication nets.

The complexity, organization, and beauty of brain development are amazing. Things can go wrong at every step of this process: The structural division of the brain into lobes may not succeed; the brain may not acquire critical mass; the neurons may get lost on the way to their assignments or they may get stuck in preexisting layers of neurons. In addition, adjacent neurons may misinterpret the identities of their neighbors and form faulty nets. And here we have considered only the most elementary unfolding mechanics of brain development!

All this machinery takes shape in the environment of the womb, which itself is another crucial variable in the equation of brain development. To appreciate the power of the womb, let us turn to a recent report published by *New Scientist* magazine. Victor Denenberg and his colleagues at the University of Connecticut in Storrs and the Jackson Laboratory in Bar Harbor, Maine, worked with a genetically identical group of mouse embryos suffering from an autoimmune disease similar to lupus in humans. (Lupus is an autoimmune disease that in milder forms causes skin irritations and in severe forms can attack internal organs and cause grave illness or death.) The researchers left one-third of the mice in their native mothers, transplanted one-third of the embryos into mice without the disease, and put the remaining third of the mice in the wombs of other autoimmune-deficient mice. To control for the variation in upbringing, all mice were brought up with healthy mothers. When the mice were weaned, researchers administered to them a battery of five learning tests.

Denenberg and his colleagues found that mice from genetically identical embryos implanted in different wombs performed mental tasks at different levels. Mice that had developed in the womb of a mouse with no autoimmune disease performed better, even though they had inherited the brain abnormalities associated with the autoimmune disease.

Equally important is a finding reported by Dennis McFadden and Edward Pasanen of the Department of Psychology and The Institute for Neuroscience at the University of Texas in Austin. McFadden and Pasanen have claimed that homosexual and bisexual females' prenatal exposure to higher-than-normal levels of androgens (male sex hormones) produced a partial masculinization of both peripheral auditory systems and some brain structures involved with sexual orientation. The behavioral effect in adults is that the inner ears of homosexual and bisexual women show less ability to detect weak sounds than do the inner ears of heterosexual women. Because fetal androgen exposure also has been linked to the development of homosexuality in women, the Texas researchers wondered if patterns of inner-ear function might mirror patterns of sexual orientation.[4] Whether it will be verified or not, this particular finding illustrates the point we are trying to make—each individual realization of brain development is the result of a complex interplay between the unfolding genetically controlled machinery of the embryo's cell differentiation and the environmental influences in the womb.

Having concluded this brief overview, let us return to the main query of this chapter, namely, what do we think we know about the reading brain?

At this point, scientists know relatively little about the mechanisms of brain development that are disrupted when an individual experiences reading problems. Most research today is carried out with developed brains, that is, with the brains of adults. The assumption is made, however, that whatever is wrong with the adult brain (assuming there has been no secondary injury such as brain trauma or stroke) is an outcome of some kind of dysfunction of brain development.

Scientists entertain two ideas about such possible dysfunction. The first idea is that there is something wrong with the structure of the brain in people with dyslexia. This point of view assumes that something unexpected happens during brain development that causes certain parts of the brains of people with dyslexia to be somehow different in shape or size from the brains of people without dyslexia. The corresponding hypothesis is that these structural differences result in poorer performance by individuals with dyslexia on reading-related tasks. A scientific methodology has been developed to verify this hypothesis. In so-called *structural* brain studies, scientists measure the brains of people with and without dyslexia and quantify group differences.

The second idea is that the structure of the brains of people with dyslexia does not differ significantly from that of the brains of people without dyslexia. What differs is how these brains are wired. In other words, although the brains of people with and without dyslexia are structurally similar, they function differently. The corresponding hypothesis in this case is that the differences in the wiring systems of people's brains result in the poorer performance of individuals with dyslexia on reading-related tasks. So-called *functional* brain studies seek to verify the hypothesis by comparing the functional performance of the brains of the two groups of people.

Are There Differences in the Brain Structures of People With and Without Reading Disabilities?

Studies of the structure of the brain first focused on the postmortem analysis of brains of individuals with a history of language and reading problems. It is impossible to overstate the importance of the role these studies have played in the development of brain sciences. Unlike walking and talking people, postmortem research participants do not object to having their brains stained, measured with a ruler, weighed, or surgically dissected. The only unfortunate thing about these studies is that, without the spark of life in the body, brains are nothing but strangely shaped formations of white and gray matter attached to each other. Postmortem brains are turned off and hence silent. They cannot provide useful verbal or other feedback.

The first postmortem studies relevant to our analysis were performed on the brains of four men with dyslexia. All four men showed unusual symmetry in the *planum temporale* (a brain structure located in the posterior part of the superior temporal lobe and known to be relevant to normal language function).[5] Whereas a normal individual tends to have an asymmetrical planum, the plana of the men with dyslexia were rather symmetrical. In normal individuals, the planum is larger on the left side of the brain in 65 percent of the population, whereas it is larger on the right side in only 11 percent of brains. Symmetry is rare.

Similar results have been obtained from a study of women. A postmortem study of three women with dyslexia also reported highly symmetrical plana in all three brains.[6] At the microscopic level, the brains of the people with dyslexia were found to have significantly more misplaced and unusually organized nerve cells, which, presumably, reflects the failure of neurons to reach their normal cortical targets during fetal development. The presence of unusually symmetrical plana is the most consistent finding about brain structure related to dyslexia.

What, then, is the nature of this unusual symmetry? Is the left planum of people with dyslexia smaller than the left planum of other individuals, so that the symmetry is a result of decreased (reversed) asymmetry? Or, is the right planum of people with dyslexia larger than that of people without dyslexia, so that the symmetry is a result of "overcome" (mixed) asymmetry?

Research on individuals without dyslexia has attempted to answer these questions. As most people would rather not have their brains stained, sliced, pierced with electrodes, injected with chemicals, hit with electrical shocks, or even slightly re-arranged by surgery, technology has been crucial to the study of living brains. Scientists have learned how to measure people's brains with a technique called *magnetic resonance imaging (MRI)*, which uses a huge magnet and lots of computer power to produce pictures of the living brain in cross section. This technique is described in more detail later.

Measurement studies of the plana in groups of dyslexic and normal readers obtained conflicting results: Neither of the hypotheses above could be verified with certainty. Eager to resolve the planum temporale puzzle, researchers decided to look at components of the planum by dividing it into the temporal banks (planum temporale) and the parietal banks *(planum parietale)*.[7] These imaginary dissections of the planum temporale made sense theoretically because the temporal bank is thought to be intimately involved in linguistic processing (e.g., speech and, possibly, reading), whereas the parietal bank is considered crucial to nonverbal and visual-spatial processing. This dissection turned out to be fruitful. Whereas researchers observed no differences between groups of readers with versus readers without dyslexia for the measurements of the total plana, specific patterns of findings fit previously observed results. For normal readers, the length of the left planum temporale (i.e., the usual left-larger-than-right asymmetry) appears to be associated with language-performance scores, so that those with a relatively longer planum tend to do better on language tasks. For readers with dyslexia, the length of the right planum temporale is negatively related to language-performance scores, so that those with a relatively longer planum tend to perform worse on language tasks. In other words, it appears that the bases of variation in language performance differ for individuals with and individuals without dyslexia. The difference in the length of the left planum temporale determines the variation in language abilities in normal readers, whereas the difference in the length of the right planum temporale determines the variation in language abilities in readers with dyslexia.[8] These findings suggest that there are indeed different sources of variation at work in readers with and readers without dyslexia.

How have scientists tried to explain the nature of the larger right planum in people with dyslexia? Albert Galaburda and his colleagues hypothesized that the enlargement of the right planum occurs during fetal development and results from abnormally reduced cell death, which leaves an excessive number of surviving neurons in the right planum.[9] These extra neurons form anomalous connections, resulting in a miswiring of the brain. Thus, according to this hypothesis, dyslexia is an outcome of anomalous neural development, presumably triggered at the prenatal stage of development.

Furthermore, these scientists have suggested that dyslexia might have its roots in the interaction between the prenatal chemical environment and the maturation rate of the relevant areas of the brain. Some particular interaction between the two could result in anomalous cell migration and organization. Such anomalous cells have been noted in the thalamus, a brain structure consisting of a mass of gray matter near the base of the cerebrum (gray matter indicates the presence of cell bodies; white matter is made up of neuronal connectors—axons and dendrites). The thalamus contains distinct nuclei, which serve as transmitting stations for incoming sensory signals. Specifically, it has been shown that neurons in various structures of the thalamus of a person with dyslexia are smaller than average.[10]

More recently, scientists have considered another possible biological basis of dyslexia. Specifically, they have suspected small vascular events and other injuries observed in the brains of people with dyslexia as being related to the dyslexia.[11] This hypothesis grew out of the observation that a number of postmortem brains had a net of scars and malformations spread throughout language-related areas. Researchers proposed that these injuries were produced by autoimmune damage of vessel walls (for example, such damage could be caused by arthritis), leading to cortical injury that resulted in malformations and scars and, as a result, disrupted blood flow.[12] The development of malformations is linked to the middle of pregnancy, whereas scars appear approximately in the second half of gestation or even postnatally.

To summarize, researchers trying to identify structural differences between the brains of people with dyslexia and the brains of people without dyslexia have focused primarily on plana temporale. The initial discovery of the unusual symmetry of the left and right plana in individuals with dyslexia still holds generally, even though more precise measurement techniques, introduced by MRI technology, have allowed researchers to zoom in on smaller subparts of the plana. The current hypothesis is that, even though variability in language skills in both normal and dyslexic groups is linked to the size of the plana, the nature of this link differs, depending on whether an individual is a normal reader or a dyslexic reader. In normal readers, the left planum is typically larger than the right planum; the larger the left planum is, relative to the right planum, the better the person's linguistic skills. For readers with dyslexia, the left planum is typically about the same size as the right planum; the larger the right planum relative to the left planum, the poorer the person's linguistic skills.

In addition to unusual planum symmetry, the brains of dyslexic readers appear to have two other distinct features. First, they have significant numbers of scars and malformations. The hypothesis is that these brains might have experienced some kind of autoimmune damage at the early stages of development. Given that the three sites of the genome that are currently being investigated as potentially linked to dyslexia are all located in the neighborhoods of major genes involved in the human autoimmune system (HLA, Rh, and ß-2 microglobulin; see Chapter 7), this hypothesis appears plausible. Finally, brain-tissue neurons of dyslexic readers appear to be smaller than average, at least in some areas of the brain (e.g., the thalamus). This thalamic neuronal "stuntedness" might well be linked to abnormalities seen in both the visual and the auditory systems of individuals with dyslexia.

To conclude, even though the findings presented here should be considered only suggestive of the potential structural differences between readers who have and readers who do not have dyslexia, the fact that researchers consistently find developmental anomalies in the brains of people with dyslexia is a rather strong indication of the plausibility of the structural-difference hypothesis as suggesting one kind of biological origin of dyslexia.

The Reading Brain in Action: Functional Studies of Readers With Versus Without Dyslexia

In addition to attempting to identify structural differences between the brains of readers with and those of readers without dyslexia, scientists have tried to look directly at the brain using a variety of techniques that can register the reading brain in action. Again, as with structural studies, these studies have provided information relevant to understanding the neurobiology of dyslexia.

In a technique widely used with both adults and children, electrodes are pasted all over the scalp, and the participant's electroencephalogram (EEG) is recorded as he or she performs various reading-related activities. The registered electrical signal is not stable or flat; it is variable and reflects the dynamics of brain activity. This signal can be decoded so that various peaks in it are identified and classified based on the time that passes between the moment a stimulus is administered and the moment the peak appears. These peaks, which emerge because the participant has been engaged in a certain reading-related task (e.g., single-word recognition or rhyming words), are referred to (when averaged to reduce error) as *evoked potentials.* The idea behind studying evoked potentials is to figure out whether there are any group differences between readers with and readers without dyslexia in the patterns of electrical activity in the brain.

For example, a number of studies were designed to gain some insight into dyslexia-specific associations with evoked potentials in response to performing tasks involving phoneme separation.[13] Results of childhood electrophysiological studies showed a clear physiological deficit in children with dyslexia. These deficits were manifested as longer latencies in evoked potentials and reduced amplitudes of a number of latencies.[14] In other words, children with dyslexia take longer to generate an evoked potential in response to a stimulus to be read, and the magnitudes of the responses of their brains are lower. These lowered patterns of electrophysiological brain activity register in parietal (top, rear), central, and frontal sites of the brain, and the general interpretation of these findings is that normal readers process verbal stimuli more actively than do readers with dyslexia.

Electrophysiological studies of adults with dyslexia also have pointed to reduced amplitudes and smaller differences in the waveforms of evoked potentials registered in response to words versus flashes of light.[15] In other words, the EEG-registered activity shows that, compared with normal readers, readers with dyslexia do not react to meaningful reading stimuli by engaging the brain more than they would for meaningless stimuli. In fact, the EEG responses of people with dyslexia to words hardly differ from their responses to meaningless flashes. In contrast, normal readers respond to the two types of stimuli very differently.

Amazing recent advances in neuroimaging technology have made it possible to investigate cortical regions and activation patterns associated with the performance of complex cognitive tasks.[16] Researchers are applying these new functional brain-imaging methods to test hypotheses of cortical dysfunction in both normal reading and dyslexia. This cutting-edge technology enables us to study the patterns of cortical activation (e.g., glucose utilization, blood flow, oxygen consumption) that various cognitive challenges elicit. The goal of these studies is to determine which areas of the brain are activated during reading and whether individuals with and those without dyslexia show similar kinds of activation in the brain regions involved in reading and language.

In a technique called *positron-emission tomography (PET)*, the individual is injected with mildly radioactive glucose or water or is asked to inhale radioactive gas. The radiation dosage in these studies is comparable to that of a chest X ray. After a period of rest to allow the radioactive particles enough time to distribute through the body tissues, the person places his or her head inside a ring of gamma-ray detectors. The parts of the brain that are more active burn more glucose; to do so, they "request" that the body send more oxygenated blood their way. The activity "island" accumulates more molecules carrying radioactive markers; thus, the activation of a particular brain region temporarily turns this region into a hot spot, emitting radiation. The patterns of radiation that emanate from the head are registered by computers and then decoded into functional maps of brain-glucose metabolism. Researchers can display the decoded maps on a computer screen as images of metabolic activity within any slice of brain in a set of specified coordinates. The brain image uses mainly three colors, in various shades. The more active areas are shown in bright red and yellow, and the quieter areas appear as dark indigo.

By subtracting the area of an image of the activated brain challenged by a cognitive task from the area of an image of a silent brain, the activation relevant to the task can be quantified, at least in theory. Alternatively, the participants can perform two tasks of different levels of complexity, so that two functional images can be taken. Researchers can record hot spots when they subtract the activation pattern characteristic of a lower-level activity (e.g., in the letter-recognition task) from the activation profile specific to a higher-level activity (e.g., in the word-recognition task). The researchers interpret these hot spots as being charged by those components of the higher-level activity that were not present in the lower-level activity. This method of the consecutive administration of increasingly difficult tasks so that researchers can subtract one brain map from another is called the *subtraction method.*

This technique is probably the most precise one available in the field now. The resolution of the maps obtained in this manner is state-of-the-art. The technique is invasive, however, in that it requires the introduction of radioactive material into a person. Thus, by default, the method limits the subject pool to adults only.

Another modern brain-mapping technique, called *functional magnetic resonance imaging (fMRI)*, is an extension of the MRI technique mentioned earlier. The fMRI technique does not require any bodily invasions and, thus, allows us to include children in experimental work. As is often the case, however, this loosening of the methodological requirements also diminishes the quality of the data obtained. The precision and accuracy of this method are yet to be determined. Currently, however, fMRI is the leading (i.e., most commonly used) tool of brain mapping. The technique is based on computer tomography, magnetic-based pictures of brain activity as indicated by various characteristics of water (its particular chemical and physical parameters) in engaged versus unengaged areas of the brain as well as in white and gray matter and blood vessels. Certain parameters of water are more informative than are others, depending on the particular brain activity or brain tissue under consideration.

In fMRI, as in PET, the first picture obtained after a participant is placed in a magnetic camera is that of the brain at rest—no activities or tasks are offered to the participant. Next, the participant is challenged by various reading-related tasks (single-word recognition, rhyming, etc.). Responding to a given challenge, the brain activates itself at specific locations (presumably, those where the cognitive function engaged by the task "maps"). Any activation requires energy. Brain cells obtain their energy from the process of glucose oxygenation, which uses oxygen and produces water and carbon dioxide. Activated brain cells want oxygen; responding to the demand, the organism delivers oxygen to them through the blood vessels. Then the activated cells consume oxygen and the local oxygen level goes down. Oxygen is delivered to the activated cells by hemoglobin molecules whose ferrous component is charged; these oxygenated hemoglobin molecules make our blood red. However, as soon as oxygen is taken off the hemoglobin molecule, the charge of the ferrous atom of the molecule changes and the blood turns dark and bluish. The changes in the valence of the ferrous component produce changes in water, determining its specific parameters. The change in the state of water in the magnetic field is exactly what gets registered by the computer as the image of the brain. So, while participants attempt assorted tasks, scientists watch the participants' brains in action. As with PET, when the first picture (the brain-at-rest image) is subtracted from the second picture (the brain-in-action image), the difference should indicate the locations where the activity took place.

The selection of the particular tasks administered to the participant in the fMRI camera is the point at which biophysics and biochemistry cease to play a role and psychology steps in. The goal is to find a set of related tasks such that the localization of brain activity will be as specific and yet as informative as possible. In essence, the best task is something incredibly basic, like the mere tapping of a finger (this task, however, would not allow us to build any exciting psychological theories). The introduction of any complication to a task can result in an explosion of unrelated brain activity. For example, olfactory studies show that administering a sample of low or moderately intense odor to a rat results in specific local activation of certain areas of the brain, but merely increasing the intensity of the odor (so that nothing changes except that the sample smells stronger) leads to rapid dissemination of activation and the loss of specificity.

So, the selection of tasks for subtraction-methodology studies is the central unresolved issue for fMRI studies. Each incremental task should be nothing more than the previous task plus the target process—the process that is being mapped. But we do not yet know for sure whether we are choosing these tasks correctly—or whether we merely believe that we are doing so. Thus fMRI studies may be making assumptions that do not quite hold up in reality. But then, many other kinds of scientific studies do the same.

Having discussed the methodologies used in modern functional brain studies, let us look at which brain areas appear to be engaged in reading.

Brain Areas Engaged in Reading

As expected, most of the hot spots generated when a person attempts to perform a language- or reading-related task are on the left side of the brain. Let us zoom in and look closer at the left-hemisphere structures involved in reading and related language-processing tasks. (As a guide to engaged brain areas, refer to Figure 6.1 on pages 138–140.) Studies involving language processing in normal individuals consistently point to left temporal activation (i.e., registered hot spots in the left temporal lobe) during the execution of language tasks (tasks related to word decoding, phoneme monitoring, word repetition, and reading aloud). In addition, left inferior parietal regions—including the supramarginal and angular gyri—also have been implicated in normal phonetic processing, word retrieval, word viewing, and oral reading.

In particular, findings from recent studies seem to be converging on the involvement of Brodmann's Area 37 (an area located in the inferior temporal-occipital part of the brain) in object recognition (the object category can include letters and words).[17] Another group of researchers has extended these findings by applying PET methodology to register brain activity during performance of a letter-recognition task.[18] The remarkable implication of this study is that the left Brodmann's Area 37 and the left angular gyrus generate metabolic activity that is inversely related to task performance.

This link between better performance and less activation suggests three possible meanings for increased activation. First, it may indicate inefficient processing, which could be related to a certain failure to inhibit competing activity. Second, it may suggest the utilization of resources in excess of what should be

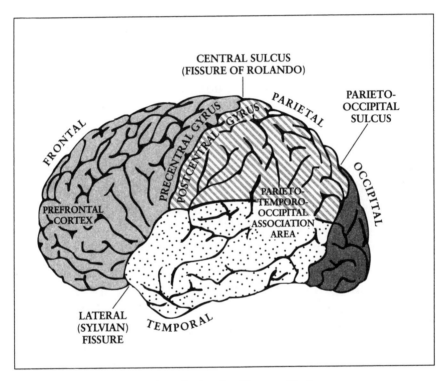

Figure 6.1   Major Landmarks in the Human Brain.

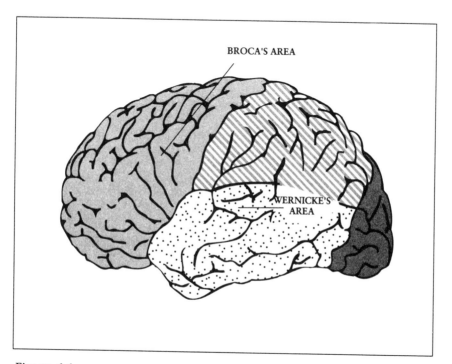

Figure 6.1

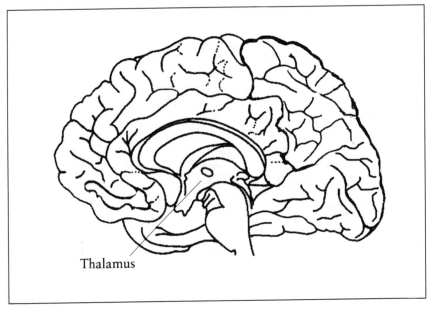

Figure 6.1

necessary for a given task. Third, it may suggest the brain's immaturity, because the brain cannot activate locally rather than globally.

Several investigators have used subtraction methodology with fMRI. Some researchers[19] decomposed the holistic process of reading into a number of distinct visual and linguistic processes involved in a variety of cognitive tasks (i.e., line, letter case, letter and nonword rhyme, and semantic category judgments). They then investigated whether these processes employed different cortical regions. The five tasks were ordered hierarchically.

The first, lowest-level task consisted of line-orientation judgments. The adult participants were presented with a task containing two stimuli (e.g., [\\] and [\\]) and were asked whether these stimuli matched each other. This task was aimed at tapping visual-spatial processing (the ability to make orientational judgments) without making any orthographic (spelling) demands.

The second task involved letter-case judgments. The participants were presented with two combinations of letters (e.g., [FFff] and [FfFf]) and were asked whether these combinations matched in patterns of uppercase and lowercase letters. (In this example, the two patterns do not match each other.) This task was considered to involve only one more process than the previous task: It supposedly added an orthographic-processing demand (working with real letters), but no phonological-processing demand, because the stimuli consisted solely of consonant strings and, therefore, represented combinations of letters that are phonologically impermissible (unpronounceable) in real language.

The third task, presented at the third level, added yet another process as an additional layer of complexity. This task was single-letter rhyme. The participants were shown two letters and were asked whether these letters rhymed, based on the vowel sound produced when naming the letters. For example, when the letters [K] and [P] are shown, the correct answer is no ("kay" does not rhyme with "pee"), but when the letters [P] and [T] are shown, the correct answer is yes ("pee" rhymes with "tee"). The scientists argued that this task, on top of the visual-spatial and orthographic processing required by the previous two tasks, involved yet another cognitive process, namely, the phonological process of translating the letters into phonological structures and then determining whether these letters rhymed or not.

The fourth-level task involved rhyming nonwords (pseudo-words). The participant was presented with a pair of nonwords (strings of letters that look like words, but do not have any meaning, e.g., [gret] and [juek]) and was asked whether these words rhymed. This task, presumably, engaged phonological processes at a higher, decoding level.

The final and most complex task required that the participant determine whether two real words (e.g., [cat] and [dog]) belonged to the same semantic category. Performance of this task supposedly required the involvement of all four cognitive processes engaged by the earlier tasks, plus the initiation of semantic processing (in that the presented words should be categorized and their categories should be compared with each other).

The researchers examined six cortical regions located in the frontal, temporal, and occipital lobes.[20] The frontal-lobe areas included the inferior frontal gyrus (centered in Broca's area), the prefrontal dorsolateral gyrus, and the orbital gyrus. The temporal-lobe areas included the superior temporal gyrus and the middle temporal gyrus. Finally, in the occipital lobe (see Figure 6.1), the extrastriate region was investigated. The study made different visual- (i.e., line and letter-case recognition) and linguistic-processing (i.e., rhyming and semantic judgment) demands on different areas of the brain. Thus, orthographic processing (as captured by the letter-case matching task) made maximum demands on the extrastriate region of the occipital lobe; phonological processing (as captured by rhyming tasks) activated both the inferior frontal gyrus and the temporal lobe; and semantic processing (as captured by the categorization task) engaged the superior temporal gyrus more heavily than did either phonological or orthographic processing.

In sum, brain studies of normal individuals suggest that many brain areas become engaged during the reading process. However, the broader relationships of language tasks to brain regions are far from simple. In particular, a wide variety of regions, both unilateral (lit up in only one hemisphere) and bilateral (lit up in both hemispheres), are activated by language stimuli. For example, numerous left-hemisphere regions, other than the temporal areas, respond to such reading-related processes as viewing words, reading pseudowords, and judging rhyme. Moreover, some of these tasks also activate right-hemisphere or bilateral regions, demonstrating that the left hemisphere is not alone in the processing of language-related stimuli.

Furthermore, studies of normal individuals utilizing tasks requiring nonlexical processing also show activation in some of the same left-hemisphere regions activated by language and reading-related tasks. For example, the left inferior parietal lobe, consistently implicated in language and reading-related tasks, is also activated by the task of attending to shapes.

One of the most exciting directions of brain research on reading focuses on finding links between patterns of metabolic brain activation stimulated by certain cognitive operations and independent behavioral measures on tasks viewed as reflecting those same cognitive operations. For example, Kenneth Pugh and his colleagues found strong associations between patterns of brain activation and peculiarities of performance in a lexical-decision task—a task that requires the participant to differentiate real words and pseudowords (as noted earlier, these are combinations of letters lacking meaning).[21] Specifically, individuals who showed greater extrastriate and inferior frontal right-hemispheric activation tended to be slower to reject non-words and responded faster in reaction to the phonetic regularity of real words. Amy Garret and Frank Wood detected strong relationships between variation in thalamic metabolism, especially in the left hemisphere, and variation in single-word reading.[22] In other words, individual differences in brain metabolism registered in various areas of the brain during reading-related task performance appear to be predictive of individual differences in performance on other reading-related tasks. Even though this line of research has taken shape only recently, one might speculate that these results are (1) indicative of the presence of some general cause that produces individual differences in brain metabolic profiles and (2) predictive of performance on a wide variety of reading-related tasks.

Interpreting the Complexities of Findings About the Brain

Scientists currently studying the basis of language processing in normal brains face the challenge of interpreting the following complexities. First, different types of language- and reading-related tasks may activate the same left-hemisphere regions, including both classic language areas and others. Second, a single language task may activate bilateral or isolated right-hemisphere regions. Third, nonlanguage tasks also may activate the same left-hemisphere regions activated by language tasks. Thus, what may appear to be straightforward neuropsychological interpretations of neuroimaging data are sometimes anything but straightforward.

The diversity of findings in the literature can be explained in part by several factors. First, there can be variation in stimulus parameters and difficulties related to the creation of appropriate tasks that avoid engaging the whole of the language apparatus. In other words, a task that should, in theory, engage only one aspect of language functioning may in fact engage others, rendering questionable any straightforward interpretations of the results. Second, there may be differences in recording techniques that are not clearly articulated, leading different researchers to think they are measuring the same thing when actually they are measuring different things. Third, the very nature of the subtraction technique, which is the dominant methodology of such studies today, is open to serious question. Let us consider this last problem further.

The subtraction technique assumes that the difference between tasks A and B is only in the engagement of the processes being mapped. In theory, the two tasks differ by just one distinct process. But it is unlikely that our knowledge of how tasks are solved is so refined that we can say with certainty that their execution differs only by one specified process. The inappropriateness of even one assumption in understanding the chain of processing of successively more complex tasks would undermine the whole enterprise.

Thus, we need to be healthily skeptical of recent studies of associations between brain regions and various procedural components of reading in accomplished readers that link subcomponent processes of reading to different brain regions. Indeed, we have to retain a healthy measure of skepticism in interpreting the results of any single kind of measurement technique. In general, these findings support the old assumption that reading is carried out primarily in the left hemisphere rather than in the right hemisphere. But what, precisely, the brain is doing while an individual is reading is still an open question.

Studies of Brains of People Identified as Having Dyslexia

Imaging studies of brains of people identified as having dyslexia originated conceptually with an early PET study by Herbert Lubs and his colleagues. This study was inspired by work in which a region on chromosome 15 (see Chapter 7 for details) was implicated as a putative locus for dyslexia.[23] Lubs and his colleagues compared profiles of the brain-glucose metabolism of six familial readers with dyslexia while reading aloud with the profiles of normal readers who either read aloud or viewed pictures. When the two groups of readers read aloud, the readers with dyslexia differed from the normal readers by having lower left perisylvian and higher occipital glucose metabolism. In general, the profiles of people with dyslexia that were registered during reading were more similar to those registered for controls when they viewed pictures. This finding was interpreted as suggesting that readers with dyslexia process less of the lexical or phonetic characteristics and more of the visual or pictorial characteristics of written words.

Subsequent studies of the same group extended this finding, revealing greater bilateral activity in the lingual gyri of the occipital lobe in the people with dyslexia; the activity was especially pronounced on the left. Whereas the evidence of left-hemisphere dysfunction in dyslexia was convergent with earlier anatomical evidence, the studies by Lubs and his colleagues suggested that the regions of excess or deficient activity in dyslexia might extend far beyond the left perisylvian region and might encompass more the posterior cortex regions usually implicated in visual rather than auditory processing.

Later studies resulted in a range of findings. Individuals with dyslexia were found to differ from controls by demonstrating a lower activation in (1) the left superior posterior perisylvian, supramarginal/angular gyrus, posterior frontal region, the right anterior hemisphere, and the left insular region (all for rhyme-detection tasks); and (2) the middle temporal gyrus (for reading either aloud or silently). Compared with controls, people with dyslexia were also found to exhibit greater activation in (1) the left sensorimotor strip (for rhyming tasks); (2) the left angular gyrus (for orthographic tasks); and (3) the bilateral medial temporal lobes (for phoneme-discrimination tasks). Moreover, control versus dyslexic group differences also extended to the right hemisphere. Thus, when performing a tonal-memory task, people with dyslexia activated the left hemisphere normally but showed a lower right temporal and posterior frontal activation. This finding points to a possible inefficiency in nonverbal functions of people with dyslexia, resulting in deficient rapid serial processing. In addition, individuals with dyslexia tended to show deficient activation of the right hemisphere while attempting a phonological-memory task.

In sum, although it appears on the surface that left perisylvian and posterior activation by language tasks is altered in dyslexia, the patterns are neither simple nor straightforward. Furthermore, there is no convergence on a single mechanism or region of abnormal activation. There is abundant evidence that the brain metabolism or blood flow in dyslexia can be abnormal during a wide variety of experimental tasks or control conditions of inactivity. The methodologies currently in use allow us to speculate and even to draw tentative conclusions, but not to draw certain conclusions.

Finally, the most crucial piece of evidence for the argument that the brains of readers with dyslexia differ structurally and functionally from the brains of normal readers comes from comparative brain-metabolism studies of normal and dyslexic readers. Only a few comparative studies have been conducted utilizing the functional neuroimaging (fMRI) methodology. Two early studies reported differences in the brain responses to cognitive tasks of individuals with dyslexia and individuals without dyslexia, but the findings were not sufficiently definitive to conclude that left-hemisphere activity is abnormal in dyslexia.[24]

Other researchers found that individuals with dyslexia, when reading, demonstrate metabolic activity that is spread unevenly throughout the brain, whereas metabolic activity in normal individuals tends to be more equally distributed.[25] Other patterns of metabolism in individuals with dyslexia are also different from those found in controls.

Amy Garret and her colleagues compared patterns of brain metabolism in accomplished readers with the metabolic patterns of readers with dyslexia and found metabolic differences in the thalamus and the posterior inferior-temporal cortex.[26] Specifically, readers with dyslexia showed decreased metabolism in two right-hemispheric regions, Brodmann's Area 37 and the thalamus.

Utilizing subtraction methodology in fMRI, Sally and Bennett Shaywitz and their colleagues used a series of increasingly complex reading tasks (described above) and compared the performance of individuals with dyslexia with that of individuals without dyslexia. As participants in the study lay in the fMRI magnet and performed one task after another, scientists watched the patterns of activation of different brain areas.

The activation pattern typical of normal readers involved superficial brain structures, and the activation pattern moved from the back of the brain to the front. The first activation point was in the primary visual cortex (the occipital lobe). This area registers and processes the information collected by the eyes. The next step was performed by the visual-association area (the angular gyrus), where symbols and signs perceived by the eyes are translated into language. The area that engaged last was the superior temporal gyrus (the so-called Wernicke's area). In this area the magic of converting the sounds of language into words takes place. In this study individuals with dyslexia barely used the three-step process utilized by normal readers. Instead, they activated a totally different area of the brain, the interior frontal gyrus (Broca's area); in individuals with dyslexia, the entire act of reading was completely carried out through the activation of this one area.

A Tentative Interpretation of the Findings from Functional Studies of the Brains of Normal Readers With Versus Without Dyslexia

Interpreting the results of findings from functional studies of readers with versus without dyslexia, Frank Wood of Wake Forest University suggested a model that might serve as a foundation for future brain-mapping work on reading. According to Wood, the present state of the art in brain research on dyslexia is centered on the hypothesis that one or a few relatively circumscribed cognitive impairments selectively impede the learning and execution of a range of reading and reading-related skills. Major contemporary models of dyslexia, whether stressing phonological deficit, visual-processing deficit, or some other deficit, share one major assumption—that dyslexia reflects the selective disruption of a cognitively identifiable system. In other words, the assumption is that a specific area of the brain is responsible for a given cognitive process (e.g., decoding or single-word reading) involved in reading and that a disruption of this brain area is reflected in a *specific* disruption of that reading-related cognitive process.

Wood and his team have put forward an alternative point of view, suggesting that a more general disruption occurs. According to this view, a definable anatomical territory in the brain suffers damage, disease, or some other compromise of its structure or function of a certain severity, and, consequently, all behavioral processes depending on tissue in that territory are affected, at least to some extent.

Work by Albert Galaburda and his colleagues seems to indicate the potential validity of this model. Galaburda's research emphasizes the diffuse changes in neuronal connectivity that are one outcome of cortical ectopias (malformations arising in areas where "lost neurons"—neurons that did not make it to their final destination—concentrated) formed at early stages of brain development. According to this view, the resultant cognitive deficits are expected to be diverse and unpredictable and to extend well beyond any particular cognitive process. Yet another possibility of an anatomical territorial impact would be a lesion in a specific region crucial for the function of a given neurotransmitter (a so-called neurotransmitter projection system). Such a lesion could have diffuse consequences throughout the brain, causing a wide range of functional disturbances.

Whether an anatomical disruption leads to a local, regional, or diffuse outcome is most often unpredictable. However, the assumption that brain metabolic abnormalities will result in some cognitive (behavioral) dysfunction seems plausible. The underlying assumption of Wood's model is that it may not be possible to understand the cognitive deficits (and sometimes, emergent psychiatric conditions) as arising from a common, underlying, "brain-wired" disorder. It might be that dyslexia (in its cognitive manifestations) is one of many manifestations of an anatomical disruption. If so, one might hypothesize the existence of other, in particular behavioral, manifestations of the same anatomical syndrome.

An analogy for such a situation is a stroke, which results in impairment in a diverse collection of psychological processes, unified only by their separate dependence on the affected tissue. A mild left-frontal stroke, for example, could induce halting speech and depression. The model offered by Wood and his colleagues recognizes the need to study the holistic individuality of a reader with dyslexia, including his or her cognitive as well as behavioral profile.

Thus, schematically, the model can be described as a system of events resulting in complex behavioral manifestations. According to the model, a gene (or genes) affects the development of the brain, and some malformation (e.g., ectopia) results. This malformation, in turn, causes distinct functional patterns of brain metabolism. These brain patterns are expected to be linked to distinct cognitive profiles specific to dyslexia. Moreover, connections are expected to be found between the cognitive manifestations of dyslexia and other behavioral patterns (e.g., behavioral impulsivity, inattention, depression, anxiety).

Although the verification of this model has just begun, some pieces of evidence have already been accumulated in support; this information, however, goes beyond the scope of this book.[27]

The task of pinning down reading functions in the brain has been enormously difficult, for many reasons. First, multiple areas of the brain could be equally involved in reading efficiently. So the reader might use different pathways of reading depending on a number of as yet unknown factors. Second, the brain is equipped with an enormous capacity to compensate. If a given pathway malfunctions, the brain will try to build a different pathway. In our search for *the* pathway of reading, and our mission to map this pathway to *particular* structures in the brain, we use an image of a hardwired, fixed structure. The brain, however, cannot be completely hardwired for the simple reason that it must learn. Experiences, memories, and emotions all shape and reshape, assemble and disassemble its circuitry, strengthening those synaptic connections that fire often and letting others weaken.

But hope springs eternal. There is always a hope for better brain maps, resulting in better localization of mental functions. As we noted before, the major emphasis now is on technology. Perhaps soon the major emphasis will turn to an integrated theoretical understanding of the mind in all its aspects.

Apes, Mice, Frogs, and
Other Creatures with Dyslexia

Our brains and behavior distinguish us from all other animals. The human brain is about three times as large as that of a primate of human size. Although chimps share most of our DNA, none of them can speak or read. Attempts to show that animals can talk, draw, write, or read are admirable for the amount of effort expended, but otherwise they have led largely to dead ends. Author Samuel Butler, who was educated at the same institutions as Charles Darwin (the Shrewsbury School and Cambridge University), but who turned out to be a committed anti-Darwinist, once remarked on an attempt to teach a dog sign language: "If I was his dog, and he taught me, the first thing I should tell him is that he is a damned fool!"

Nobody has suggested that we teach apes how to read so that we can study normal and deficient reading. However, scientists have developed numerous animal models for studying dyslexia. This idea is not crazy at all; the scientific reasoning behind these models is logical and fairly simple. As of today, we can state with certainty that dyslexia is associated with changes in the brain, among which are (1) structural anomalous deviations in language areas, (2) minor cortical malformation, and (3) smaller neurons (at least in the thalamus). Some of these features of dyslexic brains, especially the appearance of cortical malformations, can be successfully modeled in animals.

Animals might help us explore the first set of findings presented in this chapter—that is, the significance of structural brain differences (e.g., the anomaly in asymmetry and the cortical malformations) for different characteristics of animal learning. The second part of this chapter addressed functional differences between brains of people with and without dyslexia; animal research might help scientists investigate how minor malformations resulting in disrupted metabolic profiles could lead to noticeable and even persistent disorders of cognitive functioning. Finally, studies of the changes in sizes and numbers of neurons and patterns of connectivity that can be viewed as the bases for functional changes are possible in animal models only.

Finding associations between animals' cortical malformations and their learning abilities is apt to prove useful in human studies of dyslexia. There is nothing foolish in studying animal models of dyslexia so long as we set reasonable goals. When we reach the point at which we attempt to teach animals to read *The New York Times*, we almost certainly will have passed the point of setting such goals.

Do not be misled by what might look like overwhelming evidence that there is something definitely amiss with the brain of a person with dyslexia. At this point, scientists are inclined to think that this is the case, but so far nobody can say for sure what is happening in dyslexia. All we can say is that the brains of people identified as having dyslexia generally appear to be different from the brains of people not so identified.

The human brain is an interesting organ. It comes into the world with an excess of potential, an array of possibilities so vast that many will never be used. When an infant is born, his or her genes have created a huge abundance of synapses connecting the neurons (nerve cells). There are way too many of them, more than anybody could ever need. As the baby matures, that number of synapses dwindles. The synapses that do not get used are simply trashed; the connections between neurons are eliminated, so that the neurons themselves, having lost their links to the neuronal web, are essentially buried alive in the matter of the brain.

That very excessive power of opportunity given to a baby's brain makes the dyslexia puzzle even more interesting. What goes wrong so that the brain of an individual with dyslexia loses its chances for proficient reading? Might there be biological or other interventions as yet unknown that will provide or restore these chances? Pasko Rakic, a neuroscientist at Yale University, compares the process of brain maturation to sculpture: "You are constrained by the size and shape of the stone, but within that size and shape, you can make an infinite number of figures." Perhaps the day will come when we learn how to work with this stone to maximize the brain's reading potential.

Chapter Seven

The Genes of the Child with LD

Genetic Bases of Reading and Reading Disabilities

Meet the Millers. At first glance, the Millers are a typical American family. John is a construction worker and Kate is a nurse. They have four children: Rod, age sixteen; Natalie, age fourteen; and twins Amy and Josh, age six. What makes the Millers different from many families is that several of them have trouble reading. They will serve to illustrate points we make about reading disabilities throughout this chapter.

The Millers' Tale

When John was a child, more than twenty years ago, he hated going to elementary school. He was slow with every school activity and always behind because it took him several times as long as it took his classmates to read the instructions for whatever the class was doing. Sometimes he would work and work on something only to discover, when the work was done, that he had done something completely different from what was expected because he did not understand the written instructions correctly. John did just fine if someone explained orally what to do, but he failed and felt stupid whenever reading was involved.

Fortunately, John's parents had enough money to send him to a special reading teacher, with whom he met once a week for about five years. This private instructor helped John learn how to read. John made it through high school but did not even consider going to college. He did not like the idea of wading through all the books and journal articles one is expected to read in order to get a college degree.

Now John's oldest boy, Rod, has similar problems. Rod becomes extremely upset when his mother tries to talk him into going to college. He says that she wants him to suffer for the rest of his life. Kate keeps saying that Rod needs to work harder, but John understands Rod. John understands that, for his son, reading does not get easier with more work. For both John and Rod reading is laborious, slow, and no fun.

On the other hand, John's oldest daughter, Natalie, seems to be doing great. She earns straight A's at school and just loves reading. The other two children, the twins, are too young to be evaluated for reading disability. John says that he is worried about them, though. Rod is getting help, but this extra instruction is expensive, and it would be difficult for the family to manage if the twins also needed help with reading. School resources help a lot, but the special-education teacher at the school has fifty students, and there is not enough time in her schedule for her to work individually with each student even once a week. John will do anything in his power to help his kids learn how to read; after all, his family did so for him.

John says that his dad was always very supportive of him. John's father had a brother and sister who experienced difficulty reading and writing. John's aunt, Gloria, is still alive, and, within the family, her Christmas cards are notorious for the number of spelling mistakes they contain. John's cards would not have been any better. He simply does not write them, though; Kate does them instead. Strangely enough, Gloria married a man, George, who also had difficulties reading. Gloria and George always said that they were very thankful that their next-door neighbor helped them with their paperwork.

John also remembers quite well how, in childhood, he would visit Uncle Jim with his father. Uncle Jim was a great storyteller and often made up wonderful tales right on the spot. Uncle Jim's wife read newspaper highlights out loud every morning, and Uncle Jim would often make up a story based on one of these news highlights. Everybody would laugh at how different Uncle Jim's stories were from what was said in the newspaper. Uncle Jim always said that he would rather make up his own story than struggle through reading an article in the newspaper; he said he saved a lot of time that way. Uncle Jim had five children, four of whom received a college education, and one who, just like John, always had difficulties with reading.

John's brothers, David and Mike, did very well at school. David, the oldest, is a lawyer. He has a daughter who shows no signs of having difficulties with the written word. She is only five, but she already knows how to spell the word *silhouette*. As a child, Mike, the youngest brother, went to see the same reading teacher who taught John. These lessons helped Mike a lot. Mike is an engineer, but both of his daughters did not do well in school. Ann never made it through high school, and her son is also having difficulties with reading. Mary graduated from high school but refused to go to college. At school she had to work really hard to get through reading and writing assignments. She put a lot of time into her homework and always complained that everything that involved reading and writing took too long.

The Millers are not a real family, even though they possess numerous characteristics shared by many families in which reading problems are transmitted from generation to generation. The Millers are not modeled after any one particular family struggling with reading-related problems, but they have something in common with each of them. Families like the Millers have led scientists to consider whether certain types of reading problems run in families and therefore may be hereditary.

In this chapter, we will explore what scientists have learned about dyslexia by working with such families. We offer an overview and our interpretation of recent findings from genetic research on individuals who show either normal or dyslexic reading.

Like My Dad and Me

The tendency for dyslexia to run in families was first observed a long time ago and was part of the early descriptions of the disorder. Dyslexia was first described at the end of the nineteenth century; only about ten years later, several reports of familial concentrations appeared. Most of these reports were studies of single families; one described an extended family with three affected generations. In 1950, these scattered initial observations were reviewed by Bertil Hallgren, who is usually credited with formulating a hypothesis of the heritable nature of dyslexia.[1] This hypothesis attracted the attention of researchers, who then set off on a hunt for a "reading gene."

Early studies of dyslexic tendencies within families consistently showed that substantial numbers of children with dyslexia had relatives with dyslexia, with a recurrence rate as high as 30 percent. In other words, about 30 percent of the relatives of children with dyslexia were identified as having dyslexia themselves. A question arose, however, as to whether such a high concentration of affected individuals was really just an unintended and essentially meaningless consequence of the selection process; that is, the high recurrence rates may have been due to the way the families with dyslexic tendencies were selected. All these families were selected through clinics or special-education services, and these selection schemes could have reduced the variability of reading skills, compared with what would have been observed in the general population (i.e., the total population of the country or the whole world). Moreover, in these studies, information about family members and their reading problems came from individuals' own reports about themselves or their family history, or from unstructured interviews. Results may have been biased because the sources of the information were subjective or unreliable.

These concerns turned out to be well-grounded. Researchers noticed two kinds of biases in particular. Some relatives of affected individuals tended to overestimate the presence of relevant symptoms in their own behavior because they were overly sensitive to the experiences of the relative. Others' relatives, in contrast, ignored obvious similarities between their behavior and that of the affected individual—perhaps a sort of denial reaction.

To what extent, then, did these early findings hold true for the general population? In the late 1960s and early 1970s a number of studies used samples of children from the general population to answer this question. The researchers in these studies worked with large groups of randomly selected children (e.g., some researchers recruited all the children from a certain number of grades from a certain number of schools), rather than searching for dyslexic families using special-education schools or neurological clinics. In addition to changing the sampling strategy, the researchers took advantage of a new development in the field: Instead of using clinical records and subjective accounts to determine the presence of reading and spelling problems among relatives, they used formal psychological tests. These first large-scale studies, like the earlier studies,[2] reported significant recurrence of reading problems among relatives of affected individuals. Thus, scientists concluded that the familial nature of reading problems could not be simply a coincidence resulting from sampling or evaluation biases.

Since then, quite a few family studies have been conducted in order to understand and quantify the effects of genes on the development of both dyslexia and normal reading skills. The tendency for dyslexia to concentrate in families is now well established. Some studies have advanced several steps further and attempted to address five main issues: (1) the quantifiable degree of risk that relatives of readers with dyslexia either had, have, or will have dyslexia; (2) the specific mode by which dyslexia is transmitted from generation to generation; (3) the familial nature and heritability of normal reading skills; (4) the co-contributions of genes and environment to the development of dyslexia and normal reading skills; and (5) the specific genes involved in the development of dyslexia.

Why do scientists pay attention to this type of work? There are several reasons. First, genetic studies enable specialists to estimate the probability that a child will have a learning disability, given that one or both parents do. Second, such studies enable specialists to estimate comparable probabilities based on whether the child's other relatives—siblings, aunts, uncles, and children—have a learning disability. Third, understanding the genetics of dyslexia may eventually help us devise drug treatments that will target the effects of specific identified genes and possibly help remediate the effects of dyslexia. Finally, behavioral-genetic studies of dyslexia may eventually help us understand more about environmental factors that increase or decrease the risk of a person with a certain set of genes developing dyslexia.

If I Have Trouble Reading,
Will My Child Also Struggle?

The first of these key questions concerns the degree to which relatives (who, by definition, have more genes in common than do nonrelatives) resemble each other in experiencing reading problems. Many family studies of dyslexia have shown that, if at least one member of a family has a reading disability, there is a higher-than-chance probability that other members will also have a reading disability. The exact probability depends on the degree of relatedness. The probability is higher for identical twins than for siblings, higher for siblings than for cousins, and so on. This probability also depends on the severity of the reading problems experienced by the core family member studied, the particular definition of reading problems used in the study, and the source of information. With regard to source of information, the apparent similarity between skills of relatives is higher when the relatives are assessed by researchers than when study participants report on their reading skills themselves.

The fact that dyslexia runs in families and that the recurrence risk for relatives of people with dyslexia is higher than it is for people selected at random does not mean that reading problems are genetic. Many things run in families (e.g., lullabies, recipes, and jewelry), but not all of them have anything to do with DNA. For example, one might calculate a "recurrence risk" for all daughters in a family for making outstanding lasagna, given that their mother, aunt, grandmother, and great aunt all made great lasagnas. (All these women used one family recipe passed from generation to generation.) Only a very misguided researcher, however, would look for a "lasagna gene."

But if the cause of dyslexia is purely environmental and determined by such factors as poor nutrition, lack of books in the home, lead contamination from a nearby factory, or whatever, why is everybody in the Miller family not stricken by it?

Researchers computed the average rate of reading problems among the parents of children with reading disabilities across eight family studies including a total of 516 families. The median value was 37 percent, with a range of 25 to 60 percent.[3] Fathers tended to show a higher proportion of reading problems than did mothers (46 percent versus 33 percent). In other words, at least a quarter of the parents of children with reading disabilities were experiencing or had experienced reading problems themselves.

In this analysis, researchers examined children with reading disabilities and then determined the likelihood that their parents had similar problems. But similar probabilities are found if we move in the other direction on the family tree: Biological (i.e., not adopted) children of parents with reading disabilities are more likely to experience reading problems than are children of normal readers. For example, only about 5 percent of the children of parents who are normal readers have reading disabilities. In comparison, about 36 percent of adults who had reading problems in their childhood report that at least one of their children has experienced some difficulties mastering reading.[4] Similarly, a study of children with one or two parents with dyslexia found that, by the second grade, about 31 percent of these children were identified by their schools as having reading disabilities. The rate was twice as high (62 percent) when these students were evaluated with precise psychological tests. This last finding is noteworthy. Commonly, when children are assessed through a battery of cognitive tests, the rate of reading-related problems is higher than when the rate is determined by schools without such tests.

How does one know that the tendency of reading disabilities to run in families is not due largely or wholly to environmental factors? Perhaps parents who do not read well bring up their children in environments that do not provide much support for the children to learn how to read. On the one hand, the environment clearly does make a difference. Children raised to read will probably read better, on average, than will children not raised to read. On the other hand, within families that provide roughly the same reading environment for multiple children, some of the children show reading disabilities and others do not. More than just environmental factors appears to be at work. Both genes and environment matter.

Another body of evidence supporting the claim that dyslexia is a genetically influenced condition comes from studies that compare different types of twins, namely, identical (monozygotic, or MZ) twins and fraternal (dizygotic, or DZ) twins. The main premise here is that both types of twins share the same family environment, but that MZ twins differ markedly from DZ twins in genetic similarity. Monozygotic twins develop from one egg fertilized by the same sperm, whereas dizygotic twins develop from two different egg-sperm couplings; MZ twins share all their genes, whereas DZ twins share, on average, only half their genes. Thus, assuming that the environments of monozygotic and dizygotic twins are similar enough, researchers can quantify the degree of similarity within twin pairs, compare these degrees for identical and fraternal twins, and thereby estimate the impact of genes on a specific trait of interest.

Here we refer to two types of twin studies: (1) concordance studies, which determine the degree to which the same trait appears in both members of a twin pair; and (2) heritability studies, which determine to what degree the similarity of traits in twins is explainable by genes or environments.

In the first twin study of dyslexia, Knud Hermann[5] found that all ten identical-twin pairs (100 percent) were concordant (i.e., similar, demonstrating the same trait) for reading disability, in contrast to only 11 of 33 fraternal pairs (33 percent). In other words, all twins of the MZ twins with dyslexia also had dyslexia, whereas only 33 percent of the DZ twins of twins with dyslexia had specific reading problems. Subsequent studies supported these findings. Generally, MZ twins showed a higher degree of concordance (varying between 84 percent and 100 percent), whereas the concordance of DZ twins was significantly lower (varying between 20 percent and 55 percent).

Thus, unless there is something about being MZ twins besides having identical genetic makeups that could lead to the co-occurrence of reading failures in both twins (which is possible, in theory, but no researchers have suggested what this something might be), these studies all suggest that genetic factors are important in dyslexia. The findings of rather high MZ concordance rates in comparison with substantially lower DZ concordance rates indicate the presence of genetic influences in dyslexia.

Perhaps the high concordance rate for MZ twins is due to a stronger tendency to report concordant rather than discordant twin pairs.[6] Maybe twins and their parents tend to be more open to the idea of the twins' being recruited for a study if the twins are similar rather than dissimilar. A group of Colorado researchers made an effort to avoid such a referral and recruitment bias. First, they identified all the twins in grades three through twelve in the cooperating school districts in Colorado and selected those pairs in which at least one twin had low reading achievement scores. Second, they assessed the performance of both twins through an extensive battery of psychological tests in the laboratory.[7]

Using such a sample, researchers reported that the unbiased concordance rate for reading disability was 68 percent for MZ and 38 percent for DZ pairs.[8] In other words, even if previously reported samples were biased, the concordance rates obtained in those studies were still in the right ballpark.

Taken as a whole, concordance studies of reading disability show that genes contribute significantly to the development of dyslexia. These studies, however, do not help us estimate the relative magnitudes of genetic and environmental influences.

Another way to estimate the probability that a child who has relatives with dyslexia will be affected is to figure out how dyslexia is passed on from one generation to the next. What genetic mechanisms underlie the transmission of dyslexia? If we know both the means of genetic transmission for a given trait and the relevant family history, we can predict the likelihood that a given child will be affected.

Some Basic Concepts of Genetics

Research on the transmission of dyslexia has been shaped by certain ideas central to the field of genetics.[9] The fundamental scientific premise of genetics has not changed much in the 130 years since Gregor Mendel, an Augustinian monk from Bohemia, crossbred pea plants and figured out that living beings carry hereditary "elements." In modern terminology these elements are called genes. Every adult organism has two alleles (instantiations) of its genes for each trait. These two alleles may be the same (e.g., both code for brown eyes) or they may be different (e.g., one codes for brown eyes and the other codes for blue eyes). When one allele of the gene dominates the other, it is referred to as dominant and the other is referred to as recessive. For example, the allele of the gene for eye color that produces brown eyes dominates the allele that produces blue eyes. For the dominant trait (e.g., brown eyes) to be expressed, the individual can have either both alleles code for the dominant trait or one allele code for the dominant trait and the other for the recessive trait (e.g., brown-brown, brown-blue, or blue-brown). For the recessive trait (e.g., blue eyes) to be expressed, however, the individual must have both alleles coding for that trait (e.g., blue-blue). The principles of dominant and recessive transmission (the passing on of genes from generation to generation) are fundamental laws of genetics. These laws are used to interpret patterns of human inheritance.

We do not carry out breeding experiments with our fellow *Homo sapiens* the way Mendel did with peas. For one thing, such experiments would take too long; for another, they would be very expensive; and, most important, they would be unethical. Instead, scientists capitalize on the "experiments" humans carry out voluntarily in the process of fulfilling their sexual instincts. To do so, scientists use family trees (pedigrees).

Pedigrees differ in size, complexity, and number of generations. For example, some pedigrees from rural areas in Nepal include hundreds of individuals (since most of the inhabitants of these villages are related in some way). Other pedigrees, such as the pedigree of the Romanovs, a family of Russian czars, go back to the middle 1500s and include representatives of all major royal families of Europe. The pedigree of the average European usually includes two or three generations and five to eight individuals.

The first pedigree used in a genetic study at the beginning of this century was that of a family from a Norwegian village. This family was of interest because many of its members had shortened hands and fingers. The pattern of inheritance (transmission) of this trait was very distinct: (1) it never skipped a generation—all short-handed people had either one or two short-handed parents; (2) a short-handed individual who married an individual with hands of normal length had half normal-handed and half short-handed offspring; and (3) normal children of a short-handed and normal-handed person who married normal people had normal children—from then on there was no short-handedness in that branch of the family. This pattern of gene transmission is just what is expected for a dominant mode of inheritance. The dominant allele of the gene determines which trait will be expressed.

In contrast, the recessive mode of inheritance refers to a situation in which two recessive alleles are needed to express a trait. For example, in diseases transmitted recessively, most often both parents have one copy of the defective gene and look absolutely normal. The classic case of recessive inheritance is albinism. For example, in some Native American populations, one person in 150 is an albino (i.e., he or she has no pigment in the eyes, hair, or skin). Most albino children are born to parents with normal color pigmentation. According to the recessive mode of transmission, for this to be the case, each of these parents must have a single allele of the albino gene matched with another normal allele that produces normal pigmentation. However, half the sperm and half the eggs of these parents carry the albino gene. Should such sperm and egg meet, the child will have two alleles of the albino gene and will be an albino. Given that a child inherits specific genes, what do these genes do in terms of operating the biochemical processes of the body? The majority of the biochemical processes in our bodies (including brain activity) are controlled by proteins (biological products encoded by genes). In addition, proteins are the building blocks of human organisms. The specification and construction of proteins is guided by genes, which are sequences of bases (molecular letters) in the double-spiraled DNA (deoxyribonucleic acid) strings located in a chromosome. The full genome, when and if ever printed out, would take up two hundred volumes, each the size of a telephone directory with a thousand pages. (It will probably just be recorded on CD-ROMs.) DNA is made up of four chemicals: adenine (A), cytosine (C), guanine (G), and thymine (T). The human genetic makeup consists of 3 billion molecular letters, packed into genes. These molecular letters are arranged into words. All words are of the same length—they all include only three letters (e.g., TAT or AGG). These three-letter words are instructions to make amino acids, the bricks with which proteins are built. The movie *GATTACA* uses the analogy of an instruction manual to describe the role of molecular letters—the sequences of these letters tell our bodies and minds what to do. Substituting just one letter for another can sometimes mean the difference between health and disease—a person who suffers from hemophilia, for example, is a carrier of such a single-letter spelling mistake.

Not all genes function at a given moment in time. Quite a few of them are silent much of the time. A gene is turned on by a variety of regulatory molecules. These molecules latch onto a sequence of molecular letters at a precisely defined place on a gene and "unzip" a neighboring stretch of letters, allowing the gene to be decoded by specialized molecules of RNA (ribonucleic acid), which, in turn, orchestrate the production of protein. Usually the regulatory molecules are proteins themselves, so the process of an organism's development is a series of stages in which DNA makes proteins, some of which interact with other DNA so other proteins get made, and so on. This system, although incredibly efficient in terms of making certain proteins only when they are needed, is thoroughly dependent on its own perfection and precision. Even minimal deviations from the planned timing and quantity of some proteins in the course of development can have adverse effects on the organism.

The bottom line here is that a single gene rarely specifies some identifiable part of the body or behavioral trait. What a single gene does is control the production of a specific protein during specific developmental periods, or start, continue, or end a certain biochemical pathway that also is affected by many other genes. The whole operation is similar to following a very complex recipe in which the quality, amount, and timing of the mixing of the ingredients are crucially important. The recipe is especially complex for the development of the human brain, the most advanced organ of the human organism. Researchers estimate that about thirty thousand human genes are involved in the development and maturation of the brain and nervous system. With all these genes, some organization is needed for them. How are all these genes organized?

The human genome is organized in terms of chromosomes. A chromosome is a long strand of genetic material, called DNA, which contains thousands of genes in a protective package. Each individual has two copies of each chromosome—one copy from the mother and one from the father. There are twenty-three pairs of chromosomes in all human cells except for sperm and egg cells; each sperm and each egg receive only one copy of each chromosome. Twenty-two chromosomal pairs are identical in male and female organisms; these chromosomes are called autosomes. The twenty-third pair determines sex. Sex chromosomes in men and women are very different. Females have two (large) X chromosomes; males have a single X and a (smaller) Y. Many inherited diseases are carried on the X chromosome. In females, the presence of a defective gene on one X chromosome can be hidden by a normal gene on the other X chromosome. Males, however, because they have only a single X chromosome, do not have the luxury of hiding their defective gene. For this reason, sex-linked abnormalities are seen more often in males than in females. Consequently, when an unequal sex ratio is observed for a specific trait, the first hypothesis is most often that the trait is X-linked.

How Is Dyslexia Genetically Transmitted?

Scientific inquiries into the transmission of dyslexia first investigated whether the observed patterns of transmission fit into either of the two major types of inheritance—dominant or recessive. However, biology is never simple. More complicated modes of inheritance than those discovered by Mendel (i.e., the dominant and the recessive) were also tested. The idea was the same, however—to investigate families in which dyslexia runs from generation to generation to determine whether the distribution of affected individuals in different generations would correspond with the distribution expected for one of the theoretical modes of transmission.

The field of study that focuses on the mode of transmission of dyslexia was pioneered by Hallgren,[10] who analyzed ninety families of dyslexics and concluded that the pattern of transmission in these families corresponded to the dominant mode of inheritance. Hallgren also speculated that transmission of dyslexia is influenced by sex (i.e., it differs for males and females), even though he did not test this hypothesis formally. The major criticism of Hallgren's work was that he used clinical diagnosis (i.e., clinicians' subjective opinions on whether patients had dyslexia or not) rather than cognitive tests (i.e., largely objective standardized instruments that refer to the age-appropriate population norms for reading achievement) to establish the presence of dyslexia. Moreover, Hallgren's computational methods were unsophisticated by today's standards, although they were advanced by the standards of the 1950s.

To everybody's surprise, the gist of Hallgren's findings (the hypothesis that dyslexia is transmitted dominantly) held true in subsequent studies. Hallgren's work set a precedent, and a number of later studies concentrated on two major issues: (1) whether the mode of transmission of dyslexia is sex dependent, that is, different for males and females; and (2) whether transmission of dyslexia involves one gene or a group of genes.

Are There Really More Males
Than Females with Dyslexia?

It has been common knowledge for a long time that there are approximately four times as many boys as girls identified as having dyslexia. Some evidence gathered in special-education schools and neurological clinics supports this claim; in particular, clinicians and reading specialists work with more boys than girls. Moreover, researchers have documented a consistently higher gender ratio (1.7:1 of boys to girls) in the affected siblings of children with dyslexia.[11] Hence, researchers have investigated the possibility that the root of reading disabilities is different for males and females.[12]

The first hypothesis was that something in boys' prenatal environments makes them more susceptible to dyslexia. For example, researchers noticed a predominance of affected males in families with language-impaired mothers.[13] Scientists suggested that dyslexia might be linked to the male hormone testosterone[14] and that the affected mothers had higher levels of testosterone at the time of conception than did nonaffected mothers.[15]

The major investigation of the unequal sex ratio, however, unfolded around the hypothesis that there is something about the genetic transmission of dyslexia that differs in males and females. In other words, researchers suggested that sex affects the way dyslexia is passed from generation to generation. Four different types of sex effects on transmission were proposed.[16]

Two of these hypotheses considered the involvement of one of the sex chromosomes, the X chromosome, and two others assumed other effects of sex.

First, researchers suggested that dyslexia might demonstrate X-linked inheritance, as do color blindness and hemophilia.[17] For example, none of the children of a color-blind father and a non-color-blind mother will have color blindness. But all the sons and none of the daughters of a color-blind mother and a non-color-blind father will have color blindness. All males with an abnormal X exhibit its detrimental influences, but in most females, the gene is hidden by a gene for normal vision on the second X chromosome. For this reason, color blindness is seen more frequently in boys than in girls. Similarly, if the dyslexia gene is located on the X chromosome, reading problems should be more common among boys than among girls. Moreover, if the gene is indeed X-linked, there should be no (or very little) transmission of dyslexia from a father with dyslexia to his children.

A second hypothesis suggests that dyslexia is a sex-influenced disorder. An example of this type of disorder is male baldness. This type of inheritance does not assume that the relevant gene is located on the X chromosome; the gene is thought to be one of the autosomal (not sex-linked) chromosomes, but the gene's particular influence depends on the sex of the carrier as a result of some other nongenetic, sex-specific biological mechanism.

A third hypothesis is that transmission of dyslexia is mitochondrial. (Mitochondria are the only independent structures in a cell, besides the nucleus, that have their own packs of DNA. When the egg is fertilized, much of its cytoplasm, including the mitochondria, is passed on to the developing embryo. Sperm, however, pass on almost no mitochondria. Hence, mitochondrial DNA has its own pattern of transmission—it is passed down the maternal line.) There are many examples of such inheritance, including some forms of blindness due to destruction of the optic nerve. Because the egg, and not the sperm, carries mitochondrial DNA, mitochondrial transmission occurs only between mothers and offspring. Mothers pass the gene on to sons and daughters, but only the daughters pass it on to the next generation.

Finally, a fourth hypothesis implicates a genetic phenomenon called imprinting in the transmission of dyslexia. Imprinting occurs when the effects of a particular gene depend on whether it is passed on by the mother or by the father. Imprinted genes—genes that have an effect determined by their origin—can be located on any non-sex chromosome (i.e., any autosome). Each parent seems to stamp the gene personally when it gets transmitted to his or her offspring. A gene passed on by a mother to her son differs in its impact from the same gene when it is passed by this son to his own children. It appears that the transmitted gene is marked by the sex of the transmitter, and the mark reverses its sign whenever the line of transmission changes from one sex to the other. Examples of imprinted diseases are Prader-Willi/Angelman syndromes, which produce mental retardation. The symptoms of these disorders are so distinct that initially they were thought to be completely different from each other. In fact, they are caused by the same gene. The difference lies in whether the mother or the father passed the gene to the child. Children with an abnormal gene from their father develop Prader-Willi syndrome, whereas those who receive the same gene from their mother develop Angelman syndrome. Children with Prader-Willi syndrome are fat, whereas the Angelman children are of normal weight, but children with both syndromes exhibit mental retardation.

In sum, four hypotheses sought to account for the greater observed identification rates of dyslexia in males than in females. These four hypotheses are X-linked inheritance, sex-influenced inheritance, mitochondrial inheritance, and imprinted inheritance. To test these four hypotheses, researchers scrutinized the rates and the severity of transmission for each of the possible combinations of parent and child sex characteristics (boy-mother, girl-mother, boy-father, and girl-father). There were many pairs of affected fathers and sons, so the first hypothesis of X-linked transmission was rejected. Moreover, the transmission rates for mothers and fathers were essentially equal; therefore, the hypothesis of mitochondrial transmission did not hold either. Similarly, both the high frequency of the disorder in the general population and the almost equal transmission rates for mothers and fathers argued against the imprinting hypothesis. Sex-influenced transmission, however, remains a possibility because of the slight excess of affected males.

Thus, of the four tested hypotheses, described above, regarding the transmission of dyslexia, only sex-influenced transmission fits current data from family studies. This hypothesis is yet to be verified.

Recent large-scale studies of the sex ratio of affected individuals in random samples (as opposed to individuals selected through clinics) often show that the proportion of affected boys and girls is not substantially different from 1:1 (i.e., there are approximately equal numbers of boys and girls among children with dyslexia), although across multiple samples from different studies, including smaller-scale studies, the male-female ratio is somewhat higher (1.5/1.0).[18]

Two types of alternative environmental explanations have been suggested for the predominance of boys among children with dyslexia. These explanations are referral bias and greater susceptibility of boys to detrimental environmental influences.

The excess of males in referred and clinic samples of children with reading problems may be due to an ascertainment bias: Boys referred to clinical services may have manifested, in addition to reading problems, behavioral difficulties that made them more disruptive in the classroom than girls.[19] Many researchers have reported that teachers tend to refer a disproportionate number of boys for problems related to reading disabilities, compared with the ratio of boys and girls with dyslexia determined through random samples when the assessment of reading skills is carried out by a psychologist.[20] For example, in a longitudinal study of Connecticut children in kindergarten through grade three, many more boys (13.6 percent) than girls (4.2 percent) were identified by the school system as eligible for special services, whereas according to test-based research criteria, about 9 percent of boys and 7 percent of girls were classified as having reading disabilities.[21] In general, it has been demonstrated that struggling male students are more likely to be referred for evaluation by teachers than are female students with comparable abilities and achievement levels.[22]

According to the second environmental hypothesis, boys may be more affected than girls by such environmental influences as quality of teaching, social-class differences, and external societal pressures.[23] Genetic analyses showed that the environmental influences on reading skills tend to be higher for boys than for girls.[24] However, more precise identification of the environmental factors that are relevant to the development of reading problems in males will be a challenging endeavor.

Despite the inconsistencies in empirical data with regard to the exact ratio of males to females among people with dyslexia, in all studies there appears to be a slightly higher rate of dyslexia among males. As we have discussed, four hypotheses have been suggested to account for this phenomenon: (1) a selection bias, which results in more boys than girls being referred to services; (2) the presence of certain biological factors in dyslexic parents (e.g., certain hormones) that elevate the number of male births in these families; (3) a greater genetic susceptibility to dyslexia in boys than in girls; and (4) a greater environmental susceptibility to dyslexia in boys.[25] These explanations are not mutually exclusive, but at this point there is not enough evidence to favor any specific one or combination of them. So, for now, two key questions—whether there is indeed an unequal sex ratio and if so, why—still remain in a "dyslexia fog."

Does Transmission of Dyslexia Involve One Gene or Many?

To address the second issue—whether dyslexia is transmitted by one or multiple genes, and what kind of mode of transmission best explains dyslexia—let us consider the results from family studies that used formal statistical approaches (called *segregation analyses*) for studying patterns of transmission of dyslexia. There have been three of these studies: one by Finucci and his colleagues;[26] one by the Colorado group;[27] and a collaborative study that included families from three sites—Iowa, Colorado, and Washington.[28]

Formal statistical programs, designed to find the mode of transmission of a studied disorder, allow the researchers to estimate the correspondence (the fit) between the expected and observed rates of the disorder among relatives of affected individuals. The situation resembles trying to put a purchase (i.e., the observed rates of the disorder) back into its original package (the expected rates of the disorder). Each original package corresponds to one of the theoretical modes of transmission, according to which each family of a given structure and size should have a certain number of affected individuals. The task is to try out all the available "packages" and figure out which one was the original from which the "purchase"[29] was initially removed. Thus, researchers compare fits between various theoretical models and actual data and select the transmission mode that best corresponds to the outcome.

Of the three studies, only the study by Childs and Finucci[30] supported the initial hypothesis that dyslexia is transmitted as a major-gene autosomal (not sex-linked) dominant condition. A family study of dyslexia conducted in Colorado did not show any support for the involvement of a single major gene, and no best fit was found for any of the tested modes of transmission. However, when the researchers divided their sample into different subsamples (e.g., a sample of the families of affected boys and a sample of the families of affected girls), they found that different genetic modes of transmission fit the data in different subsamples. This finding allowed the researchers to theorize that there is no single mode of transmission of dyslexia and that the disorder is transmitted differently in different families. This hypothesis is known as the hypothesis of the genetic heterogeneity of dyslexia, and at least one other study has offered evidence in support of this idea.[31]

The third study we mentioned, by Bruce Pennington and his colleagues, is the most compelling study of patterns of transmission of dyslexia done so far.[32] According to this study, the data best could be explained by a sex-influenced autosomal dominant mode of transmission, with the disorder manifesting itself with a probability of 100 percent in males (i.e., every male who inherits the gene[s] develops the disorder) and approximately 65 percent in females (i.e., only about 65 percent of females carrying the gene[s] develop the disorder). Moreover, this model assumed the presence of a major gene (i.e., a major contribution from different forms of a single gene).

Thus, of these three studies of dyslexia, two offer robust evidence in support of both the sex-influenced dominant mode of inheritance of dyslexia and the involvement of a major gene. Having established that dyslexia is robustly familial, that at least some of this familial nature can be attributed to the genetic similarities of family members, and that affected family members might have a dominant "reading gene," we can now attempt to estimate more precisely how much the familial nature of dyslexia is influenced by environmental factors and how much it is shaped by genetic influences.

Normal Reading: Half Genes–Half Environment

So far we have been considering dyslexia and dyslexic families. From the very beginning of this chapter we assumed that the Millers and families like them constitute a special subgroup of a general population and that, in order to understand the roots of dyslexia, researchers needed to study this subgroup. This opinion, however, is not accepted by all scientists. On the contrary, some researchers believe that the roots of dyslexia may not be distinct from the foundation of normal reading skills.[33]

Keith Stanovich, for example, stated that dyslexia falls on a certain spectrum of reading abilities and that, therefore, the boundary between disordered and normal functioning may be somewhat arbitrary. Continuing this argument, some researchers have suggested that causal factors resulting in dyslexia should be essentially the same in type, if not in degree, as those important for the development of normal reading performance. Often, however, researchers have conflated two different issues. The first issue concerns the nature of the distribution of reading-performance scores, that is, whether there is a distinct group of poor readers whose scores converge on a specific low range of the overall spectrum and, therefore, form a gap in relation to normal readers' scores. This question can be addressed experimentally by studying large unbiased samples.

The other issue is whether the roots of dyslexia are fundamentally distinct from the roots of normal reading performance. The answer to this question is independent of the answer to the first question, because it is possible to find, when the general population is sampled, that there is no gap between scores of deficient and normal readers, even though reading skills in these two groups might have distinct roots.

A clear example of such a situation comes from studies on mental retardation. It is well known that, in the general population, IQ is distributed on a normal curve. If, however, we zoom in on the lower tail of this distribution, we find that the roots of low and very low IQ scores are very much distinct from the roots of average IQ scores. In particular, many single-gene diseases result in low and very low IQ scores, whereas average IQ scores involve influences from many different genes. However, when the IQ scores of these average-IQ and low-IQ individuals are plotted among other scores from the general population, there is not a visible gap between the scores of the two groups. Today the question of two distinct roots for the same trait cannot be addressed experimentally.

As often happens, the opinions of scientists on this matter are divided. Some scientists say that to understand the basis of dyslexia we have only to study subsamples of people with dyslexia from the general population, whereas others say that to understand poor reading we have to study normal reading.

So, what is known about the genetics of normal reading performance? Is normal reading, like dyslexia, familial and heritable? If so, what is the mode of transmission, and does it differ from that for dyslexia?

As is the case for many cognitive functions, reading skills tend to be similar among primary relatives (i.e., those relatives who share 50 percent of their genes: child-parent and sibling-sibling pairs). Likewise, researchers have found a high degree of similarity between MZ twins and significantly lower correlations between DZ twins (median correlations over six studies were 0.89 and 0.61, respectively), suggesting that about half the variance describing individual differences in normal reading is due to genetic influence.

Some researchers have investigated the degree of heritability for specific cognitive subprocesses involved in reading. Just as they distinguish different processes in children's *acquisition* of reading skills (Chapter 5), scientists distinguish different components of *developed* reading. Currently, developed reading is characterized by two clusters of cognitive processes, one of which focuses on the accuracy of reading and writing (i.e., the accuracy of phonological awareness, phonological decoding, and spelling and orthographical processing) and the other of which focuses on the fluency or automaticity of reading (i.e., the speed of reading and the ability to process written symbols quickly).

Scientists found that only certain reading-related processes appear to be heritable. Spelling, short-term memory, phonological decoding, phoneme awareness, and word recognition (i.e., the skill of reading a single word presented out of context) show significant heritability, whereas orthographic coding (i.e., sound-symbol association) and reading comprehension (i.e., the ability to comprehend a piece of reading material and answer questions relevant to the read piece) seemed not to be heritable.[34] For example, for word recognition, heritability has been estimated at 45 percent,[35] meaning that about half of variation across individuals in this process is explained by genetic differences (for more details on heritability, see Chapter 2). Heritability estimates for spelling ability have ranged from approximately 21 percent to 62 percent.[36] Altogether, for various reading factors, heritability estimates range from 79 percent[37] down to 10 percent.[38] Some of these findings have been revised along the way as researchers have accumulated more cases in their samples. For example, initially, orthographic coding did not appear to be heritable, but when the sample was enlarged, reanalyses showed the presence of significant genetic influences.[39]

Overall, current results obtained by the Colorado group suggest that genetic influence appears to be somewhat higher for phonological decoding and phoneme awareness than for word recognition and orthographic coding.[40] The impact of environment appears to be significant for all reading-related processes and especially strong for word recognition. In particular, researchers have found that both word recognition and spelling are substantially influenced by genetic (46 percent and 48 percent, respectively) and environmental (45 percent and 37 percent, respectively) influences, whereas, for reading comprehension, environmental influence is high (52 percent) and genetic influence is low (27 percent).

Because various reading components tend to operate in conjunction with one another and, therefore, are highly correlated, it is plausible to assume that these correlations could indicate a full or partial overlap of the genes influencing these components. Indeed, researchers have found a significant genetic link between word recognition and phonological decoding. The genetic correlation for word recognition and orthographic coding is significantly lower. One could conclude from these results that word recognition and phonological decoding are influenced by the same gene(s), whereas orthographic coding appears to be influenced by different genes.

The Colorado research group also has studied the genetic and environmental causes of the association between reading performance and verbal short-term memory.[41] Results of the group's analyses indicate that both reading ability and verbal short-term memory are highly heritable and that a substantial proportion of their comanifestation is due to common genetic influences.

In summary, all twin studies indicate that at least some components of normal, developed reading performance, most likely its accuracy components, show high heritability estimates, which suggests the involvement of genetic factors. However, it is important not to be misled by what looks like convincing evidence of genetic influences on reading skills. All in all, these influences account for, on average, about 50 percent of the observed variation in reading performance. The other 50 percent is attributable to environmental influences. The implication of these results for remedial training will be considered in Chapter 8.

Notice that estimates of heritability (and, conversely, estimates of the contribution of environmental factors, so-called *environmentality*) have varied across studies and measures. These findings should be interpreted cautiously for at least three reasons. First, within each study, heritability estimates are specific to certain sampling constraints. Most of the studies done today rely on participants representing a fairly narrow range of socioeconomic statuses and educational backgrounds.

The studies use predominantly white middle-class families. If a broader range of reading environments—representing the spectrum from poverty to wealth of families—were utilized, heritability estimates most likely would be lower, whereas environmentality estimates would be higher, as a result of the greater observed variation in the trait (i.e., people from different socioeconomic backgrounds are expected to vary from each other more in terms of reading-related characteristics as a result of differences in their education as well as in the amount of reading material available in their respective homes). In contrast, sampling twins from more narrowly defined environments (e.g., college-preparatory schools only) would artificially increase heritability estimates (because it would be expected that in a homogeneous sample of prep-school students almost everybody would read quite well, and, due to the similarities in education, the observed differences in reading would be attributable primarily to genetic differences).

Second, the very definition of the trait of reading achievement, as well as the definitions of the traits corresponding to reading-related components, vary from study to study. Some definitions of the trait include general, composite scores of reading performance, whereas others include specific reading processes. Thus, the discrepancy in heritability estimates in these studies may be attributable to discrepancies in definitions.

Finally, the base rates of reading disabilities could differ for twins when compared with single-birth children. For example, in a 1975 nationwide study of school performance in Australia, David Hay and his colleagues showed that by the age of fourteen only 42 percent of twin boys had achieved adequate standards of literacy, compared with 71 percent of single-born boys.[42]

Having established that the heritability of normal reading skills is fairly high, the next logical step is to look for specific modes of transmission for reading skills. Only one family study to date has conducted a formal segregation analysis aimed at identifying the mode of inheritance.[43] As with the procedures used in dyslexia-transmission studies, researchers compared the fits between a number of theoretical genetic models and the observed data. The best-fitting model was a major-gene autosomal dominant model of inheritance (i.e., suggesting that a single gene of major effect located on a non-sex chromosome is involved).

This finding was actually quite surprising. The best-fitting model for transmission of normal reading skills matched the best-fitting model for transmission of dyslexia. Some scientists have concluded that this finding supports the idea that normal and deficient reading skills share the same roots. Other scientists argue that this finding suggests that, as with the transmission of dyslexia, normal reading skills appear to be transmitted dominantly with a significant effect from a major gene. Whether the genes involved in dyslexia and normal reading are the same is yet to be determined.

In Search of the Reading Gene

One step remains to complete the argument that individual differences in reading and reading-related processes are determined, at least partially, by variability in people's genetic makeups. If this argument is true, behavioral differences are, to a certain degree, due to specific identifiable genes. Disrupt these genes, and reading should suffer, while other linguistic and intellectual processes carry on.

Before we venture into the details of this argument, some clarification of terms is necessary. Our use of the term *reading gene* does not imply that there is a gene that reads for an individual. However, it does imply that there is a gene that affects the normal course of reading-skill acquisition. The search for a reading gene is inspired by the inference that there is a gene (or genes) responsible, at least in part, for the observed distribution of reading disabilities in families. This gene (or genes) is thought to disrupt reading, but does not necessarily control reading.

The evidence presented in the following paragraphs comes from studies conducted on samples of relatives and families of individuals with dyslexia. As should be obvious from our previous consideration of sampling biases, these particular groups feature much higher concentrations of people with reading problems than would a randomly selected sample. To our knowledge, so far, nobody has looked for a gene for normal reading skills.

What have we learned up to this point through our inquiries into "reading genes"? Do these genes really exist, or is the idea a misguided notion? If reading genes exist, what do they do?

The reading genes could be those genes that code for proteins or start the transcription (decoding) of another coding gene. The produced proteins might guide, attract, and incorporate neurons into networks and, therefore, be important to the development of the brain. Or these proteins might determine the efficiency of neuronal connections and, therefore, be important to the synaptic tuning that occurs during learning (i.e., the tuning that occurs between nerve cells). Or these proteins might be part of a totally different system, such as the human immune system, which is intimately related to the functioning of the whole organism in general and of the brain in particular.

No one has located a reading gene, but the search is on. The leading hypothesis now is that dyslexia may be caused by many genes, of which one or very few have a major effect, in interaction with profound effects from the environment.

The ultimate goal of a genetic study of a monogenic (single-gene) condition is the exact physical localization and isolation of the gene in question. The absence of the expression of this gene in individuals with a given trait, or the direct demonstration of a correlation between genes and specific manifestations in the organism, constitutes powerful evidence that the gene plays an important role in the development of the studied char-

acteristic. Once located, the encoded protein may permit a physiological explanation for the gene's role in normal processes or
diseases. Research may eventually lead to the development of
new interventions (both biological and nonbiological) that may
lessen the effects of dysfunctional products of genes.

Finally, the isolation of a gene may allow for gene therapy,
which involves replacing a "defective" mutant gene with a normally functioning copy or introducing another genetic agent
designed to conquer the disease. The former could be done
through the insertion of laboratory-made copies of "healthy"
genes into a living cell, either with the help of a virus or by fir-
ing DNA into cells from a minuscule "gun." The latter could be
done by introducing genes that stimulate the immune system's
defenses against the disease (in the case of cancer, for example,
this could be accomplished by providing cancer cells with the
means of their self-destruction or by making these cells susceptible to particular drugs).[44]

Using current molecular techniques and specialized statistical
computer software, investigators have carefully studied selected
family trees (pedigrees) of dyslexic individuals in which developmental dyslexia recurs in different generations. The results of
one early study suggested that a major gene for dyslexia is located on chromosome 15.[45] David Fulker and his colleagues followed up these findings by selecting from the original
extended-family study a sample of siblings who represented
lower (more extreme) levels of reading ability.[46] Their analysis
of this restricted subsample also pointed to chromosome 15.
However, subsequent genetic studies, which included the same
dyslexia pedigrees, refuted the original findings.[47] Independent
investigators who examined Danish families with an autosomal
dominant pattern of transmission for dyslexia also were unable
to replicate the chromosome 15 finding.[48]

A screening of other regions of the genome revealed chromosome 1 as a locus for dyslexia.[49] Coincidentally, German researchers have identified a family in which dyslexia and

delayed speech development were observed in individuals with a balanced translocation (rearrangement of chromosomal material) between chromosomes 1 and 2.[50] One of the possible hypotheses was that the dyslexia gene was located on chromosome 1. Subsequent genetic studies have produced conflicting results. At least one study yielded no evidence for linkage at any location of the short arm of chromosome 1.[51] Another study, however, showed linkage between the reading-related process of phonological decoding and a region on chromosome 1 that is located very close to the Rh (human rhesus factor) gene (which determines the Rh factor in blood type).[52]

Several investigators have hypothesized a possible association between dyslexia and various disturbances of the immune system (e.g., autoimmune disorders such as asthma, allergies, etc.).[53] Results of their studies have suggested that rates of autoimmune diseases are elevated in relatives of people with dyslexia and that the incidence of dyslexia is increased in relatives of those having autoimmune illnesses. Although the causal basis of the association is unknown, the evidence for association from these independent studies points to the human leukocyte antigen (HLA; a gene that is tightly linked to the function of the human immune system) complex located on chromosome 6 as a candidate region.[54]

Data from two independent samples of 114 sibling pairs with at least one sibling with reading disability revealed evidence for linkage between reading disability and the HLA region on chromosome 6.[55] Analyses of corresponding data from an independent sample of 50 dizygotic twin pairs also provided evidence for linkage to the HLA complex. However, the continuous reading index used in this study was based exclusively on perceptive vocabulary (the ability to recognize words and find corresponding pictures) and verbal IQ measures. Thus, the analyzed trait, even though it is associated with a specific reading disability, may reflect an overwhelming influence of verbal IQ.

Both earlier genetic findings (regarding chromosome 6 and chromosome 15) have been replicated in an independent sample of dyslexic families.[56] What is especially interesting is that all three genetic regions—the chromosome 6 region (located in the neighborhood of the HLA complex), the chromosome 15 region (located in the vicinity of the ß-2-microglobulin gene), and the chromosome 1 locus (located in the neighborhood of the Rh locus)—are loci implicated in human autoimmune disorders. This link suggests that some autoimmune disturbance of the developmental organism may be a primary insult to the brain, which, in turn, results in disturbances of blood flow to various regions of the brain, including those engaged in reading.

In summary, genetic studies hunting for a reading gene have pointed to some regions of interest that are spread across a number of chromosomes throughout the human genome. None of these findings can be referred to as the true result, and more research in the same regions is needed. When these findings are applied at the level of individual readers with dyslexia, such as the members of the Miller family we considered earlier, three important observations can be made.

First, differential linkage of various manifestations of dyslexia to different chromosomal regions may indicate the genetic heterogeneity of dyslexia. In other words, the genetic cause of reading problems in John's family may be different from the genetic cause of dyslexia in the family of Gloria's husband, George. Moreover, there could be different genetic causes of dyslexia within John's own family. Such genetic heterogeneity might be the reason for the different behavioral manifestations of reading problems among the Millers.

Second, similar remedial training within a given family might have differential success. Whereas Mike completely compensated for his childhood reading problems, John carried them, though to a reduced degree, throughout his life. These individual differences in receiving and responding to remediational help are questions for special investigation.

The third crucial observation concerns the degree of severity of dyslexia, even within one family. As is obvious in the case of the Millers, severity varies. One more unanswered question is why.

What, then, is the significance of these findings? Two main purposes underlie the hunt for the reading gene(s). The first goal is to identify and understand the specific gene(s) involved in dyslexia so that effective biological interventions can be developed. An example of successful pharmacological intervention through the manipulation of neural transmitters is the treatment of some disorders within the attention-deficit spectrum with Ritalin. The second goal is to identify children at risk so that interventions can be started before rather than after disabled reading becomes a major problem in the children's lives. It soon may be possible to use reliable DNA information to identify children from families with a history of reading difficulties who are at high genetically based risk for reading disabilities. As we will show in Chapter 8, properly structured early intervention can lead to amazingly effective remediation of reading problems, even in very severe cases, but children with dyslexia need to be identified early, well prior to experiences of failure and frustration in school.

Is there a need to screen everyone genetically for dyslexia? Of course not. We are far from advocating genetic screening for everything (as in the 1997 movie GATTACA, in which Ethan Hawke's character goes to a job interview and the company analyzes his DNA instead of talking to him).

Educators are often wary of behavioral-genetic, genetic, and brain studies. They are concerned that evidence from these biological studies will be used to claim mistakenly that the deficit is not remediable—and, therefore, does not warrant the investment of limited resources—or that these biological differences account for poorer reading performance among individuals in disadvantaged racial or ethnic groups.

One of the causes of this wariness is the common misperception that DNA creates life on its own. In every living cell, DNA interacts with its molecular environment by way of enormously complex systems of chemical reactions. DNA is extremely sensitive and responds to various chemicals caused by emotional reactions, eating, and breathing. Every biological event in the body, every emotional or intellectual reaction, every organismal experience, from mobilizing the antibodies of the immune system for an attack against viral intruders to experiencing love, is possible through and orchestrated by an interaction with DNA.

Yet this interactive nature of DNA is commonly overlooked. Complex problems often get reduced to simplistic explanations. In the popular mind, as *Village Voice* columnist Mark Schoofs noted, there is a "gene for everything." There is a gene for Huntington's disease, there is a gene for criminality, there is a gene for novelty seeking . . . you name it. Dorothy Nelkin, the author of *The DNA Mystique*,[57] quoted a newspaper clip stating that women are genetically predisposed to be in the funeral industry!

Even identifying a gene does not explain much. In essence, the identification of a gene responsible for a given disorder is just the beginning of a whole other story—the story of what this gene is responsible for, how it acts, what environments trigger its expression, and what factors prevent its expression. For example, it is a well-established observation that individuals who carry a certain form of the APOE (apolipoprotein E) gene are at higher risk for Alzheimer's disorder. However, only about 50 percent of those who have this mutant gene develop the disorder. Why? We do not know the answer.

The belief that destiny is hidden in a fertilized egg is mistaken. Even after a child becomes an adult, DNA continues to interact with the environment, and new generations of cells reflect and assimilate the effects of that interaction. As Tom Bouchard, a famous twin researcher, said, "Without an environment to grow up in, DNA is just a moist spot on the floor."

The more researchers know about dyslexia, the more apparent it becomes that the data accumulated within three paradigms of study (cognitive, as discussed in Chapter 5; neuropsychological, as discussed in Chapter 6; and behavioral-genetic, as discussed in this chapter) converge—that findings from one paradigm contribute to progress in another paradigm and that the multi-disciplinary efforts of researchers help advance our understanding of the workings and the course of dyslexia. These convergent efforts are undertaken in hopes of maximizing the benefits of remedial help, which we address in Chapter 8.

Part Three

Learning Disabilities in the School, Courtroom, and Society

In Part II, our focus was on the individual, in particular, on the cognitive, neuropsychological, and genetic origins of learning disabilities, with emphasis on reading disabilities. In Part III, our focus shifts to the environmental context in which the individual lives—the home, the school, and the societal legal system that regulates what happens in the school. We discuss here learning disabilities in general, because whereas scientific work has focused very largely on reading disabilities, educational, legal, and societal institutions in general have had to deal extensively with all the different kinds of learning disabilities.

Chapter Eight

Getting
a Better Ticket
LD in the School

In an oft-repeated anecdote,[1] famous psychologist William James once spoke with an old woman about the structure of the world. According to this woman, we live on a layer of earth spread over the back of a giant turtle. Because James was a gentleman and thought it appropriate to show interest in the woman's speculations, he continued the conversation and inquired what the turtle was standing on. The woman replied that she was impressed with his question, had thought about it, and had an answer. "The first turtle stands on the back of a second, far larger, turtle, who stands directly under him," she said. James, not satisfied with her answer, proceeded to inquire what was under *that* turtle. To this the old woman crowed, "It's no use, Mr. James—it's turtles all the way down."

Time for a Change

This anecdote calls to mind the dangers of infinite decomposition, the possibility of endless regression in explanation, the problem of looking for ever-evasive, absolute truth. When do we stop?

In the previous chapters we summarized the current state-of-the-art scientific views on specific reading disabilities (dyslexia). These views, as well as the reality that underlies reading disability, are rather complex. The danger with these explanations is that they can multiply endlessly—we can keep discovering one turtle underneath another. All these sophisticated scientific results and interpretations are practically useful only to the extent that they enable us to answer three major questions: (1) Do we know why reading disability develops? (2) Do we know what the course of reading disability is? And (3) Do we know how to remedy reading disability?

At this point we do not have definite answers to these questions. We do know enough, however, to help individuals who are at risk for or who have a reading disability to become better readers. As complex and unresolved as some of our questions about dyslexia are, scientific research has been of tremendous practical significance. This chapter will show how the scientific knowledge accumulated over the last decade of intensive research on reading disability has shaped, in a few cases, and could shape, in many more cases, the preventive and remedial programs offered to children with dyslexia.

Most of the results presented in the three previous chapters were obtained through research programs supported by the National Institute of Child Health and Human Development (NICHD). The NICHD initiated its program on learning disabilities in 1965, and since then it has funded the research of over a hundred scientists in medicine, psychology, and education. All these scientists have worked to further our understanding of the nature and course of learning disabilities. Because a large proportion (about 80 percent) of learning disabilities involve reading problems, the majority of these NICHD studies have focused on dyslexia. Besides accumulating scientific knowledge about dyslexia, one of the main agendas of the NICHD-funded research was to develop a set of intervention techniques that would link the frontiers of scientific knowledge to the practical needs of children and adults with dyslexia. Much needs to change.

The most famous monument in Highgate Cemetery in London is that of Karl Marx. The words inscribed on it are well-known: "Philosophers have only interpreted the world. The point, however, is to change it."

There is a desperate need for change in the way we teach reading, in both regular and specialized classrooms. The whole system is in crisis. First, the numbers of children with inadequate reading skills as well as those identified as having reading disabilities are rising. Second, there are insufficient numbers of special-education teachers, and their training has been and remains very costly. Third, students in regular classrooms have such a wide range of abilities that the teachers need to be equipped to teach at least three or four different grade levels simultaneously. Fourth, many parents have resorted to obtaining costly supplemental materials and private instruction in reading to augment what is done in school. Fifth, the school systems have been challenged by numerous lawsuits accusing them of failing to provide appropriate educational programs.

Beginning in the 1980s, we have made great advances in learning what is essential for success in reading and how those who are at risk for failure can be helped to succeed. As always, science has been slow to filter into everyday practice. In this chapter, we will review major conclusions drawn from the NICHD-supported intervention studies and consider the implications scientific findings have for teacher-preparation programs and parental practices.

Let us start with an improved definition of dyslexia based on recent research findings in the field and developed by a collaborative group of scientists, practitioners, and advocates from the National Center for Learning Disabilities and the Orton Dyslexia Society.

Several of the ideas embedded in standard definitions of dyslexia are important for the following discussion (see Chapters 1 and 2). First, as has been stated throughout the book, the core indicators of dyslexia are difficulties in decoding and analyzing phonemes within words. Second, the difficulties people with dyslexia have are specific—people with dyslexia walk normally, talk normally, and comprehend oral language normally, yet they have problems processing written symbols. Third, reading problems often coincide with writing and spelling problems. Finally, dyslexia is assumed to be of constitutional origin, that is, it has a biological foundation. We will return to these important points over the course of the chapter. Now, however, we start with the last issue, which has major implications for education.

This is the issue to which we keep returning. If dyslexia is in part biological, is there any hope for remediation? The answer to this question is both straightforward and certain: Yes. Educational intervention is now the only hope of readers with dyslexia. Moreover, if adequate help is not offered, their reading deficit will only remain or worsen. In a sense—even though this analogy is somewhat extreme—denying a reader with dyslexia proper instruction is like leaving a child with a high fever outside in the cold instead of putting that child into a warm bed.

How do we know that it is possible to compensate for the biological liabilities of readers with reading disabilities? To our knowledge, there has not been a single study that quantifies the degree of biological impairment in people with dyslexia and that simultaneously measures how much remediation is required to achieve grade-matched reading standards. In addition, studies investigating a number of different behavioral traits show that compensation for an individual's biological deficits is possible.

The following study illustrates the possibility of such compensation. Finnish researchers studied the relationship between modifiable and nonmodifiable factors influencing people's longevity. This study is one of many that have tried to

address the importance of genetic history relative to the importance of exercise and remediation for the risk of developing a
particular condition. At the study's conclusion in 1994, there
were 434 sets of twins in which one sibling had died of natural
causes—usually heart disease or cancer—and the other had sur-
vived. In 173 of those 434 sets, the twins had exercised at different levels. Specifically, the researchers found that occasional
exercisers (those who took some, but fewer than six, brisk
walks or jogs each month lasting about thirty minutes each)
were 30 percent less likely than their sedentary twins to have
died. Vigorous exercisers (those who took at least six brisk
walks or jogs each month lasting about thirty minutes each)
were 44 percent less likely to have died. In response to this
study, Steve Farrell, an exercise physiologist and associate director of the Cooper Institute for Aerobics Research in Dallas, said,
"Even if you have bad genes, this study strongly suggests that
increasing physical activity can help you live longer."[2]

As this study illustrates, "biological" does not mean engraved
in stone. On the contrary, "biological," according to *Webster's
New Collegiate Dictionary*, 7th edition, means "pertaining to life
and living processes." If biological is about the living, then it is
inherently about change. Living is never static; it is always dy-
namic. Popular views regarding the hopelessness of improving
upon anything that is biological are based on misconceptions.

The biological foundations of dyslexia should be taken into
account as one of the factors contributing to a particular outcome—a child's acquisition of reading skills. But the origins of
dyslexia are complex, potentially involving educational environment and family reading traditions. Thus, the realization
that dyslexia has a partially biological basis should not obviate
remedial training; on the contrary, this realization should
make it clear why such intervention is needed.

As Finnish researchers have shown, people who shape their
activities and their environments to suit themselves instead of
sitting around and waiting for their biological liabilities to

catch up with them tend to live longer. The same can be said of reading. The more proper instruction that is provided to the youngster while he or she learns to read, the more the child will read and the less likely it is that he or she will become a reader with a disability.

One of the most well-traveled pathways to poor reading is a biologically predetermined early failure at reading enhanced by environmentally imposed frustration with reading. In other words, early difficulty with reading material leads to slowed growth of reading skills, and, consequently, to avoidance of the practices of reading. At the prereading stage, the biological "weakness" of a poor reader is often not noticed, so the child is viewed and treated by parents and peers as no different from any other child. Once the child starts to learn how to read, however, he or she quickly begins to experience multiple failures; unlike his or her friends, this child finds reading a highly frustrating undertaking. What is more, the child can progress quickly and quickly become as good as or better than the other kids in many other domains (computer games, sports, drawing, etc.). So, whereas time spent with Nintendo's Dr. Mario is rewarding (the child can rescue the princess and victoriously eliminate all the bad guys along the way), time spent with reading is unrewarding, unpleasant, and frustrating. Without proper instruction offered in a timely manner, this child may never read for enjoyment. It is impossible to overestimate the importance that structured, targeted, and effective reading practice, systematically offered at school and supported by parents, plays in overcoming this crescendo of frustration.

In many families, parents do not involve their preliterate children in reading by reading together with them, showing them pictures in a book, reading aloud to them, or encouraging them to rhyme words that sound similar. This parental response is not unreasonable. After all, the thinking goes, this is the kind of thing schools are for—they will teach the child to read when the time comes.

Even parents who have provided appropriate early reading experiences for their children with dyslexia often wonder if there is something else they could have done. When a child does not master reading as well as his or her peers, even though the child's parents and school have provided an environment that has been adequate for the reading development of the child's classmates, many parents experience a high level of guilt. Statements such as "I should have noticed it earlier," "I should have been more concerned about it," and "I should have handled it better" indicate that parents often feel they have failed to provide their children with a "good" environment for reading development. Strangely enough, the discovery that the problem may have originated in the child's "miswired" brain or with "problematic" genes often relieves parental anxiety about failing to place a child in the right reading environment.

A feeling of relief is not enough to correct the problem, however. What really needs to be understood is that, in severe cases of reading disability, a normal environment for reading development is not sufficient, and extraordinary instructional effort may be required. Scientists are working hard to determine whether some medical intervention is possible, but our best bet right now lies in educational efforts.

These educational efforts can be classified into three categories: (1) special types of prereading and early reading instruction as well as remediation, when necessary, carried out by appropriately trained teachers; (2) a significantly greater amount and intensity of conscious and accurate reading practice (e.g., through computer-based exercises and reading practice;[3] and (3) increased parental awareness of the ways in which they can help develop their children's prereading skills, encourage and stimulate the poor reader's practice of reading, and ensure the continuity of the remedial effort. Thus, the most successful treatment is based on and involves three components—the school (by providing specialized, professional instruction in reading), the student's practice reading, and the family's ongoing support of the process. The coordinated effort of all three elements offers the most hope for success.

In 1997 the NICHD published some sobering numbers addressing the effectiveness of reading instruction in the United States. According to the institute's research-based estimates, about 40 percent of children in the United States encounter reading problems, for whatever reasons, severe enough to hinder their enjoyment of reading.

This figure should be a call for immediate action. We believe that all 40 percent of these children can be helped. Does this mean that all of them should become clients of special-education services? Of course not. If special services are offered to 40 percent of the population, they are no longer special and their quality may deteriorate rapidly. This number indicates that reading curricula as they now exist are not working adequately for many children. Therefore, the country's entire system of reading education needs to be changed. This startling statistic should be a wake-up call and should motivate us to restructure regular classroom teaching and retrain reading instructors.

Twenty-five years of reading-disability research funded by the NICHD has documented many teaching and intervention techniques that can help produce the skills students need to master reading. The problem, however, is communication of this information to teachers. According to the Orton Dyslexia Society,

> . . . most teachers are not being given the content and depth of training needed to enable them to provide appropriate instruction. Altering current practice in teacher training will require a fundamental change in how reading instruction commonly is viewed. In contrast to the erroneous and damaging belief that little preparation is necessary to be able to teach reading,

we need to promote awareness that literacy instruction is a complicated task. The professional demands of teaching reading must be acknowledged, and, in turn, much-improved training opportunities must be available to prepare teachers better for the challenging task of teaching children to read. (p. 1)[4]

To meet the demands of nationwide reading failure, the professional preparation of teachers should include four elements. First, it should include fundamental knowledge about the correspondence between written and spoken language and language structure. Second, preparation should involve transmission of knowledge regarding what basic skills are required for children to master reading. Third, familiarity should be developed with leading methodologies of reading education, such as whole-language and phonics methodologies. Balanced views should replace sweeping rejections of or rigid commitments to a particular methodology. Ideally, teachers should use a balanced and informed approach based on the instructional technique that will best address a given component of reading at a particular time. Fourth and finally, instruction should impart to teachers a basic knowledge about how to diagnose the types of reading problems that students are likely to experience.

These changes in teacher preparation will not be free, but they will be significantly less costly than educating an increasing number of special-education teachers to play catch-up to a constantly growing population of poor readers. Although special-education teachers will still be needed to teach the more severely impaired readers, many poor readers can be taught successfully in the regular classroom.[5]

Teaching Reading: Down to Specifics

Before we present the specific strategies investigated by researchers in their intervention studies, we introduce two general principles for reading instruction.[6] First, children profit most from reading instruction that is explicit, systematic, and sequential. Second, as is the case for all teaching, reading instruction is most effective if it is active and engaging and based on discovery and understanding, even as it allows room for practice and exercise. Although some would say that these different components are alternatives and reflect the very contradiction between different modern leading approaches to teaching reading, we think that effective reading instruction has to include these multiple elements.

An example of the importance of structured self-practice comes from a study conducted by Barbara Wise and Richard Olson.[7] These researchers selected a group of second through fifth graders who scored in the lowest 10 percent of their classes on a test of single-word recognition. These children were trained in half-hour sessions over a semester (for a total of twenty-five hours) during their regular reading periods. The children were asked to read interesting stories on the computer. The stories were chosen to match or to be slightly ahead of a given child's reading level. The children were told to select with the computer mouse any difficult word they encountered. A computer-synthesized voice would then read the word to ensure the accuracy of the child's reading. This structured reading practice brought significant gains on several measures of word recognition.

This study permits us to draw two conclusions. First, structured and accurate reading is very beneficial to poor readers. Second, the amount of instruction in accurate reading these children received during the training periods was significantly greater than most of these readers would have received in their regular classrooms.

However, when researchers returned to the same group of children two years after the end of training, they discovered that the students' word recognition had returned to the slow rate experienced before training.[8] The lesson here is that the training of reading accuracy should be structured, continuous, and, most important, sustained.

The importance of direct reading instruction was also shown by Rebecca Felton in her longitudinal study of poor readers. Felton followed a group of poor readers from the third to the eighth grade. The students were evaluated at the beginning and end of the study, as well as in the fifth grade. When Felton compared reading improvements over time, she found that poor readers made more gains in all aspects of reading from the third to fifth grades than from the fifth to eighth grades. In other words, poor readers made less progress in middle school than in elementary school. Felton attributed this difference to the decrease in direct-reading instruction that students experience when they progress from elementary to middle school.[9]

Our own research (see Chapter 5 for details) has convincingly shown that the format of teaching is very important. Teaching should be organized to fit students' individual profiles. The ideal, of course, is to individualize teaching so that every child receives the maximum possible benefit. However, this ideal is no more likely to be attained now than it was when first proposed in Rousseau's time. What can be done is to organize teaching in such a way that it meets the needs of children who differ in terms of three main types of abilities—analytical, creative, and practical. According to Sternberg, people have different ability profiles, and the most successful outcomes over a life span are seen when a person finds a match between his or her set of abilities and the requirements of the outside world.[10]

Traditionally, most teaching around the world emphasizes memory and, to a lesser extent, analytical reasoning, which primarily benefits students with a memory-oriented or analytically oriented profile of abilities. In our work, we have shown that everything (even reading!) can be taught triarchically—in a way that addresses all three types of abilities, analytical, creative, and practical. Our research findings demonstrate that, as a group, children taught triarchically (to think analytically, creatively, and practically while learning) outperform children taught only for memory or only for analytical thinking.[11] This superior performance is seen not only on specialized tasks (e.g., those that are creative and practical), but also on traditional analytical activities and even on multiple-choice memory tests at which one would expect the more traditionally instructed children to excel.

In its summary research statement, the NICHD reviewed leading intervention studies in the field of specific reading disability and proposed six major principles for early reading instruction.[12] Notice that these principles, discussed in the following numbered sections, closely match a definition of dyslexia we presented earlier.

Underlying these principles is the idea that instruction should be targeted at reading, given that the other cognitive skills of the child are in accordance with typical development. Instruction should be aimed at the improvement of phonological (e.g., phonemic awareness and phonological memory) and decoding skills, which have been shown to be central to the enhancement of single-word reading. Reading instruction should also address spelling skills, as poor spelling is assumed to be closely linked to the development of reading problems. In the following pages, we will use examples from scientific research to explain and illustrate fundamental principles.

1. We need to teach phonemic awareness directly, starting in kindergarten.

As noted earlier, phonemic awareness is the ability to recognize and analyze the individual sounds (called phonemes) in words; children who are able to recognize and identify individual sounds in words are phonemically aware. It is important to remember that phonemic awareness and phonics are different concepts. Phonemic awareness refers to the mastery of the skill of analyzing the individual speech elements within a word. Often young children attain a great degree of awareness of the sounds within words (for example, rhymes) prior to acquiring any knowledge regarding specific sound-letter (or sound-spelling) correspondence. Phonics is about this correspondence—the representation of sounds with letters.

For the majority of normal readers, phonemic awareness as well as other phonological skills (e.g., phonological memory) further develop as a consequence of learning how to read. Some of these skills develop in normal readers even when these children are not given explicit instruction in this area. In other words, normal readers become adept at analyzing the sounds within words and understanding the relationship between letters and sounds as they learn to recognize words in print.

However, without direct instruction in phonemic awareness, many readers with dyslexia fail to develop such understanding even though they learn to recognize some individual words. Thus, these poor readers cannot benefit from the alphabetic system of English and are forced to rely on other cues for reading—memory of how words look, pictures, clues from the meaning of the story, and so on. Although all these cues play a role in reading, to be a proficient reader in English requires understanding that words are made up of individual sounds and that these sounds are represented by letters or strings of letters. Phonemic awareness can be developed through a variety of activities in which the student actively engages in analyzing the sounds of words (rhyming games, songs and poetry, categorizing words based on sounds). Research has unequivocally established the importance of phonemic awareness to the mastery of reading, through three major pieces of evidence. First, kindergarten and first-grade children who were behind in mastering phonemic awareness were found to be at risk for having problems learning to read.[13] Second, the phonemic awareness of older children and adults who are poor readers has been found to be limited.[14] Third, teaching strategies aimed at fostering phonemic awareness have been found to be an important component of successful instructional programs.[15]

All students need a firm foundation of phonemic awareness prior to receiving formal instruction in reading. Therefore, kindergarten programs should include well-organized and carefully sequenced phonemic-awareness instruction for all students. Some students, including those at risk for difficulty learning to read, will require additional structured training in phonemic awareness to prepare them for reading and spelling instruction. Furthermore, when reading and spelling training begins, training in phonemic awareness should not stop. Many intervention studies have shown that teaching phonemic awareness and sound-spelling relationships simultaneously accelerates the development of reading skills. For older poor readers, assessment should include evaluation of phonemic-awareness skills and instructional programs should include skills that have not been mastered. The following box provides examples of tasks that may be used to evaluate phonemic awareness.

Most children in kindergarten or higher grades are developmentally ready to receive phonemic-awareness instruction. Moreover, direct phonemic-awareness instruction appears to be the most powerful tool to help those children who fall behind. Although not giving direct phonemic-awareness intervention to these children puts them at risk for falling further and further behind, giving them this instruction, however, does not magically transform them into normal readers. Researchers have suggested that, whereas the integration of phonological skills into higher-level reading operations is automatic for normal readers, children with dyslexia have difficulty integrating their mastered phonological skills and turning them into automatized components of higher-order reading.[17]

In this context, it is important to appreciate the observation made by many scientists, child-development practitioners, and educators that *all* children require some level of instruction to master reading skills. Reading skills do not develop naturally; virtually no child will read if he or she is not taught how.

Examples of Tasks of Phonemic Awareness[16]

Phoneme deletion
What word would be left if the /s/ sound were taken away from
  sad?
Word to word matching
Do *cat* and *cowboy* begin with the same sound?
Blending
What word will you get if you put these sounds together: /b/,
  /a/, /g/?
Sound isolation
What is the first sound in *nose*?
Phoneme segmentation
What sounds do you hear in the word *hat*?
Phoneme counting
How many sounds do you hear in the word *candy*?
Odd word out
What word starts with a different sound:
cook, cat, car, or *dust*?
Sound to word matching
Is there an /l/ in *tulip*?

2. We need to teach sound-spelling correspondence explicitly.

Thus far, the main conclusion to be drawn from intervention studies is that explicit, direct instruction, including matching of sounds with corresponding letters (or sounds with corresponding letter combinations), is more beneficial than asking a child to derive the sounds for the letters by giving clues. Researchers have found evidence that many children have difficulty identifying the individual sound-spelling correspondences if they hear them only embedded in words or word parts. Students should be taught to read and spell words by utilizing the letter-sound associations they have been taught.

Explicit phonemic instruction begins with bringing the student's attention to a speech sound (phoneme) in isolation and may include information about how the sound is produced. Next, the letter or combination of letters that represents that sound in English is taught directly. For example, to introduce a new phoneme, the teacher would produce the sound and ask the children to make the sound, emphasizing the correct pronunciation. The teacher also might lead students in a discovery of the phoneme in different positions within words (first sound, last sound). The teacher would then show the children the letter used to represent the sound that had been introduced. Beginning readers should practice new phonemes and those already learned by using them to read and spell words.

3. We need to teach the most frequent and highly regular sound-spelling relationships directly and systematically.

English has about seventy highly frequent sound-spelling pairs. Research has shown that if these pairs are taught systematically, the benefit for reading is substantial. Systematic teaching means that instruction in sound-spelling correspondences is closely linked to the material children are given to read and spell. The closer the match between the two components (the sound-spelling correspondence and the reading and spelling material), the higher the probability of a successful outcome. Systematic also means presenting letter-sound associations in a logical order, beginning with the most regular and proceeding to the more irregular. Some regular sound-letter relationships are shown in Table 8.1 on the next page.

Many teachers are both attentive to details and creative when designing their class lessons. As one elementary-school teacher pointed out, if the first sound-spelling relationships introduced to children were *a*, *b*, and *c*, then the only two real words the children could read would be *ba* and *cab*. If, however, the first sound-spelling relationships are introduced by the letters *a*, *c*, *e*,

Letter	sound (as in)	Letter	sound (as in)	Letter	sound (as in)
a	cat	g	gap	v	velvet
m	mix	l	limp	e	bet
t	tea	h	horse	u-e	mule
s	sun	u	umbrella	p	pocket
i	hit	c	cap	w	wet
f	fun	b	baby	j	jar
a-e	make	n	nickel	i-e	ripe
d	dog	k	kiss	y	yoke
r	rose	o-e	role	z	zebra
ch	check	ou	loud	kn	know
ea	meat	oy	joy	oa	loaf
ee	heel	ph	photo	oi	coil
er	stern	qu	quit	ai	paid
ay	May	sh	show	ar	far
igh	light	th	think	au	maul
ew	drew	ir	dirt	aw	dawn

Figure 8.1 Sound–letter relationships

and *r*, the variety of words available to the children is larger (*arc,
are, car, rear, race, era, acre, ace, care,* and so on).

4. We need to teach children how to sound out words.

The mastery of as few as two or three sound-spelling correspondences should be followed immediately by teaching children how to blend sounds into words. Children should be taught how to move sequentially through the words from left to right in order to sound out the word. The training should be consistent in that only those sound-spelling relationships that have been mastered should be used in these exercises.

For example, the word *sun* includes three sounds (*s, u,* and *n*). The teacher should help the child realize this by asking him or her to divide the word into sounds and to pronounce the word sound-by-sound.

5. Students should practice the learned sound-spelling relationships using connected, decodable text.

Nothing is free, including reading. The results of much intervention research emphasize how important it is for children to practice applying their knowledge of sound-spelling relationships to the task of reading. Only *decodable* text—that is, text that matches the level of sound-spelling correspondence mastered by students—should be used for teaching students who are developing their skills in using spelling-sound associations to read unfamiliar words. This is true both for beginning readers and for those who have failed to develop these skills and who require remediation. The higher the level of mastery of sound-letter relationships, the more sophisticated in meaning the decodable texts should be. However, the initial level of decodable texts should be very low, so that students can have the opportunity to practice their newly acquired skills. Following is an example of sentences from a decodable story used after students have been taught the sounds for a set of consonants, short vowels, and the *ee* spelling of the long *e* sound: "See the seed. Plant it deep. Feel the sun."

Less-decodable texts require children to use prediction or context to read words that they have not yet been taught to decode or that are not yet in their sight vocabulary. Whereas much evidence supports the importance of prediction skills in reading to determine meaning (such as predicting the next event or outcome), this strategy is not considered useful in word recognition.

To understand the challenge introduced by the prediction strategy, consider the following sample of Jack London's writing. A "regular" sixth-grade reader was able to decode approximately 80 percent of this text.[18] The passage shows how the sixth grader sounded out the text. The dashed slots represent the parts of the words that the child was not able to decode accurately. Now, draw on your own personal experience to consider how easy it would be for you to understand this piece.

He had never seen dogs fight as these w-ish c-r-t-s, and his first ex-t-t him an unf-able l-n. It is true, it was a vi- ex-, else he would not have lived to pr-it by it. Curly was the v-. They were camped near the log store, where she, in her friend- way, made ad- to a husky dog the size of a full- wold, th- not half so large as–he. –ere was no w-ing, only a leap in like a flash, a met- clip of teeth, a leap out equal- swift, and Curly's face was ripped open from eye to jaw.

[He has never seen dogs fight as these wolfish creatures, and his first experience taught him an unforgettable lesson. It is true, it was a vivid experience, else he would not have lived to profit by it. Curly was the victim. They were camped near the log store, where she, in her friendly way, made advance to a husky dog the size of a full-grown wolf, though not half so large as she. There was no warning, only a leap in like a flash, a metallic clip of teeth, a leap out equally swift, and Curly's face was ripped open from eye to jaw.

No doubt, some of the unknown words in this passage could be determined using context or a prediction strategy. However, simply making the right prediction—without decoding—does not transfer to real reading. Children can practice most effectively when they are provided with decodable texts early in instruction and until they have mastered a basic set of decoding skills. Then, predictable texts can be used to encourage reading further and to allow students to augment their reading-related self-efficacy.

We emphasize the importance of teaching and practicing decoding skills because poor word recognition is the major hallmark of a person with a reading disability. To compensate for their limited recognition skills, poor readers tend to rely more on context and to use guessing and prediction strategies. Many scientists have noted that poor decoding skills in elementary school are highly predictive of limited comprehension and inaccurate and slow reading in the later grades. Direct instruction in decoding along with practice using decodable texts is a critical component of remedial programs for students with reading disabilities.

6. To develop language comprehension, teachers should use interesting and culture- and age-appropriate stories.

It would be wrong to conclude that everything we have said so far rules out the use of interesting and engaging authentic stories in the teaching of reading. What is ruled out unequivocally, however, is the use of these stories as reading material for students with extremely limited word-identification skills, whether they are nonreaders in grade one or very poor readers in grade five. As discussed, in the early stages of reading, the use of texts that are controlled for both decodability and vocabulary is crucial. However, more complex texts, texts that build motivation and passion for reading, should be read out loud by the teacher. These materials will build students' oral-language comprehension, which is closely linked to reading comprehension. It is important to remember, though, to view texts with story-based materials as what they really are—the enhancers of comprehension—rather than as vehicles for teaching decoding skills.

For reading instruction to be effective, it is crucial that both comprehension and decoding skills, described in sections 1 through 5, be taught directly. Good readers read words accurately (using a variety of word-analysis skills, including the effective use of spelling-sound associations) and employ a variety of methods to determine the meaning of words and text. Instruction for young readers and older, poor readers must include a balance of techniques designed to build both word-identification and comprehension skills. Research indicates that teaching each of these components directly and systematically is the most effective instructional practice.[19]

At the early stages of reading acquisition, there is a notable discrepancy between children's oral-language comprehension and their reading comprehension. Their ability to comprehend orally is more fully developed. Therefore, the text material used for enhancing and promoting children's comprehension skills should be based on their oral-language rather than on their reading skills. These materials should be of a high enough level to build children's vocabulary and comprehension strategies and verbal reasoning.

In contrast, the material used to build decoding skills should focus narrowly on accomplishing that goal. Although the texts used should be as interesting and engaging as possible, the initial primary goal is to develop decoding skills rather than comprehension or vocabulary skills.

We Know What to Do—But When and How?

Now that we know how to help, when should we start and what role can concerned parents play? Common sense suggests that the intervention should start as soon as the child begins to fall behind. But within the field of reading instruction, professionals and researchers have been debating two major positions. According to the first position, the "developmental-lag" approach, teaching should be aimed at students performing at the mean of the class, and those that fall below this mean should not be helped or pushed but rather given time to catch up naturally. Institutionally, this position is reflected in educational policies that suggest retention without intervention. These are wait-and-see or wait-for-failure practices.[20]

According to the second position, the cognitive processes of children with reading difficulties do not, as the developmental-lag hypothesis supposes, simply develop at a slower rate through the same sequence experienced by normal readers. Rather, severely impaired readers are characterized by a deficit (i.e., the absence of a component of a process or a whole process or some failure to meet the developmental standard), and, therefore, they fail to develop appropriate reading skills. Rather than gradually catching up with their peers who do not have dyslexia, most such students fall further and further behind. A number of longitudinal studies have shown that 70 to 80 percent of children who are poor readers in third grade remain poor readers in ninth grade.[21] Scientists supporting this position argue that special measures should be undertaken to screen prereading children for the possibility of a future deficit, and preventive remediation should start prior to the formation of the deficit.[22]

The data unequivocally support the second position. Empirical studies of children with dyslexia do not show that reading disability results from developmental lag; on the contrary, much evidence supports the deficit model by demonstrating that deficiencies in phonological processing form obstacles to the development of reading and spelling. Therefore, it is clear when we need to intervene. We cannot wait. We need to construct programs for the primary grades that expedite the phonological development of future normal readers and prevent the formation of the deficit in those children who are at risk for dyslexia.

These findings have a number of implications for parents. First, it is clear that early identification and treatment of students at risk for having problems in reading provides the best opportunity for success. Children whose families have a history of reading difficulties should be carefully evaluated in kindergarten to determine whether risk factors (such as poor development of phonemic-awareness skills or failure to learn letter-sound associations) exist. If risk factors are present, interventions should begin immediately. Although some parents may worry about labeling their child as having a reading disability by documenting and treating the problem early, the alternative of waiting to see if a problem develops is far too risky.

It is also very important that the educational treatment be appropriate for the student and in line with the principles described here. The following case is given as an example of *inappropriate* early intervention for a student with a severe reading disability.[23]

Jacob (not his real name) was identified in first grade as having difficulties with reading and was given individual tutoring using predictable books. He was taught a number of strategies for reading words in stories, including looking at the pictures, skipping unknown words and using context to see what would make sense in the sentence, and using partial phonics cues (such as looking at the beginning letter of the word and thinking of a word starting with that sound that would make sense). Jacob received this type of instruction during the first and second grades, but his progress was limited and the decision was made to retain him in second grade. At this time, he was tested to determine eligibility for special-education services as a student with learning disabilities in reading. Testing showed that Jacob had significant deficits in phonemic awareness and decoding (using spelling-sound patterns to read unfamiliar words). He had learned only a few sight words and was unable to read the predictable books that he had appeared to have mastered in the first and second grades. Unfortunately, Jacob's early-intervention program had failed to target his particular needs and was ineffective.

Given that many children are not identified or properly taught early in their school careers, what can parents expect from remedial efforts? The case of Kathryn is informative in this regard.[24]

Kathryn seemed to be learning to read well in first grade. Her parents were both professionals and had provided her with ample prereading experiences. She was able to learn words as sight words easily and effectively used context to determine the meaning of stories. However, in second grade it became clear to her parents that Kathryn was not developing strategies for reading words that she had not memorized as sight words. Rather than sound out such words, Kathryn typically made a guess based on some of the letters in the word (e.g., *house* for *horse*). She seemed not to notice the importance of the order of letters within words (e.g., *present* for *perfect*), and her spelling skills were so poor that it was difficult to tell what she was trying to write. When her parents expressed concern, Kathryn's second-grade teacher suggested that she would develop these skills given time—the important thing was that she was enjoying reading and gaining meaning from text.

By third grade, Kathryn's reading and spelling skills had begun to have a negative impact on her school performance, and she became frustrated. Her parents obtained a comprehensive assessment that showed that Kathryn had significant weaknesses in phonemic awareness and decoding. Following this assessment, Kathryn began receiving regular tutorial instruction in those areas identified as weaknesses. This instruction has continued into middle school. She has become much more accurate in word identification and spelling skills, but she continues to require direct instruction in higher-level word analysis (e.g., root words, prefixes, suffixes) and in spelling more complex, multisyllable words.

Along with obtaining remedial instruction, Kathryn's parents pursued appropriate accommodations for her, which they discussed with her remedial tutor. With these accommodations, which included having extra time for tests requiring reading skills and being allowed to use spell checkers to correct her written work, Kathryn has improved her reading performance significantly and has had a chance to learn from her own mistakes. Appropriate remediation and accommodations that take into account her progress and are remedial in nature have enabled Kathryn to perform successfully in regular education classes and to plan to pursue a college education.

These cases illustrate the importance of assessments that include phonemic awareness and decoding, appropriate instruction that is targeted to the individual student's deficits and is carried out until the student becomes proficient, and appropriate accommodations for as long as they are needed.

A Note of Caution

Although the findings and recommendations discussed above are clear and well documented, we must add a cautionary note to this praise of early phonology-based intervention programs. As always, the truth is a little more complex than one might expect. As Benita Blachman[25] put it, "'phonological awareness' has become one of the educational buzzwords of the 1990s" (p. 411). It is important, as excited as we may be about the potential impact of science on educational practices, not to forget that many unanswered questions linger.

For example, studies have shown that socioeconomic class plays a significant role in determining parents' attitudes toward preliteracy activities with their children.[26] Children in middle-class families are often read to daily from the time the children are a year old. When they enter first grade, these children are not yet readers, but, on average, they are well prepared to become readers. These children are usually good at language rhymes; they know how to separate words into sounds; they understand what print is for; and they know how books work.

In contrast, many children from low-income families do not experience this preliteracy preparation. Therefore, on average, they come to school with less-developed phonological skills and they know much less about written words and books. These students are at risk for experiencing difficulties while learning how to read. This observation is important for kindergartens making decisions regarding their preliteracy curricula. Although all children most likely would benefit from early phonemic-awareness instruction, the greatest beneficiaries would be students from lower-income families and students at biological risk for reading difficulty.[27]

Moreover, scientists have found that not every child profits equally from early-intervention programs. Some children find it very difficult to perform phonemic-awareness tasks ("Do *plane* and *train* sound like each other?" "Sure, you can go places in both").[28] Such children may not respond to the type of instruction that is effective for most students. Early-intervention programs can help identify these "treatment-resistant" children so that more appropriate instruction can be offered at the very early stages of the child's development.

Another word of warning is in order regarding the assumption of the centrality of phonological-skill deficits to reading disability. Even though the best-described and most common subtype of dyslexia is one that is phonologically based, there may be other types of reading disabilities.[29] Therefore, we should expect to see some cases in which phonology-targeted intervention is not appropriate. Because many poor readers (up to 70 percent) profit from phonology-based intervention, early intervention efforts could help us identify those children whose deficit appears to be more complex or different.

Some researchers have suggested that phonological deficit is not the whole story underlying reading disabilities.[30] Support for this viewpoint comes from two lines of research, genetic studies and brain studies on dyslexia (Chapters 6 and 7). Both types of studies suggest that, whereas at the behavioral level there are significant links between different reading-related processes (e.g., phonological skills, single-word reading, and orthographic coding), there may be differential biological foundations for these processes.

The intriguing story of unique biological signatures for specific deficits in reading-related processes is only beginning to unfold. But there is enough preliminary evidence to attempt the verification of hypotheses that different genetic and functional brain pathways result in specific deficits (e.g., orthographic, phonological, or single-word reading). If these hypotheses hold true, these findings would explain why phonological training does not always yield a high degree of success and why there are children who resist treatment.[31]

The second part of this book has attempted to summarize the current state of knowledge regarding able and disabled reading acquisition. The scientific understanding of these issues has progressed immensely within the last decade, and, given its rapid development, there is good reason to hope that the gaps still existing will be filled in rather soon. What is also very exciting is that scientific ideas are now influencing the actual teaching of reading. However, because any educational innovation affects millions of children, it is necessary to be careful.

Recently, states such as California have started moving toward changing the whole-language practices that have dominated the teaching of reading for the last decade.[32] These states are attempting to promote balanced beginning-reading programs that include literature-based reading and writing instruction along with instruction in phonological skills (e.g., phonemic awareness, sound-spelling correspondence, alphabetic coding). It remains to be seen, however, how teachers will implement these new modes of instruction. Good ideas work only when they are well executed.

Children learn best when instruction corresponds to their current reading level. Children might not learn well when instruction is not attuned to their stage of mastery. For example, phonics instruction will not benefit students who do not yet possess sufficient levels of phonemic awareness to recognize that words are composed of individual sounds. Similarly, teaching phonics to a child who has already figured out the alphabetic principle and who reads Mark Twain for pleasure is diminishing his or her reading development. Thus, we have to find the golden middle. We should not bore children by making them endlessly divide words into phonemes; neither should we become so preoccupied trying to foster students' appreciation of authentic texts that we neglect to teach them to read the words accurately. The convergent evidence from research suggests that most children, including those at risk for reading failure, gain from developmentally appropriate instruction targeting specific reading skills.

Understanding the nature of the reading failure of a significant portion of the U.S. school population is a complex task. Scientists believe that this disability is of mixed origin and encompasses reading problems due to inappropriate instruction, lack of reading stimulation in children's families, cultural devaluation of the significance of reading for intellectual development, and so on. The quest to understand the various sources of reading failure in this diverse group of children could result in a "turtle game"—once we account for a certain percentage of reading failure, we might find that there is yet another reason why these children fail to reach grade-level standards. However, even though we do not know how many turtles there are "all the way down," we can say that most of these children will do much better in regular classrooms if the system of reading education in these classes changes.

Scientists have demonstrated that most children who might have been classified as having a reading disability prior to early intervention would not have been classified as such following intervention. Scientists, in collaboration with various advocacy groups, have suggested how regular instruction should be changed to help American children read better.[33]

Within the 40 percent of American pupils experiencing difficulty in mastering reading at school, however, there is a significantly smaller group of children (about 5 to 8 percent of the school population in the United States) who represent a distinct category of students whose development of reading skills needs special attention. We refer to these children as those who have a biological liability for dyslexia.

Improving the teaching of reading in regular classrooms will have a positive impact on all poor readers by providing a crucial component for those children who need better structure and stronger skill-oriented, directed instruction to master reading. Moreover, it will help address the need for special-educational support for the most severe cases of reading disability by minimizing the demand imposed on special education by the vast numbers of poor readers.

Hippocrates, in the fourth century B.C., was the first to systematize various ill-health symptoms accurately enough so that diseases could be diagnosed with some certainty. According to the ancient Greek doctor, his patients had diphtheria, tuberculosis, and influenza. None of his records, however, describe manic depression, smallpox, bubonic plague, or dyslexia. New civilizations bring new sets of challenges. In order for dyslexia to be recognized, we, as a civilization, had to reach a stage of development at which we could afford to expect all our citizens to read. Now we have to match our expectations with opportunities. Why lose more children? The time truly is now.

Chapter Nine

There Are No Jackpots

LD in the Courtroom

So far we have discussed definitional, scientific, and educational aspects of learning disabilities. Yet much of the action in the field of learning disabilities right now is occurring neither in the laboratories nor in the classrooms. It is occurring in courtrooms, usually when unhappy students or parents sue a school in response to what they view as inadequate services. We describe in this chapter some of the major court cases and their outcomes. The court cases show that in the courtroom, as in the LD lottery, there are no clear winners and no clear losers. They also attest to the need for scientists and educators to reach informed decisions about how to serve children with learning disabilities. Judges cannot be expected to make these decisions in a way that takes into account the accumulated body of knowledge about LD; by placing decisions in their hands, we are asking them to make decisions they were never trained to make.

LD and Litigation

The United States ranks as one of the most litigious societies in the world, and may well occupy the number one place. Many forces in U.S. society drive people toward litigation.

First, there is an extremely high proportion of lawyers relative to the total working population. Some of these lawyers need litigation as a means of staying in business.

Second, some individuals in the workforce have found that litigation can pay beyond their wildest dreams. Well-publicized, extremely generous settlements for some people may encourage other people to litigate matters that they might otherwise have sought to resolve by other means.

Third, there appears to be some potential to manipulate the system to win. Jury consultation has become a major business enterprise, and some people believe that with the right jury consultants to help litigants choose the right jury, almost any case can be won.

Fourth, U.S. society in some respects encourages people to view themselves as victimized. In another country, a person who stumbles and falls on the street might be viewed as careless in not looking where he or she was going. In the United States, any accident represents a potential lawsuit. Of course, in some instances a town, state, or whatever entity owns a street *is* careless in its upkeep, and so some argue that a lawsuit is the appropriate course of action.

The same considerations apply to the treatment of children with learning disabilities. Some lawsuits are frivolous; others are not. It is no easy task to separate the frivolous lawsuits from the serious ones that seek to redress a real wrong.

These issues become paramount because many issues of learning disabilities—which once were primarily psychological and educational issues—have now become legal issues. A discussion of three recent court cases will illustrate the kinds of issues that are raised in courtrooms and how they have been resolved.

Unfortunately, court proceedings pit against each other parties that ideally should be working with each other to produce a solution that is fair and will benefit all concerned. Instead of trying to achieve viable compromises and wise solutions that take all competing interests into account, court proceedings encourage a perverse mentality. As a result, organizations may actually support schools (or individuals) whose handling of a situation was poor, but whose loss in the court proceeding is seen as potentially punishing even to those who handle a situation well. Thus, even if a school district handled a particular situation poorly, other schools may see a loss by the school district as undermining schools' ability to handle their own situations well.

Because it pits against each other parties that should be working together, an adversarial system is *not* the best way to resolve issues regarding learning disabilities. Yet sometimes individuals or organizations believe they have no choice but to seek redress of perceived injustices in the courtroom.

Elizabeth Guckenberger, et al. *v.* Boston University, et al.

The Facts of the Case

The facts presented here are based on the actual findings of the court in this case, including paraphrasing of the court decision.[1]

A class-action suit was brought against Boston University (BU) by a group of students identified as having attention-deficit hyperactivity disorder (ADHD), attention-deficit disorder (ADD), and various learning disabilities. The basic claims were threefold: first, that BU was establishing unreasonable criteria by which students would qualify as disabled; second, that BU failed to provide reasonable procedures for reviewing and then evaluating students' requests for accommodations in their educational programs; and third, that BU prohibited, across-the-board, course substitutions in the areas of foreign language and mathematics. The university claimed that its eligibility criteria were reasonable, that its review and evaluation processes were fair, and that, as a university, it was within its rights in deciding what requirements to set for the conferral of a degree.

As background for its decision, the court pointed out that before 1995, BU was viewed as a leader among educational institutions in seeking to provide services to students diagnosed as having learning disabilities. BU's program was so comprehensive as to attract students with such problems. BU even had a brochure that advertised its accommodations, such as note-taking assistance and extended time on examinations. Whereas in 1990–1991, 42 students with self-proclaimed learning disabilities applied to BU, in 1994–1995, 348 students with LDs applied, 233 (two-thirds) were accepted, and 94 enrolled at BU. By late 1995, there were 429 such students applying to the university, and the university had enrolled 480 students identified as having learning disabilities.

In addition to in-class note takers, tape-recorded textbooks, and time and a half on final examinations for students with documented learning disabilities, course substitutions in mathematics and foreign languages were sometimes allowed. For example, a course on the anthropology of money could be substituted for a mathematics course, or a foreign-culture course could be substituted for a foreign-language course.

Before 1995, a standard process was in place by which a student would apply for accommodations. The student with an LD would submit a description of the need for accommodations, a statement of a history of accommodations, and a current professional evaluation. University staff would determine whether the request was appropriate and then act on it. The staff making the decision consisted for the most part of professionals with training in the LD area.

In the spring of 1995, the provost of BU, Jon Westling, apparently discovered what was going on—in particular, that students with LDs were allowed to make substitutions for mathematics and foreign-language courses. Previously, he had accepted BU's policies on students with LDs, apparently without giving them much thought. He now was not sure the policies were appropriate. Westling asked an assistant, Craig

Klafter, who apparently had no specialized qualifications or advanced training in the field of LD, to investigate whether there really existed a disability that would prevent a student from learning a foreign language. Klafter concluded that there was no such disability, nor was there a disability that would prevent a student from learning mathematics.

In June 1995, Westling effected a change in policy by which all letters granting accommodations would have to be approved by his office before they went out to students. He decided unilaterally to end course substitutions, without consulting experts in the field of learning disabilities or discussing with faculty members the importance of the mathematics and foreign-language requirements for the students' general education.

At about the same time, Westling started giving speeches in which he denounced what he called the "learning-disabilities movement." Westling questioned the rapidly and steadily increasing numbers of children who were being diagnosed as having learning disabilities and accused advocates of fashioning disabilities that were not scientifically supported. As quoted in the court decision, Westling viewed the learning-disability movement as "a great mortuary for the ethics of hard work, individual responsibility, and pursuit of excellence, and also for genuinely humane social order."2

In our opinion, Westling's strong ideology probably affected his judgment and resulted in his making statements that, if less extreme, might have been helpful rather than inflammatory. The result was that the issue of accommodations was not satisfactorily addressed.

The issue society has to face is that it generally is not willing to provide in the world of work the same accommodations it is willing to provide in the world of school. Students therefore may be set up in school to succeed in a system that they will never enter, because it does not exist in the world of work. Doctors are put to a difficult test when they need to treat patients where they are, sometimes in noisy and anxiety-provoking circumstances. They do not always have a quiet, stress-free room, such as that provided for some students for taking tests. Business executives have to make important, sometimes quick decisions under stressful circumstances, often with the affected people right there. Lawyers cannot leave the courtroom to ponder the rapid-fire legal tactics they may need to adopt in the courtroom.

In an address delivered on July 22, 1995, Westling spoke of a student named Samantha, whom he identified as a freshman in one of his classes at the university. Westling told of how Samantha had approached him on the first day of class and "shyly yet assertively" presented him with a letter from the Disability Services Office of BU. The letter stated that Samantha would need time and one half on all tests; double time on midterms and final examinations; examinations in a separate room; copies of lecture notes; and a seat in the front of the classroom. According to the letter, Samantha also might fall asleep in class, and it would be Westling's responsibility to fill her in on any material she missed while asleep. Westling labeled this student "Somnolent Samantha" and argued that the learning-disabilities movement actually interfered with students with learning disabilities, encouraging them to underperform rather than to work hard to overcome their academic difficulties. Moreover, he argued, these policies demoralized other students, who felt that a hoax was being perpetrated on the university, to their own disadvantage.

The issue of Somnolent Samantha blew up in Westling's face when the student turned out to be his own invention. There never was any Somnolent Samantha. Moreover, Samantha was not even a combined or averaged prototype of students whom Westling had encountered. Rather, she represented some kind of idealization of the kind of student whom Westling apparently had come to believe existed and needed to be put in her proper place. The court pointed out that Westling's belief notwithstanding, there had been no documented instances at BU of falsifications of learning disabilities for the purpose of obtaining accommodations.

Somnolent Samantha, as Westling called her, probably did more damage to Westling's and BU's case than did any other single issue. To this day, no one seems to know why Westling invented Samantha. Perhaps Westling himself does not know. But this invention suggested to some that Westling was substituting fiction for fact.

Westling discovered that his directive that all accommodation letters be approved by his office was being disregarded by the learning-disabilities office. Westling ordered the files of all students for whom the disabilities office had prepared but not yet delivered accommodation letters to be delivered to his office, where he and members of his staff, none of whom had any apparent specialized advanced training in the nature or evaluation of learning disabilities, reviewed them. Westling and his staff concluded that only a few of the students had sufficiently documented disabilities to merit the accommodations that were about to be granted.

At this point, Westling made yet another apparent mistake. According to the court transcript, Westling sent a letter to the learning-disabilities office that accused the staff of incompetence and of willfully and knowingly undermining university policies and standards. Westling may have believed that students were being given accommodations they did not need. But it is not clear why, if he insisted that evaluators have the highest level of credentials, he would assign people with questionable credentials to make decisions about accommodations. This inconsistency could only hurt BU's case.

The letter Westling wrote did not seek to deny any accommodations, only to make such accommodations substantially less likely to be made and to restrict the kinds of accommodations that would be made. Westling insisted that corrective action be taken immediately and that requests for accommodations would have to include (1) current evaluations (i.e., evaluations no more than three years old); (2) actual test results supporting the proposed accommodations; (3) documentation regarding the credentials and competence of the professional evaluator who had labeled the student as having a learning disability; and (4) a detailed analysis by the disability-office staff, including an academic history of the student. In addition, Westling instituted a change in procedure for accommodations whereby students would be informed that course substitutions for mathematics and foreign language would not be available.

The credibility of these directives was compromised by the fact that the directives were made without a thorough study by competent professionals representing a diversity of viewpoints. Whether the directives were justified in view of BU's educational goals is almost beside the point. The directives did not result from a process of deliberation that would appear sufficiently credible to the faculty, to the students, or to the legal system that eventually would sit in judgment.

Westling's directive was followed, but apparently at least some staff at the learning-disabilities office told worried students to ignore the letters they were receiving. The result was chaos. A letter went out from the learning-disabilities office, without Westling's approval, issuing new, stricter guidelines. Disapproving of the letter, Westling had another letter sent to students that emended the earlier letter. By the end of 1995, few people could figure out what BU's policy really was.

By early 1996, several employees in the disabilities office had resigned, and, curiously, the Office of the Provost became responsible for deciding what accommodations, if any, would be granted to students with learning disabilities. Although professionals, including those left in the disabilities office, were consulted, the responsibility for the decisions lay with the Office of the Provost. Eventually, a new director was hired for the learning-disability support services, and responsibility devolved to her to make decisions.

The lawsuit filed by Guckenberger and her fellow students was based on their experiences at BU. For lack of space, we do not attempt to relate the experiences of all the students, but to relate the experiences of the primary plaintiff, Guckenberger, as described in the court decision.

Elizabeth Guckenberger was diagnosed as dyslexic (i.e., as having a reading disability) in 1990, when she was a college freshman. The college she was attending, Carleton, provided her with a variety of accommodations, including double time on examinations, exemption from the school foreign-language requirements, and the option of having a note taker take notes for her. Guckenberger also received accommodations when she took the Law School Admission Test (LSAT). Ultimately, she was admitted to the Boston University School of Law.

The BU Law School was aware of her reading problem, and the letter of admission stated that she would receive accommodations to the full extent required by the law. Guckenberger submitted her materials to the learning-disabilities office at BU, with the result that the office determined that she had "problems with both visual and auditory processing." It was recommended that she receive note-taking assistance, a reduction in course load, priority registration for afternoon classes, and time and a half on examinations, which would be administered in a distraction-free room. For her first year of law school, Guckenberger received these accommodations.

During the first semester of her second year at BU, Guckenberger went to verify that she would receive accommodations on examinations she was about to take. She was informed that she would need to be completely retested for dyslexia before examinations began. Guckenberger asked for names of specialists whose evaluations would be acceptable to Boston University and was told that no list was available. She further was told that she could not be provided with a formal statement of the new policy at BU.

Guckenberger sought a new evaluation, but neither of two doctors was able to schedule the evaluation until after the examination period would be over. Although at first she was told that she would need to have the retesting done quickly, she later was granted a deferral until August of the following year, which would enable her to take the examinations with the usual accommodations.

In the ensuing months, Guckenberger met with a university official, whose attitude was not encouraging. This official expressed concerns that some students might be "faking" learning disabilities for the purpose of obtaining accommodations, and he also indicated that he thought it significant that those getting diagnoses were primarily "rich kids." He further apparently referred to some licensed specialists in the field of learning disabilities as "snake-oil salesmen."

Eventually, Guckenberger was retested and received the identical diagnosis with the identical recommendations. In fact, throughout her time in law school at BU, Guckenberger always received all the accommodations she requested. But Guckenberger, in addition to her learning disability, had a history of emotional problems, and the court decision states that she experienced anxiety during the 1995–1996 school year because her accommodations were threatened. Thus, the harm done to her was not with respect to her learning disability, but with regard to the anxiety she claimed to suffer as a result of the situation.

The Ruling of the Court

The court decision comprised thirteen points. The decision noted that federal law prohibits universities—public or private—from discriminating against students with specific learning disabilities. The court further noted that the requirement of retesting was unacceptable because it tended to screen out students with specific learning disabilities. But as BU policy had since changed, the issue had become moot. The court also viewed BU's policy of not accepting evaluations by persons with only a master's degree as unacceptable, again because it tended to screen out students with specific learning disabilities. According to the court, BU did not demonstrate that individuals with only a master's degree would be unable to make an adequate diagnosis of learning disabilities. The court accepted, however, that the rendering of evaluations of persons with ADHD or ADD could be restricted to individuals with a doctorate.

The court further found that BU violated the law in changing its policy regarding accommodations without giving any advance warning to eligible students. The court found that Westling and his staff had formulated and implemented a procedure based on uninformed stereotypes about individuals with learning disabilities.

The court held that federal law does not require a university to modify its degree requirements by permitting course substitutions if the university determines that those requirements are a fundamental part of its academic program. However, the decision stated, BU's refusal to modify its degree requirements was based not on such considerations, but on uninformed stereotypes. At the same time, the plaintiffs failed to demonstrate that a request to modify degree requirements in mathematics was necessary, given current scientific knowledge. In sum, according to the court decision, BU breached its contract with the students by failing to honor its commitments to them with regard to the documentation of learning disabilities and the appropriate accommodations to be made for them.

The outcome was that BU was ordered by Judge Patti B. Saris to pay Guckenberger $5,800 and to pay five other plaintiffs amounts ranging from $1 to $13,000. The total payouts to the plaintiffs were just under $30,000. Later, in 1998, the court ruled that BU did not have to make a substitution for foreign-language requirements if the university believed the learning of a foreign language to be an essential part of students' education.

Who won? It is difficult to say. The students won financial settlements, but these settlements were small relative to the time
and effort the students put into the lawsuit and relative to the
probable costs of the litigation to all parties. Some of BU's policies were overturned, but others were upheld, leaving the university in a position in which it, too, could say it had won. To
the extent that either side won, it was a Pyrrhic victory at best.

Boston University's greatest error may have been its confusing, inconsistent, sometimes poorly motivated, and rapidly
changing policies. The court decision is unlikely to result in
much stabilization, either for BU or for any other institution.
The question of what to do about alleged foreign-language disabilities and the taking of foreign-language courses was unresolved and probably cannot be resolved in a courtroom. The
decision regarding mathematics disability and mathematics
courses was also left as largely unresolved.

What kinds of accommodations are really appropriate under
what circumstances? The court decision did not address this
question clearly. Indeed, it is hard to see how this court decision could have much generalization beyond the specifics of
the particular case. This is a problem with many court decisions, and yet another reason why matters of policy are better
decided rationally in schools than in courtrooms. For example,
the judge allowed that a university could uphold its academic
standards and mission by requiring a foreign language, or
whatever, but she also stated that BU's requirements of the LD
students did not serve to uphold such standards. Requiring a
doctorate on the part of a diagnostician to diagnose ADD or
ADHD but not LD seems an arbitrary decision on the part of
the court. For the most part, the people who have the training
to diagnose attention deficits will be the same people who
have the training to diagnose learning deficits.

The idea that psychological and educational issues should be
decided in a courtroom is unfortunate from almost any point
of view. BU practically invited legal action by the inconsisten-

cies in its policies and by the seeming arbitrariness of the policy decisions it was making. Yet school districts are likely to become more and more afraid to follow what they believe to be educationally justifiable guidelines for fear of being sued. Moreover, such lawsuits apparently can be filed successfully even by people who do not necessarily suffer from lack of accommodations, but who get anxious or depressed over negotiating for these accommodations.

Pain-and-suffering complaints have become common in the U.S. legal system. Whether justified or not, they tend to obscure the real issues, because they can result in litigating not the procedures themselves, but whether these procedures caused pain and suffering.

We have reviewed the Guckenberger case in detail because it raises so many issues about learning disabilities and the law. How should students be identified as having learning disabilities? Who should be allowed to do the identifications? What kinds of accommodations should be made, and under what circumstances? How should schools react to requests for accommodations? Every one of these issues confronts students and school administrators every day. We review next some other cases in less detail. They raise important issues, but perhaps not so many and diverse issues as the Guckenberger case.

The Guckenberger case involved students at the graduate level; some lawsuits have pertained to students much younger in age. One such case is the earlier case of *Florence Country School District Four* v. *Shannon Carter*.

Florence County School District Four
v. Shannon Carter

We describe this case in less detail than we described the Guckenberger case, giving its flavor rather than trying to present it in all its aspects.[3] In 1983, Florence County School District IV of South Carolina evaluated Shannon Carter, who was fifteen years old at the time, as unmotivated in her studies, and urged her parents to get her to work harder. This diagnosis was based on an evaluation made by an uncertified evaluator who had used suspect procedures for evaluating Shannon.

Shannon's parents began to push Shannon harder, but Shannon became severely depressed and potentially suicidal. In 1985, a licensed clinical social worker tested Shannon and found that she had both a learning disability and an attention-deficit disorder. The school district then gave Shannon an extensive set of tests and reached the same conclusion. At this point, Shannon was well behind her peer group academically and, according to the report of her lawyer, was functionally illiterate.

Shannon's parents now found themselves in disagreement with the school district. The district proposed to place Shannon in a partial special-education program that would involve three hours of special work each week. Shannon's parents, based on advice from experts, argued for a self-contained LD classroom. The district did not have such a classroom, however, and was unwilling to set one up. Nor was it willing to pay for Shannon to be placed in the self-contained LD classroom of a neighboring district, District One. In May 1985, representatives of the school district basically told Shannon's parents that they had made their final offer and that there was nothing more to discuss.

Shannon's parents requested a due-process hearing, arguing that three hours per week of special education was insufficient for their child. A hearing was held, and the hearing officer maintained that the proposal of the school was adequate. Shannon's parents, unwilling to accept this decision, pulled Shannon out of the public schools and enrolled her in a private school that they believed would make adequate provisions for her.

In the fall of 1985, a reviewing officer upheld the decision of the hearing officer. The Carters then filed suit. A series of court hearings was held, and the case eventually made its way to the Supreme Court. Although the case involved just one individual, a great deal was at stake. The issue was whether the Carters should be reimbursed for Shannon's education at the private school. School districts from all around the country realized that they had a stake in the decision, because if the local district lost, they, too, might find themselves bearing substantial costs for the education of children identified as having either learning disabilities or attention-deficit disorders. Given that, in some districts, the number of identified students had reached 20 percent of the student population, school districts feared that a decision in favor of Shannon's parents could force them into extreme financial exigency.

By the time the case reached the Supreme Court, the whole U.S. educational establishment was watching. Friend-of-the-court briefs were filed in favor of the local school district by seventeen states, as well as by a number of other organizations. The identities of the organizations that filed briefs also say a lot. These organizations included the National League of Cities, the U.S. Conference of Mayors, the Council of State Governments, the National Association of Counties, the National Governors' Association, the National School Boards Association, and the National Association of State Boards of Education, among others. Briefs in favor of Shannon were filed by the United States Department of Justice, the National Head Injury Foundation, Inc., the National Alliance for the Mentally Ill, the National Association of Protection and Advocacy Systems, and the Learning Disability Association of America, among others.

The number of organizations involved in this lawsuit shows how deeply issues of learning disabilities permeate U.S. society. These organizations have somewhat different interests in this and related cases. Basically, those filing for the school system were concerned about the cost and other resource implications that would ensue if the school district lost. These organizations were concerned about the general implications of the case, not about whether the school district handled the situation correctly. The organizations filing for the plaintiff were concerned with protecting the individual rights and privileges of students identified as having learning disabilities.

The Supreme Court made its decision in a mere thirty-four days. In a decision written by Justice Sandra Day O'Connor, the Court ruled for Shannon. According to the Court, school systems must provide children with an appropriate special education. It was not sufficient to adopt an attitude of "take it or leave it." The special education also had to be free.

We believe that all children should be provided with an appropriate education, special or not. To the extent that the school district did not provide an appropriate education, its response was inadequate, regardless of the particular circumstances. We are concerned, though, that a system is evolving that pressures school districts to provide an appropriate education only if children are identified as having a disability of some kind. It is therefore little wonder that so many parents are seeking to have their children labeled as having a disability. In essence, we are creating a scheme whereby a school will invest more resources in a child, but only if the child is certified as having something wrong with him or her. An alternative approach, and the approach we advocate, would be to say that all children, regardless of whether they are labeled or not, must be provided with an appropriate education.

Not all cases go to court. Some are heard by other kinds of officiating bodies.

The Case of Matthew P., a Student in the School District of Philadelphia

We discuss here the result not of a court decision, but of a recent special-education due-process appeal review panel in the state of Pennsylvania.[4]

Matthew C. was an eight-year-old student residing in the Philadelphia school district who had been found to be eligible for special-education services and other related services. First classified as learning disabled in 1992, his diagnosed disabilities included visual perception and visual processing, visual memory, auditory processing, and attention-deficit disorder.

In September 1995, Matthew's parents arranged, at their own expense, for him to receive one hour of tutoring per week in a method called the Wilson Reading System, which involved phonetically based reading taught by a multisensory approach. By the fall of 1996, Matthew was showing some limited progress in the development of basic reading skills.

In June 1996, the school district proposed an individualized education program (IEP) for Matthew for the following school year which would use an alternative reading program. Matthew's parents were asked to sign a form approving this program. They refused, asking that the IEP designate the Wilson Reading System as the prescribed one for Matthew. Now the district refused, insisting on the alternative program. Following a due-process hearing of five sessions, the hearing officer concluded that the program proposed by the school was appropriate for Matthew. He therefore ordered the district to continue with its prescribed program.

Matthew's parents objected, stating that (1) uncontested evidence that the school's reading program was not working for Matthew had been presented to and ignored by the hearing officer; (2) the hearing officer had failed to consider additional specific recommendations relevant to Matthew's learning environment, such as provision of a separate, quiet space and daily one-on-one instruction in reading for one hour per day; and (3) the hearing officer had erred by not invalidating the IEP meeting, during which the district's representative had spent a great deal of time on the phone or out of the room.

The panel, taking into account all available evidence, ruled in favor of Matthew and his parents. Members pointed out that although Matthew had a low-average IQ, his educational progress was poor. His report card for the 1994–1995 school year revealed grades of D and sometimes of C in reading, and standardized test scores for reading showed minimal progress. As the school's program was not working, an alternative program was needed, and the panel was persuaded that the recommendation of the parents for a multisensory reading system with one-on-one instruction by a qualified instructor in a separate area was appropriate. In particular, the district would have to provide the one-on-one instruction by a certified teacher for at least one hour per day, five days per week; to designate a separate space in which to deliver this instruction; to evaluate and provide additional services as needed; to use technology such as a speech synthesizer or computer-enhanced learning programs; to use talking books or equivalent ways to supplement and enhance reading; and to have an assigned aide to serve as a scribe to help Matthew in transcriptions.

We are rapidly reaching a point that is beyond our reach. If we provided 20 percent, 10 percent, or even 5 percent of our children with the equivalent of these services, our school systems would risk going bankrupt or into great debt. The other option, of course, is to raise taxes. The question, then, becomes one of how we can fulfill the needs of our students and still stay within the resources of our school systems as they now exist. We do not have a final answer to this question, nor are we aware of anyone who does.

We all need to keep in mind that designating who needs these accommodations is largely the result of the draw of a lottery of time and place of birth. In another time, another place, good readers who could not properly aim a bow and arrow or till the fields might be those viewed as having a learning disability. In other societies, different subgroups would be in need of help.

Whatever the final answer, we are quite confident that it will not be achieved through the legal system. Legal systems are responsive to questions of law, which in turn are questions in contexts set up by legislators, not by educators or psychologists. Today, more than ever, educators with a grounding in learning disabilities need to come to a consensus as to what science knows about such disabilities and what best educational practices are. The problem is that educators have so many ideological battles themselves that no consensus is on the horizon. As a result, they have ceded control to the courts.

Court involvement has come about in much the way in which union involvement came about in industrializing the United States. Management was not always as careful of workers' rights as it should have been. In some cases, it was and continues to be downright careless, sometimes placing workers in positions of health or safety risk that the managers themselves would never enter. Unions came about to protect workers. Today, courts have entered the scene to protect students.

When one surveys the specifics of the court cases, it frequently seems that neither side is totally blameless or even clearly in the right. This is not surprising, because the legal system in the United States is adversarial, and once the legal battle is joined, the opposing sides become like enemies locked in mortal combat. There is little incentive for compromise or even for finding out the truth. Rather, the goal is for the winner to take all, and each side wants to be a winner. Yet, in practice, decisions are often split and yield neither side a clear victory.

We doubt that issues of best educational practices for children with learning disabilities can be resolved with a winner-take-all mentality. Our reading is that when cases have gone to court, it is usually fairly easy to point out decisions made by schools that were ill considered and, in some cases, deeply flawed. No one is likely to argue that the confusion that arose at Boston University regarding the identification of students with learning disabilities and the selection of appropriate accommodations for them was exactly in anyone's best interest, including that of the university. But we question whether the best interests of the students are served when these students receive accommodations that have no remedial value. These accommodations essentially allow the students to enter into job streams for which they are not fully qualified—in part because of the accommodations they have received. We believe the accommodations will make sense only if the society provides in jobs the same kinds of accommodations it is providing in the schools. As of yet, U.S. society, at least, shows no signs of willingness to bear this responsibility or expense.

Some accommodations can miss the point of just what is being accommodated. The value of note taking is not only in the studying of the notes; part of the value of note taking is in the taking of the notes. Part of the value of taking a test is in learning to work under pressure and in the kinds of conditions that later will occur on the job. These values are lost when accommodations are granted that relieve students of the responsibility for note taking or for taking tests under at least some time pressure. At the same time, no one wants children with learning disabilities to fail in situations in which they have the ability to succeed. Accommodations should be chosen that balance the ability of the child to succeed with conditions that are realistic in preparing the child for later life.

People who succeed are often those who learn to overcome various adversities. Creative people almost always are people who defy the odds and defy the crowd.[5] Thus failure in itself is not a bad thing. Part of what makes people excel is that they have overcome failure to rise above it. At the same time, people need to have successes as well, and an educational system needs to be set up so that children can both succeed and make mistakes from which they can learn.

Part Four

What Needs to Be Done

We have introduced some of the main educational, policy, and scientific issues that underlie the study of learning disabilities, as well as interventions in the schools to help children who have LDs. Where does all this information take us? In the final chapter, we summarize our policy recommendations, based on the current state of knowledge about LDs.

The LD lottery is like many lotteries in life. You get one or more tickets, and a number is called. But if your number is called and you are identified as having a learning disability, do you win or lose? A little of both. There are some skills you are identified as not having, but there are many others, perhaps creative and practical skills, you do have. Moreover, having a disability in reading or anything else may help you develop these other skills more. Often, the people whose numbers are not called have LDs, too; it's just that they are not identified as having LDs. They, too, have had to develop skills to overcome their disabilities.

Succeeding in life requires the same formula for all—figuring out strengths and weaknesses, making the most of the strengths, and finding ways of correcting or dealing with weaknesses. In this chapter we suggest ways to help people do these things.

Chapter Ten

LD: The Lottery That Everyone Wins and Loses

The richest man in the city of Leon, Mexico, was an entrepreneur who owned major shoe factories. He was interviewed by a reporter for a leading national newspaper.

It was common knowledge that he was illiterate, and this knowledge piqued the curiosity of the interviewer. She asked him how he had managed to succeed. He explained that when he was a boy, he had worked on an assembly line for a man who had once owned a shoe factory in Leon. When the owner discovered that the boy working for him was a mere illiterate, the owner fired him on the spot. He was forced to rely on his own devices.

The boy eventually became a man and also eventually bought the factory of the man who had fired him, as well as other factories. The interviewer, curious, asked whether he did not think that he would have been even more successful if he had learned how to read. "On the contrary," he answered, "if I had learned how to read, I would still be on the assembly line."

The point is important: Reading is not tantamount to success, and there are many kinds of jobs in which one can succeed without reading well, or, in some cases, without reading beyond a basic level. There are also some jobs that require no reading at all.

People seem to split into two groups with regard to their approach to learning disabilities: those who want almost unlimited services for children with learning disabilities, and those who believe that children with learning disabilities already are getting too many services, thereby taking away needed services from other students. We believe that both points of view are too extreme. They derive from a society that has created a closed system that is maladaptive not only to those with learning disabilities, but also to many, and arguably most, of those who do not have them. It is a society based on a myth that success should go to the deserving as defined by tests of reading, IQ, and related skills.

What Is Needed for Success?

We need to develop new kinds of identification procedures and new kinds of educational procedures that reflect the reality of jobs, not a fiction we have created. The tests we use do not adequately reflect the skills people need in the world of work. As a result, people with high levels of work-related skills may not do well on existing tests and people who do well on existing tests may not do well in the world of work. This point applies to those with or without identified learning disabilities.

Ask yourself this question: To what extent does the attainment of success in the job you hold (or that someone else holds) require the kinds of skills that are so important on tests of IQ, academic aptitude, or even reading? Then, go one step further: To what extent would a grade of A in the courses that were supposed to prepare you for your job truly predict success in what you do?

We have been studying the answer to this question for over a dozen years. Motivating our work is the commonsense notion that common sense—or what we call practical intelligence—is different in kind from the kind of intelligence and the kinds of achievements measured by conventional standardized tests. In other words, we have been trying to study rigorously the notion that people such as the shoe entrepreneur can be high in common sense and high in life achievement and yet rather weak in the skills measured by conventional ability and achievement tests.

In the series of studies mentioned earlier in the book (see Chapter 2), we found that people with high practical intelligence are not necessarily those with high IQ. There just is no relation. But, as we mentioned, practical intelligence predicts success on the job as well as or better than does IQ.

Even for children, practical intelligence and academic intelligence can be quite distinct. In a series of studies, Brazilian researchers found that Brazilian street children who had the practical intelligence and mathematical know-how to run a successful street business could not successfully answer the same mathematical problems they needed to solve on the street when these problems were presented in a decontextualized way through a paper-and-pencil format. The same phenomenon can be found in the United States among some children who run successful and often illegal businesses on the street. The very teachers who might view such children as having a mathematical disability would probably be less proficient in running their own businesses and in doing the math to keep them afloat.

The odd thing is that the university credentials we so much value often matter relatively little to success on the job. The United States has created a society in which schooling, especially at the university level, often serves more of a purpose of credentialing than it does a purpose of education.[1] Many students have become much more concerned with their grades than with anything they learn because they are often among the first to recognize that they are in college or graduate school primarily to get the degree and only secondarily, if at all, to learn anything. Law schools implicitly recognize this fact in requiring no special major or courses for admission. They simply require a college degree, in whatever!

The result is that many people who could be highly successful in a wide variety of jobs never get to enter these jobs because of a largely senseless closed system that puts a premium on one set of abilities in schools and then on another set of abilities in life once schooling is over. How many times have you needed the kinds of algebraic and geometric skills measured by either the SAT-I or the SAT-II, the achievement test series of the Scholastic Assessment Test? How many times have you had to read passages of the difficulty level found on the SAT?

In our Kenya study, mentioned earlier, children's practical knowledge for adapting to their environment was negatively correlated with their advanced word knowledge on tests of English vocabulary. The fact is that the kinds of words that appear on vocabulary tests, and the kinds of reading passages that appear on verbal sections of tests used for undergraduate and graduate admissions, appear only rarely in the everyday lives of the great majority of people. Obviously, some jobs require high levels of reading or mathematical skills. People who are book editors need to be highly skilled readers, just as actuaries need high levels of mathematical skill. But for the large majority of jobs, the kinds of skills needed are quite different from the kinds of skills measured by these tests.

People in a wide variety of jobs have been asked about the kinds of attributes that characterize the most successful practitioners on the job. Although the attributes mentioned vary somewhat with occupation, frequently mentioned are a sense of responsibility, enthusiasm, high motivation, an ability to work with others, patience, empathy, willingness to overcome obstacles, and sheer stick-to-itiveness. People also mention content knowledge, of course, but content knowledge often can be acquired in a variety of ways, with reading being only one of them, and often not the most important one.

Some years back, a student applied for admission to a prestigious graduate program in psychology and was turned down. She had good grades, outstanding letters of recommendation, and even had done significant published research. Why was she turned down? Because of her test scores. Her situation was ironic: Although she was unable to gain a slot in the graduate program, had she been applying for a job, she most likely would have gotten it. Why? Because application for a job would not have required her to take the graduate-school admissions test that was used. The United States is a society obsessed with tests, to the point that even when we have much better information than the tests supply, we sometimes prefer the information provided by the tests.

Our research shows that practical as well as creative abilities are largely distinct from the kinds of abilities measured by conventional ability tests. Moreover, people can excel in abstract analytical skills, and yet do poorly on tests, such as the SAT, that allow them to show their analytical skills only in the verbal and mathematical domains. Thus, it is indeed true that an individual with learning disabilities could have outstanding creative, practical, or even analytical skills, and not show it on tests of reading and related skills.

In essence, U.S. society has taken a largely arbitrarily selected set of skills and put it on a pinnacle. Some students with learning disabilities do not have these skills, so people at one extreme dismiss these students as inept, whereas people at the other extreme pretend that, despite the lack of these skills, these individuals can do essentially what anyone else can do. But these students cannot do anything others can do, especially if we continue arbitrarily to value advanced reading skills even for jobs that do not require them. The situation changes, however, if we consider only the levels of reading, math, or whatever that truly will be required on the job.

Consider a particular university professor who is a fluent speaker of German as a second language and who can read newspapers in German with no difficulty. His work could earn him a decent job in a German-speaking country, or a job as a faculty member or an administrator at a college, but he would not get into a college that required him to take an SAT-type of test for admission. Why? Because his level of German-language vocabulary and reading skill does not come up to the advanced level that college and graduate-school admissions tests measure.

We maintain that nothing is to be gained from pretending that children with learning disabilities can do almost anything. But we believe that a lot is to be gained from recognizing that they may have tremendous talents that simply are not being recognized and valued by the educational system. The students lose, but so does the society. These children may never get the chance to show what they can do, and accommodations—intended to help them—practically will guarantee that they won't. Thus, the highly creative child, instead of being directed to work that will enable him or her to capitalize on a strength, now may be directed to work in a way to capitalize on a weakness.

Why, then, are people not creating new kinds of ability tests that will recognize the strengths of children and adults with learning disabilities? Why are we not assessing their creative skills or their practical skills in terms of the theory of successful intelligence? Or, in terms of Gardner's theory of multiple intelligences,[2] why are we not measuring their spatial, musical, interpersonal, intrapersonal, bodily-kinesthetic, or naturalist intelligence, choosing instead to concentrate almost exclusively on their linguistic and logical-mathematical intelligences? The answer proves to be systemic.

The Stagnant Currents of Ability Testing

Intelligence tests have changed hardly at all since the beginning of the century because they measure the skills that schools so highly value. These skills, however, are not necessarily the ones, and are certainly not the only ones, that are crucial in the workforce. If we want to change the intelligence tests and the reading tests with them, then we need to change the schools to reflect the different kinds of abilities we measure—the ones that will matter more later on.

Almost every form of technology is changing rapidly. In five years, the computer you buy today probably will be useful only for an antiques sale. Similarly, the analog cellular phone you purchase today will probably be obsolete, as digital cellular phones will most likely have taken over the market. Innovation in almost every form of technology is astounding.

This is not true of the testing field, however. The same stale tests have been served up for close to a century. Little has changed. The Wechsler intelligence test of 1939 differs little from the test of today. It would be easy to blame the testing companies, and in part we do. They devote little or no attention to serious, basic R&D, tend to be about as uncreative as any industry, bar none, and sometimes are smugly self-satisfied when they should be beet-red with shame. But most of them do not even recognize that hundred-year-old products need more than a face-lift. If the tests were such terrific predictors of real-world success, perhaps the companies could claim that Binet, Wechsler, and others just got lucky and found the right mix of problems to put on their tests. But given that the tests predict only about 10 percent of the variation in individuals in various measures of life success,[3] no such claim to good luck can be made. The tests are predictors, but weak ones. Moreover, as we have seen, the existence of closed systems greatly inflates this percentage, because high scores on the tests in part cause success, regardless of whether the abilities they measure are relevant to the workplace or not.

Only part of the blame can go to the testing companies, however. Basically, they are doing what other businesses do—producing the products and services that will make them money.

In that fundamental respect, they are no different from any other business. If educators, psychologists, and any of the diagnosticians who evaluate children with LDs are going to buy their tests, then why should the testing companies bother to change them? As long as the market is good and the competition minimal, there is no incentive for the testing industry to change. Ironically, though, U.S. society is placing greater and greater emphasis on tests that tell very little about a person's potential truly to succeed. Thus, ultimately, we must blame the system society has created, and not just the testing companies.

There is a great deal of resistance to changing the system; too many people are benefiting from it. The people who should be at the forefront in demanding change are those who are being shortchanged by the system—for example, those with LDs who appear to lack more abilities than they do lack. But some of these individuals and their parents—especially those at the top of the societal heap—have co-opted the system so that it serves to their advantage. Thus, the people who lose most under the present system often are people of lower socioeconomic status, immigrants, and pretty much anyone who does not speak English as a native language. Sometimes these people are viewed as getting what they deserve or, perhaps, more. So the years go by, and nothing changes.

As study after study shows American students doing worse and worse in international comparisons,[4] people hear again and again a battle cry to uphold standards and to hold the schools, the administrators, the teachers, and the students more accountable. But more accountable for what? In many respects, the United States has had great success—economically, politically, and militarily. Perhaps part of this success is that some of its citizens have recognized so well that once school ends, the academic game is over. Those who continue to play it do so at their peril. Even in the so-called ivory tower of academia, the academic game is over. Professors need primarily to produce knowledge, not consume it. They have to work in the real world, too. As George Bernard Shaw said, academic politics are so vicious only because the stakes are so small.

The Plan

We have a plan. What we hope to see are ability tests, instruction, and assessment that reflect what students truly are able to do. Instruction should be geared not only to the traditionally academically able student, but to all students. Let us explain what we mean.

In our research, we have looked at the effects of teaching children not only in the traditional mode, emphasizing verbal memory and analytical skills, but also in modes that emphasize creative and practical skills. These are skills in which children with LDs are likely to show no particular deficit. Children with LDs may even show advantages in these skills, since these are the skills they had to practice to survive in a world that is, in some respects, challenging and even hostile to them. In presenting the following examples for consideration, we wish to emphasize that we are not advocating replacing traditional classroom activities entirely. Rather, we are advocating supplementing those activities, and supplementing them in ways that better reflect what people who actually work in these areas do on the job. These activities are far less likely to penalize children with LDs than are traditional classroom tasks, and they actually may benefit such children. Furthermore, they do so without the false advantages of accommodations that merely hide problems not only with the children, but with the curriculum they are being fed.

In literature classes, many kinds of activities can go beyond the sometimes limited activities that teachers may now do. In a traditional English-literature class, a teacher one of us observed did little more than ask students who said what quotations. The teacher then tested the children in their ability to recognize quotations. Obviously, students with reading disabilities will do poorly in this kind of a classroom, unless they are given special accommodations that do not require them to meet the same challenges that other students must meet. But there are other things the teacher might have done. The teacher could have had children tell their own stories, or invent alternative endings to existing stories, or develop skits, or discuss how they could apply a lesson learned by a literary character to their own lives. The teacher might have asked the students to create poems, or to draw pictures based on a text they had read, or to do book reviews. In other words, there are many possible activities at which children with reading disabilities can do well or even excel. Traditionally, however, teachers have not offered these activities. Moreover, these kinds of tasks are far closer to what literary scholars do than is the memorizing of quotations.

In science, the traditional approach, in which students read the book and memorize the facts, once again hits hard at children with learning disabilities. These are not the kinds of tasks in which they are likely to excel. But there are many other options science teachers can offer that do not disadvantage children with LDs at all. One teacher we observed took children onto the roof and had them use principles of physics to estimate where a beanbag shot off the roof would land. Another teacher took the children outside into the parking lot and, with just a bit of initial direction, had them work as a group to estimate the mass of his parked car. Students can design their own experiments and then conduct, analyze, and write up these experiments. They can do critiques of existing experiments. They can come up with their own theories, or compare and contrast existing theories. In other words, they can do tasks that are much closer to what scientists do than the tasks typically done in science class. These tasks do not put children with LDs at a disadvantage.

In a social-studies class, a teacher can go way beyond having children read a textbook and then take a test on the facts. For example, one teacher had the students in her class form their own classroom government. The students decided on the form of government, how to set it up, and how to carry it out. Another teacher had children simulate a debate between Lincoln and Douglas, so that children could better understand the alternative points of view that ultimately led up to the Civil War. Children can do simulations of historical events or projects in which they study and analyze different periods of history. They can show how events in the near or distant past might shed light on present or recent events. For example, what lessons, if any, does the war in Vietnam hold for the interventions of the United States in Serbia or Iraq? Another task children can undertake is to plan an itinerary for a trip abroad and to consider how they would deal with problems that might arise when visiting with people of another culture.

The research described in this book shows that when children are given opportunities to do *practical* mathematics, some of those who might otherwise have appeared to have a mathematical disability prove to have nothing of the sort. They can function effectively and without lapses. We thus encourage teachers to have children learn their mathematics, at least in part, through activities that focus on everyday mathematics, such as would be used in dealing with train schedules or recipes or buying tickets for an athletic event. Having children learn to work with different systems of numeration (e.g., base 3 instead of base 10) or new operators beyond addition, subtraction, multiplication, and division, (e.g., logarithms) also can help the children think more creatively about the possibilities of mathematics.

When we conducted a study among middle-school and high-school students in North Carolina, California, and Maryland, we discovered that children who were taught in ways that allowed them to think creatively and practically as well as analytically achieved at higher levels than did children who merely rote-memorized material. They also achieved at higher levels than did children who were taught for so-called critical (analytical) thinking. The children taught in the broader way performed better than did the other students even on straightforward, multiple-choice tests of memory. Ironically, therefore, the modes of learning that often most disadvantage children with LDs are not, according to our research, the best methods for helping most children learn new material.[5] Accommodations that fail to correct deficits are a cop-out, and are educationally sterile. Much better, we believe, are methods of teaching and learning that enable children with LDs to capitalize on their strengths, as well as, when possible, to correct weaknesses. These include the full range of teaching techniques discussed in Chapter 8.

We do not claim to be offering a panacea, nor do we underestimate the difficulties in teaching children with LDs. We realize that the methods we propose pose challenges of their own, and that many teachers are at present ill-equipped to teach in these new ways. They can learn to teach in these ways, but first they have to want to. They also need the support of the educational system. Many educators have been trying and will continue to make a difference in the lives of children. We believe there now are more effective ways of making such a difference. Theories of teaching and learning have come a long way. If we give them serious study so that we can adopt the best of them, we will be able to obtain much better outcomes for our children.

Recommendations

We believe that changes can start now. Here is what we can do.

1. *We must make decisions about separate services for children with learning disabilities on the basis of matched educational and social agendas.* Our goal should be to help all children make the most of their strengths and correct their weaknesses. When correction is not possible, compensation for weaknesses makes sense as well. All children, including

children with learning disabilities, should be encouraged to pursue careers for which they have or can develop the skills to excel. Existing practices, however, sometimes may lead students to capitalize on weaknesses rather than on strengths. If a society is willing to provide the same levels of accommodations in the workplace that it is willing to provide in the classroom, then those accommodations in the classroom make good sense. If the society, instead, is willing to provide those accommodations only in the classroom, then it is preparing students for a world that does not exist. It then is doing the students a disservice.

2. *We immediately must stop using discrepancy scores to identify children with LDs.* This method is psychologically indefensible, statistically invalid, and educationally counterproductive. It's got to go.

3. *We must identify children in need of assistance by level of achievement only.* We do not need IQ scores or any other ability scores to tell us if children are underachieving. Any child's achievement can be modified. If achievement is low, we should take steps to help the child improve, regardless of IQ.

4. *To the extent possible, we must prevent the full-blown development of disabilities rather than try to correct them once they have developed fully.* We now know enough about the cognitive, biological, and genetic origins of reading disabilities (see Chapters 5, 6, and 7) to be able to assess risk factors for learning disabilities of children at a very early age. Those children at risk should receive early special-educational care (see Chapter 8) before their disabilities fully manifest themselves.

5. *We must identify the interventions to be used on the basis of diagnosis of deficiencies in information processing.* Labeling a child as having a learning disability or anything else does not tell us what to do about improving the child's functioning. Psychologists and educators working to-

gether need to diagnose what the problems are and then design interventions to help with the problems. Lumping all children with language disabilities, or even with reading disabilities, together as though they had a common problem is itself a disabled form of intervention.

6. *We must target our interventions on the basis of need and motivation.* Interventions should be based on need, not on invalid systems of identification. Moreover, in deciding whether and how much to intervene, we ought to count the child's motivation to improve more than we count a bunch of test scores. If the child wants to work hard, let him or her do so. We also should devise programs to help adults with reading or other disabilities develop skills they may not have developed fully.

7. *We must permit accommodations with regard to societally necessary skills (such as reading) only when they help students correct weaknesses.* Accommodations that serve no purpose other than to let students fall further and further behind their peers ought to be stopped, at once, and permanently. These accommodations allow children with learning disabilities to fall further behind while giving them the illusion that they are succeeding. It is analogous to driving a runner to the end of the race track and congratulating him or her for finishing first. The purpose of accommodations should be to help individuals correct weaknesses, not to help them fall further behind.

8. *We must help individuals with LDs capitalize on strengths, not on weaknesses.* Individuals with LDs may excel in a number of skills outside their area of disability. They may be highly creative or practical. Many of them are musically, artistically, spatially, interpersonally, intrapersonally, or naturalistically gifted. The student with a reading disability may be brilliant in math, or the student with a mathematical disability may be brilliant in language. We need to help students make the most of their strengths and learn in

ways that take these strengths into account. Instead of concentrating largely on weaknesses in our diagnosis and instruction, we should concentrate much more on strengths.

9. *Tests of abilities must reflect the full range of abilities, not just the narrow range currently being tested.* The stagnancy of progress in our testing industry is an embarrassment, but nothing will change as long as psychologists and educators keep buying tests based on century-old ideas. Testing companies should start spending the money on research and development that will bring them past the early years of the twentieth century. It's time to let the brains come out of the pickle jar. We have the theories to produce better tests.

10. *Curriculum must be taught in a way that values the full range of learning and thinking abilities.* Instruction now values students with superior memory, and to some extent analytical abilities, primarily as exercised in the verbal and, to a lesser degree, quantitative domains. Instruction should value equally students with creative and practical abilities, abilities that will be more important in later life and job performance than are the abilities the schools now value so highly.

11. *We must reward excellence, not mediocrity—but excellence broadly defined.* Children with LDs often have enormous talents. These children need to be supported in the development of their talents and rewarded for those talents. Throw away the crutches and let the children use their wings. Help them make the most of the skills they have.

Here is our last word: Identification and instruction of children with learning disabilities should be guided by educational considerations, not political ones. It's time to do away with the LD lottery and to act in the best interests of our children. We must start right away. Give children with learning disabilities a lot of care, not a lottery.

Notes

Preface

1. Cramer, S. C., & Ellis, W. (Eds.). (1996). *Learning disabilities: Lifelong issues.* Baltimore: Paul H. Brookes. Lyon, G. R., Alexander, D., & Yaffe, S. (1997). Progress and promise in research in learning disabilities. *Learning Disabilities, 8,* 1–6.

2. Spear-Swerling, L., & Sternberg, R. J. (1996). *Off-track: When poor readers become "learning disabled."* Boulder, CO: Westview.

Part One

1. Gardner, H. (1983). *Frames of mind: The theory of multiple intelligences.* New York: Basic Books. Sternberg, R. J. (1985). *Beyond IQ: A triarchic theory of human intelligence.* New York: Cambridge University Press.

2. Grigorenko, E. L. (1995). *A family study of dyslexia.* Unpublished doctoral dissertation, Yale University, New Haven. Sternberg, R. J. (1985). *Beyond IQ: A triarchic theory of human intelligence.* New York: Cambridge University Press.

3. Lyon, G. R., Alexander, D., & Yaffe, S. (1997). Progress and promise in research in learning disabilities. *Learning Disabilities, 8,* 1–6.

Chapter One

1. Kelman, M., & Lester, G. (1997). *Jumping the queue: An inquiry into the legal treatment of students with learning disabilities.* Cambridge, MA: Harvard University Press.

2. Wong, B. Y. L. (1996). *The ABCs of learning disabilities.* San Diego: Academic Press.

3. Cummins, J. (1976). The influence of bilingualism on cognitive growth: A synthesis of research findings and explanatory hypotheses. *Working Papers on Bilingualism, 9,* 1–43.

4. Herrnstein, R., & Murray, C. (1994). *The bell curve.* New York: Free Press.

5. Sternberg, R. J., & Grigorenko, E. L. (Eds.). (1997). *Intelligence, heredity, and environment.* New York: Cambridge University Press.

6. Ibid.

7. National Joint Committee on Learning Disabilities (1999). Available Internet: http://www.ncld.org/ld/info_ld.html.

8. *Federal Register.* (1977, December 29). p. 65083.

9. Spear-Swerling, L., & Sternberg, R. J. (1996). *Off track: When poor readers become "learning disabled."* Boulder, CO: Westview.

10. Wong, op. cit.

11. Wong, op. cit.

12. Wong, op. cit.

13. Specific information regarding the current numbers of children diagnosed as having a learning disability are available from the Learning Disabilities Association of America (www.ldanatl.org) and from the National Center for Learning Disabilities, Incorporated (www.ncld.org).

14. Kelman & Lester, op. cit.

15. Kelman & Lester, op. cit.

16. Sternberg, R. J. (1998). *In search of the human mind* (2nd ed.). Ft. Worth, TX: Harcourt Brace College Publishers.

17. Wong, op. cit.

18. Orton, S. T. (1937). *Reading, writing, and speech problems in children.* New York: Norton.

19. Christensen, C. A. (1992). Discrepancy definitions of reading disability: Has the quest led us astray? A response to Stanovich. *Reading Research Quarterly, 27,* 276–278. Christensen, C. A. (1999). Learning disability: Issues of representation, power and the medicalization of school failure. In R. J. Sternberg & L. Spear-Swerling (Eds.), *Perspectives on learning disabilities* (pp. 227–249). Boulder, CO: Westview.

20. Skrtic, T. M. (1991). The special education paradox: Equity as the way to excellence. *Harvard Educational Review, 61,* 148–206. Skrtic, T. M. (1999). Learning disabilities as organizational pathologies. In R. J. Sternberg & L. Spear-Swerling (Eds.), *Perspectives on learning disabilities* (pp. 193–226). Boulder, CO: Westview.

21. Coles, G. S. (1987). *The learning mystique: A critical look at "learning disabilities."* New York: Pantheon Books.

Chapter Two

1. Ceci, S. J. (1996). *On intelligence . . . more or less.* Cambridge, MA: Harvard University Press. Gardner, H. (1983). *Frames of mind: The theory of multiple intelligences.* New York: Basic Books. Perkins, D. N. (1995). *Outsmarting IQ.* New York: Free Press. Sternberg, R. J. (1997). *Successful intelligence.* New York: Plume.

2. Perkins, D. N, & Grotzer, T. A. (1997). Teaching intelligence. *American Psychologist, 52,* 1125–1133.

3. Flynn, J. R. (1987). Massive IQ gains in 14 nations. *Psychological Bulletin, 101,* 171–191. See also Neisser, U. (Ed.). (1998). *The rising curve.* Washington, D.C.: American Psychological Association.

4. Sternberg, op. cit.

5. Tyson-Bernstein, H. (1988). *America's textbook fiasco: A conspiracy of good intentions.* Washington, D.C.: Council for Basic Education.

6. Kirst, M. W. (1982). How to improve schools without spending more money. *Phi Delta Kappan, 64,* 6–8.

7. Chall, J. S., & Conard, S. S. (1991). *Should textbooks challenge students? The case for easier or harder textbooks.* New York: Teachers College Press. Reis, S., & Renzulli, J. R. (1992). Using curriculum compacting to challenge the above-average. *Educational Leadership, 92,* 51–57. Reis, S., Burns, D., & Renzulli, J. S. (1997). *Curriculum compacting: The complete guide to modifying the regular curriculum for high-ability students.* Mansfield Center, CT: Creative Learning Press.

8. Tyson-Bernstein, op. cit.

9. Dennis, W. (1973). *Children of the creche.* New York: Appleton-Century-Crofts.

10. Rutter, M. (1996, April). *Profound early deprivation and later social relationship in early adoptees from Romanian orphanages followed at age 4.* Paper presented at the 10th Biennial International Conference on Infant Studies, Providence, RI.

11. Plomin, R. (1997). Identifying genes for cognitive abilities and disabilities. In R. J. Sternberg & E. L. Grigorenko (Eds.), *Intelligence, heredity, and environment* (pp. 89–104). New York: Cambridge University Press.

12. Carroll, J. B. (1993). *Human cognitive abilities: A survey of factor-analytic studies.* New York: Cambridge University Press.

13. Gardner, op. cit.

14. Wechsler, D. (1991). *Manual for the Wechsler Intelligence Scale for Children-III.* San Antonio, TX: The Psychological Corporation.

15. Thorndike, R., Hagen, E., & Sattler, J. R. (1986a). *Guide for administering and scoring the Stanford-Binet Intelligence Scale* (4th ed.). Chicago: Riverside. Thorndike, R., Hagen, E., & Sattler, J. R. (1986b). *Technical Manual. Stanford-Binet Intelligence Scale* (4th ed). Chicago: Riverside.

16. Naglieri, J. A., & Das, J. P. (1997). *Das-Naglieri Cognitive Assessment System.* Itasca, IL: Riverside.

17. Jensen, A. R. (1998). *The g factor.* Greenwich, CT: Greenwood.

18. Gardner, op. cit.

19. Sternberg, op. cit.

Chapter Three

1. Gardner, H. (1983). *Frames of mind: The theory of multiple intelligences.* New York: Basic Books.

2. Sternberg, R. J., Wagner, R. K., Williams, W. M., & Horvath, J. A. (1995). Testing common sense. *American Psychologist, 50,* 912–927.

3. Sternberg, R. J., & Grigorenko, E. L. (1997). The cognitive costs of physical and mental ill health: Applying the psychology of the developed world to the problems of the developing world. *Eye on Psi Chi, 2,* 20–27. Other collaborators on this study were Kate Nokes, Wenzel Geissler, Frederick Okatcha, Ruth Prince, and Don Bundy.

4. Heath, S. B. (1983). *Ways with words.* New York: Cambridge University Press.

5. Ibid.

6. Sternberg, R. J. (1997). *Thinking styles.* New York: Cambridge University Press. Sternberg, R. J., & Grigorenko, E. L. (1995). Styles of thinking in school. *European Journal of High Ability, 6,* 1–18.

7. Sternberg, R. J. (1985). *Beyond IQ.* New York: Cambridge University Press.

8. Sternberg, R. J., & Smith, C. (1985). Social intelligence and decoding skills in nonverbal communication. *Social Cognition, 2,* 168–192.

9. Cronbach, L. J., & Furby, L. (1970). How we should measure "change"—or should we? *Psychological Bulletin, 74,* 68–80.

10. Nisbett, R., & Ross, L. (1980). *Human inference: Strategies and shortcomings of social judgment.* Englewood Cliffs, NJ: Prentice-Hall.

11. *Draft Report on Special Education in Connecticut.* (1997). Hartford, CT: State Department of Education.

12. Renzulli, J. R. (1977). *The enrichment triad model.* Mansfield Center, CT: Creative Learning Press.

13. Herrnstein, R., & Murray, C. (1994). *The bell curve.* New York: Free Press.

Chapter Four

1. Sternberg, R. J. (1997). *Thinking styles.* New York: Cambridge University Press.

2. Ibid.

3. Adams, M. J. (1990). *Beginning to read: Thinking and learning about print.* Cambridge, MA: MIT Press.

4. Tyson-Bernstein, H. (1988). *America's textbook fiasco: A conspiracy of good intentions.* Washington, D.C.: The Council for Basic Education.

5. Sternberg, R. J., Conway, B. E., Ketron, J. L., & Bernstein, M. (1981). People's conceptions of intelligence. *Journal of Personality and Social Psychology, 41,* 37–55.

6. Sternberg, R. J. (1985). *Beyond IQ: A triarchic theory of human intelligence.* New York: Cambridge University Press.

7. Thurstone, L. L. (1924). *The nature of intelligence.* New York: Harcourt Brace.

8. Stenhouse, D. (1973). *The evolution of intelligence.* New York: Harper & Row.

9. Kelman, M. & Lester, G.(1997). *Jumping the queue: An inquiry into the legal treatment of students with learning disabilities.* Cambridge, MA: Harvard University Press.

10. Sternberg, R. J. (1997). *Successful intelligence.* New York: Plume.

Part Two

1. Galaburda, A. M. (1997). Neurobiology of developmental dyslexia: Results of a ten year research program. *Learning Disabilities, 8,* 43–50. Geschwind, N., & Galaburda, A. M. (1985). Cerebral lateralization. Biological mechanisms, associations, and pathology: 1. A hypothesis and a program for research. *Archives of Neurology, 42,* 521–552.

2. Christensen, C. A. (1992). Discrepancy definitions of reading disability: Has the quest led us astray? A response to Stanovich. *Reading Research Quarterly, 27,* 276–278. Christensen, C. A. (1999). Learning disability: Issues of representation, power and the medicalization of

school failure. In R. J. Sternberg & L. Spear-Swerling (Eds.), *Perspectives on learning disabilities* (pp. 227–249). Boulder, CO: Westview. Skrtic, T. M. (1991). The special education paradox: Equity as the way to excellence. *Harvard Educational Review, 61,* 148–206. Skrtic, T. M. (1999). Learning disabilities as organizational pathologies. In R. J. Sternberg & L. Spear-Swerling (Eds.), *Perspectives on learning disabilities* (pp. 193–226). Boulder, CO: Westview.

3. Sternberg, R. J. (1997, August 25). Extra credit for doing poorly. *The New York Times,* p. A27. Torgesen, J. K. (1999). Phonologically based reading disabilities: Toward a coherent theory of one kind of learning disability. In R. J. Sternberg & L. Spear-Swerling (Eds.), *Perspectives on learning disabilities* (pp.106–135). Boulder, CO: Westview. Wagner, R. K., & Garon, T. (1999). Learning disabilities in perspective. In R. J. Sternberg & L. Spear-Swerling (Eds.), *Perspectives on learning disabilities* (pp. 83–105). Boulder, CO: Westview.

Chapter Five

1. Adams, M. J. (1990). *Beginning to read: Thinking and learning about print.* Cambridge, MA: MIT Press. Liberman, I. Y., & Liberman, A. M. (1990). Whole language versus code emphasis: Underlying assumptions and their implications for reading instruction. *Annals of Dyslexia, 40,* 51–76. Perfetti, C. A. (1985). *Reading ability.* New York: Oxford University Press. Stanovich, K. E. (1991). Word recognition: Changing perspectives. In R. Barr, M. L. Kamil, P. Mosenthal, & P. D. Pearson (Eds.), *Handbook of reading research* (Vol. 2, pp. 418–452). New York: Longman.

2. American Academy of Ophthalmology. (1981). *Policy statement: Learning disabilities, dyslexia, and vision.* San Francisco.

3. Wagner, R. K., & Torgesen, J. K. (1987). The nature of phonological processing and its causal role in the acquisition of reading skills. *Psychological Bulletin, 101,* 192–212. Wagner, R. K., Torgesen, J. K., & Rashotte, C. A. (1994). The development of reading-related phonological processing abilities: New evidence of bidirectional causality from a latent variable longitudinal study. *Developmental Psychology, 30,* 73–87.

4. Bowey, J. A. (1985). Contextual facilitation in children's oral reading in relation to grade and decoding skill. *Journal of Experimental Child Psychology, 40,* 23–48.

5. Perfetti, op. cit.

6. LaBerge, D., & Samuels, S. J. (1974). Toward a theory of automatic information processing in reading. *Cognitive Psychology, 6,* 293–323. Sternberg, R. J., & Wagner, R. K. (1982). Automatization failure in learning disabilities. *Topics in Learning and Learning Disabilities, 2,* 1–11.

7. Sternberg, R. J. (1985). *Beyond IQ: A triarchic theory of human intelligence.* New York: Cambridge University Press.

8. LaBerge & Samuels, op. cit. Sternberg & Wagner, op. cit.

9. Bell, L. C., & Perfetti, C. A. (1994). Reading skills: Some adult comparisons. *Journal of Educational Psychology, 86,* 244–255.

10. Wagner, R. K., & Sternberg, R. J. (1987). Executive control in reading comprehension. In B. K. Britton & S. M. Glynn (Eds.), *Executive control processes in reading* (pp. 1–21). Hillsdale, NJ: Erlbaum.

11. Ibid.

12. Sternberg, R. J. (1997). *Successful intelligence.* New York: Plume.

13. Wagner & Sternberg, op. cit.

14. Wagner & Sternberg, op. cit.

15. Sternberg, R. J. (1985). *Beyond IQ: A triarchic theory of human intelligence.* New York: Cambridge University Press.

16. Grigorenko, E. L., & Sternberg, R. J. (1998). *ELATE: Expert Learning for All Through Teacher Education.* Unpublished reading program. Williams, W. M., Blythe, T., White, N., Li, J., Sternberg, R. J., & Gardner, H. I. (1996). *Practical intelligence for school: A handbook for teachers of grades 5–8.* New York: HarperCollins.

17. Sternberg, R. J. (1997). *Successful intelligence.* New York: Plume.

18. Farr, R. C., & Strickland, D. S. (1993). *Light up the sky.* Austin, TX: Harcourt Brace.

19. Gardner, H., Krechevsky, M., Sternberg, R. J., & Okagaki, L. (1994). Intelligence in context: Enhancing students' practical intelligence for school. In K. McGilly (Ed.), *Classroom lessons: Integrating cognitive theory and classroom practice* (pp. 105–127). Cambridge, MA: Bradford Books. Sternberg, R. J., Okagaki, L., & Jackson, A. (1990). Practical intelligence for success in school. *Educational Leadership, 48,* 35–39.

Chapter Six

1. The same is true for a significant portion of human genetics. See Jones, S. (1994). *The language of genes.* London: Flamingo.

2. Johnson, G. (1998, March 1). Tests prove that nobody's smart about intelligence. *The New York Times.*

3. Dooling, E. C., Chi, J. G., & Gilles, F. H. (1983). Telencephalic development: Changing gyral patterns. In F. H. Gilles, A. Levitan, & E. C. Dooling (Eds.), *The developing human brain* (pp. 94–104). Boston: John Wright.

4. McFadden, D., & Pasanen, E. G. (1998). Comparison of the auditory system of heterosexuals and homosexuals: Click-evoked otoacoustic emissions. *Proceedings of the National Academy of Sciences of the United States of America, 95,* 2709–2713.

5. Galaburda, A. M., Sherman, G. F., Rosen, G. D., Aboitiz, F., & Geschwind, N. (1985). Developmental dyslexia: Four consecutive cases with cortical anomalies. *Annals of Neurology, 18,* 94–100.

6. Humphreys, P., Kaufman, W. E., & Galaburda, A. M. (1990). Developmental dyslexia in women: Neuropsychological findings in three cases. *Annals of Neurology, 28,* 727–738. Hynd, G. W., Clinton, A. B., & Hiemenz, J. R. (1999). New neuropsychological basis of learning disabilities. In R. J. Sternberg & L. Spear-Swerling (Eds.), *Perspectives on learning disabilities* (pp. 60–79). Boulder, CO: Westview.

7. Leonard, C. M., Voeller, K. K. S., Lombardion, L. J., Morris, M. K., Hynd, G. W., Alexander, A. W., Andersen, H. G., Garofalakis, M., Honeyman, J. C., Mao, J., Agee, O. F., & Staab, E. V. (1993). Anomalous cerebral structure in dyslexia revealed with magnetic resonance imaging. *Archives of Neurology, 50,* 461–469.

8. Morgan, A. E., & Hynd, G. W. (1998). Dyslexia, neurolinguistic ability, and anatomical variation of the planum temporale. *Neuropsychology Review, 8,* 79–93.

9. Galaburda et al., op. cit.

10. Galaburda, A. M., Schrott, L. M., Sherman, G. F., Rosen, G. D., & Denenberg, V. H. (1996). Animal models of developmental dyslexia. In C. H. Chase, G. D. Rosen, & G. F. Sherman (Eds.), *Developmental dyslexia* (pp. 3–14). Baltimore: York Press.

11. Galaburda, A. M. (1990). Address given to the Sixteenth Annual Rodin Remediation Society Meeting, Boulder, CO.

12. Galaburda, A. M., Schrott, L. M., Sherman, G. F., Rosen, G. D., & Denenberg, V. H. (1996). Animal models of developmental dyslexia. In C. H. Chase, G. D. Rosen, & G. F. Sherman (Eds.), *Developmental dyslexia* (pp. 3–14). Baltimore: York Press.

13. Hughes, J. R. (1985). Evaluation of electrophysiological studies on dyslexia. In D. B. Gray & J. F. Kavanaugh (Eds.), *Biobehavioral measures of dyslexia* (pp. 71–86). Parkton, MD: York Press.

14. Harter, M. R., Anllo-Vento, L., Wood, F. B., & Schroeder, M. M. (1988). Separate brain potential characteristics in children with reading disability and attention deficit disorder: Color and letter relevance effects. *Brain and Cognition, 7,* 115–140.

15. Preston, M. S., Guthrie, J. T., Kirsch, I., Gertman, D., & Childs, B. (1977). VERs in normal and disabled adult readers. *Psychophysiology, 14,* 8–14.

16. Demonet, J. F., Price, C., Wise, R., & Frackowiak, R. S. J. (1994). A PET study of cognitive strategies in normal subjects during language tasks: Influences of phonetic ambiguity and sequence processing on phoneme monitoring. *Brain, 117,* 671–682. Peterson, S. E., Fox, P. T., Posner, M. I., Mintun, M., & Raichle, M. E. (1989). Positron emission tomographic studies of the processing of single words. *Journal of Cognitive Neuroscience, 1,* 153–170. Shaywitz, B. A., Pugh, K. R., Constable, R. T., Shaywitz, S. E., Bronen, R. A., Fulbright, R. K., Shankweiler, D. P., Katz, L., Fletcher, J. M., Skudlarski, P., & Gore, J. C. (1995). Localization of semantic processing using functional magnetic resonance imaging. *Human Brain Mapping, 2,* 10–20.

17. Howard, D., Patterson, K., Wise, R., Brown, W. D., Friston, K., Weiller, C., & Frackowiak, R. (1992). The cortical localization of the lexicons. *Brain, 115,* 1769–1782. Petersen, S. E., Fox, P. T., Snyder, A. Z., & Raichle, M. E. (1990). Activation of extrastriate and frontal cortical areas by visual words and word-like stimuli. *Science, 249,* 1041–1044. Shaywitz et al., op. cit.

18. Garret, A. S., Wood, F. B., Flowers, D. L., & Absher, J. R. (1997). *Glucose metabolism in the interior temporal cortex related to accuracy of performance on a letter recognition task.* Unpublished manuscript.

19. Pugh, K. R., Shaywitz, B. A., Constable, R. T., Shaywitz, S. A., Skudlarski, P., Fulbright, R. K., Brone, R. A., Shankweiler, D. P., Katz, L., Fletcher, J. M., & Gore, J. C. (1996). Cerebral organization of component processes in reading. *Brain, 119,* 1221–1238.

20. Ibid.

21. Pugh, K. R., Shaywitz, B. A., Shaywitz, S. E., Shankweiler, D. P., Katz, L., Fletcher, J. M., Skudlarski, P., Fulbright, R. K., Constable, R. T., Bronen, R. A., Lacadie, C., & Gore, J. C. (1997). Predicting reading performance from neuroimaging profiles: The cerebral basis of phonological effects in printed work identification. *Journal of Experimental Psychology: Human Perception and Performance, 23,* 299–318.

22. Garret et al., op. cit.

23. Lubs, H. A., Duara, R., Levin, B., Jallad, B., Lubs, M.-L., Rabin, M., Kushch, A., & Gross-Glenn, K. (1991). Dyslexia subtypes: Genetics, behavior, and brain imaging. In D. Duane & D. Gray (Eds.), *The reading brain: The biological basis of dyslexia* (pp. 89–118). Parkton, MD: York Press.

24. Hynd, G. W., Hynd, C. R., Sullivan, H. G., & Kingsbury, T. B. (1987). Regional cerebral blood flow (rCBF) in developmental dyslexia: Activation during reading in a surface and deep dyslexic. *Journal of Learning Disabilities, 20,* 294–300. Rumsey, J. M., Berman, K. F., Denckla, M. B., Hamberger, S. D., Druesi, J., & Weinberger, D. R. (1987). Regional cerebral blood flow in severe developmental dyslexia. *Archives of Neurology, 44,* 1144–1150.

25. Wood, F. B., Flowers, D. L., Buchsbaum, M., & Tallal, P. (1991). Investigation of abnormal left temporal functioning in dyslexia through rCBF, auditory evoked potentials, and positron emission tomography. *Reading and Writing: An Interdisciplinary Journal, 4,* 81–95.

26. Garret et al., op. cit.

27. Wood, F. B. (1998). *Regional brain metabolism studies.* Unpublished manuscript.

Chapter Seven

1. Hallgren, B. (1950). Specific dyslexia ('congenital word blindness'): A clinical and genetic study. *Acta Psychiatrica et Neurologica, 65,* 2–289.

2. For a review, see Pennington, B. F., & Gilger, J. W. (1996). How is dyslexia transmitted? In C. H. Chase, G. D. Rosen, & G. F. Sherman, *Developmental Dyslexia* (pp. 41–62). Baltimore: York Press.

3. Olson, R. K. (1999). Genes, environment, and reading disabilities. In R. J. Sternberg & L. Spear-Swerling (Eds.), *Perspectives on learning disabilities* (pp. 3–21). Boulder, CO: Westview.

4. Finucci, J. M., Gottfredson, L. S., & Childs, B. (1985). A follow-up study of dyslexic boys. *Annals of Dyslexia, 35,* 117–136.

5. Hermann, K. (1959). *Reading disability: A medical study of word blindness and related handicaps.* Springfield, IL: Charles C. Thomas.

6. Hay, D. A., O'Brien, P. J., Johnston, C. J., & Prior, M. R. (1984). The high incidence of reading disability in twin boys and its implication for genetic analyses. *Acta Geneticae Medicae et Gemellologiae, 33,* 223–236.

7. DeFries, J. C., Filipek, P. A., Fulker, D. W., Olson, R. K., Pennington, B. F., Smith, S. D., & Wise, B. W. (1997). Colorado Learning Disabilities Research Center. *Learning Disabilities, 8,* 7–20.

8. DeFries, J. C., & Alarcón, M. (1996). Genetics of specific reading disability. *Mental Retardation and Developmental Disabilities Research Reviews, 2,* 39–47.

9. Jones, S. (1994). *The language of the genes.* London: Flamingo.

10. Hallgren, op. cit.

11. James, W. H. (1992). The sex ratios of dyslexic children and their sibs. *Developmental Medicine and Child Neurology, 34,* 530–533.

12. Ackerman, P. T., & Dyckman, R. A. (1993). Gender and reading disability. *Journal of Learning Disabilities, 26,* 498. DeFries, J. C., & Gillis, J. J. (1993). Genetics of reading disability. In R. Plomin & G. E. McClearn (Eds.), *Nature, nurture, and psychology* (pp. 121–145). Washington, D.C.: American Psychological Association. Finucci, J. M., & Childs, B. (1981). Are there really more dyslexic boys than girls? In A. Asnara, N. Gerschwind, A. M. Galaburda, M. Albert, & N. Gartrell (Eds.), *Sex differences in dyslexia* (pp. 1–10). Towson, MD: Orton Dyslexia Society. Tallal, P., Ross, R., & Curtiss, S. (1989). Unexpected sex-ratios in families of language/learning-impaired children. *Neuropsychologia, 27,* 987–998.

13. Tallal, Ross, & Curtiss, op. cit.

14. Geschwind, N., & Behan, P. O. (1982). Left-handedness: Association with immune disease, migraine, and developmental disorder. *Procedings of the National Academy of Sciences USA, 79,* 5097–5100.

15. Kihl, P. (1990). Testosteronhypotesen: En ny teori om dysleksiens arsag [The testosterone hypothesis: A new theory of the causes of dyslexia]. *Skoloepsykologi, 27,* 331–340.

16. Gilger, J. W., Pennington, B. F., & DeFries, J. C. (1991). A twin study of the etiology of comorbidity: Attention-deficit hyperactivity disorder and dyslexia. *Journal of the American Academy of Child and Adolescent Psychiatry, 31,* 343–348.

17. Symmes, J. S., & Rapoport, J. L. (1972). Unexpected reading failure. *American Journal of Orthopsychiatry, 42,* 82–91.

18. Shaywitz, S. E., Shaywitz, B. A., Fletcher, J. M., & Escobar, M. D. (1990). Prevalence of reading disability in boys and girls. *Journal of the American Medical Association, 264,* 998–1002. Wadsworth, S. J., DeFries, J. C., Stevenson, J., Gilger, J. W., & Pennington, B. F. (1992). Gender ratios among reading-disabled children and their siblings as a function of parental impairment. *Journal of Child Psychology and Psychiatry, 33,* 1229–1239.

19. Shaywitz et al., op. cit.

20. Flynn, J. M., & Rahbar, M. H. (1994). Prevalence of reading failure in boys compared with girls. *Psychology in the Schools, 31*, 66–71.

21. Shaywitz et al., op. cit.

22. McGee, R., & Share, D. L. (1988). Attention deficit disorder-hyperactivity and academic failure: Which comes first and what should be treated? *Journal of the American Academy of Child and Adolescent Psychiatry, 27*, 318–325. Shaywitz et al., op. cit. Vogel, S. A. (1990). Gender differences in intelligence, language, visual-motor abilities, and academic achievement in students with learning disabilities: A review of the literature. *Journal of Learning Disabilities, 23*, 44–52.

23. Geschwind, N. (1981). A reaction to the conference on sex differences and dyslexia. In A. Asnara, N. Geschwind, A. M. Galaburda, M. Albert, & N. Gartrell (Eds.), *Sex differences in dyslexia, Orton Dyslexia Society* (pp. 1–10). Towson, MD: Orton Dyslexia Society.

24. DeFries & Gillis, op. cit.

25. After James, op. cit.

26. Finucci, J. M., Guthrie, J. T., Childs, A. L., Abbey, H., & Childs, B. (1976). The genetics of specific reading disability. *Annals of Human Genetics, 40*, 1–23. Childs, B., & Finucci, J. M. (1983). Genetics, epidemiology and specific reading disability. In M. Rutter (Ed.), *Developmental psychiatry* (pp. 507–519). New York: Guilford.

27. Lewitter, F. I., DeFries, J. C., & Elston, R. C. (1980). Genetic models of reading disabilities. *Behavior Genetics, 10*, 9–30.

28. Pennington, B. F., Gilger, L. W., Pauls, D., Smith, S. A., Smith, S., & DeFries, J. C. (1991). Evidence for a major gene transmission of developmental dyslexia. *Journal of the American Medical Association, 266*, 1527–1534.

29. After James, op. cit.

30. Childs & Finucci, op. cit.

31. Finucci et al., op. cit.

32. Pennington et al., op. cit.

33. Cf. Perfetti, C. A. (1984). *Reading ability.* New York: Oxford University Press. Spear-Swerling, L. C., & Sternberg, R. J. (1996). *Off track: When poor readers become "learning disabled."* Boulder, CO: Westview.

34. Olson, R., Wise, B., Conners, F., Rack, J., & Fulker, D. (1989). Specific deficits in component reading and language skills: Genetic and environmental influences. *Journal of Learning Disabilities, 22*, 339–348.

35. Brooks, A., Fulker, D. W., & DeFries, J. C. (1990). Reading performance and general cognitive ability: A multivariate genetic analysis of twin data. *Personality and Individual Differences, 11*, 141–146.

36. Brooks, Fulker, & DeFries, op. cit. Petrill, S. A., & Thompson, L. A. (1994). The effect of gender upon heritability and common environmental estimates in measure of scholastic achievement. *Personality and Individual Differences, 16*, 631–640.

37. Martin, N. G., & Martin, P. G. (1975). The inheritance of scholastic abilities in a sample of twins. *Annals of Human Genetics, 39*, 219–228.

38. Canter, S. (1973). Some aspects of cognitive function in twins. In G. Claridge, S. Canter, & W. I. Hume (Eds.), *Personality differences and biological variations: A study of twins*. Oxford, England: Pergamon.

39. Olson et al., op. cit.

40. Olson, R. K., Wise, B., Ring, J., & Johnson, M. (in press). Computer-based remedial training in phonemes awareness and phonological decoding: Effects on the post-training development of word recognition. *Scientific Studies of Reading*.

41. Wadsworth et al., op. cit.

42. Hay, D. A., O'Brien, P. J., Johnston, C. J., & Prior, M. R. (1984). The high incidence of reading disability in twin boys and its implication for genetic analyses. *Acta Geneticae Medicae et Gemellologiae, 33*, 223–236.

43. Gilger, J. W., Borecki, I. B., DeFries, J. C., & Pennington, B. F. (1994). Commingling and segregation analysis of reading performance in families of normal reading probands. *Behavior Genetics, 24*, 345–356.

44. Billing, P. R., Beckwith, J., & Alper, J. S. (1992). The genetic analysis of human behavior: A new era? *Social Science and Medicine, 3*, 227–238. Kidd, K. K. (1991). Genes and neuropsychiatric disorders. *Social Biology, 38*, 163–178.

45. Pennington et al., op. cit. Smith, S. D., Kimberling, W. J., Pennington, B. F., & Lubs, H. A. (1983). Specific reading disability: Identification of an inherited form through linkage analysis. *Science, 219*, 1345–1347. Smith, S. D., Pennington, B. F., Kimberling, W. J., & Ing, P. S. (1990). Familial dyslexia: Use of genetic linkage data to define subtypes. *Journal of the American Academy of Child and Adolescent Psychiatry, 29*, 338–348.

46. Fulker, D. W., Cardon, L. R., DeFries, J. C., Kimberling, W. J., Pennington, B. F., & Smith, S. D. (1991). Multiple regression analysis of sib pair data on reading to detect quantitative trait loci. *Reading and Writing: An Interdisciplinary Journal, 3*, 299–313.

47. Cardon, L. R., Smith, S. D., Fulker, D. W., Kimberling, W. J., Pennington, B. F., & DeFries, J. C. (1994). Quantitative trait locus for read-

ing disability on chromosome 6. *Science, 266*, 276–279. Lubs, H. A., Duara, R., Levin, B., Jallad, B., Lubs, M.-L., Rabin, M., Kushch, A., & Gross-Glenn, K. (1991). Dyslexia subtypes: Genetics, behavior, and brain imaging. In D. Duane & D. Gray (Eds.), *The reading brain: The biological basis of dyslexia* (pp. 89–118). Parkton, MD: York Press. Rabin, M., Wen, X. L., Hepburn, M., & Lubs, H. A. (1993). Suggestive linkage of developmental dyslexia to chromosome 1p34–36. *Lancet, 342*, 178–179.

48. Bisgaard, M. L., Eiberg, H., Moller, N., Neihbar, E., & Mohr, J. (1987). Dyslexia and chromosome 15 heteromorphism: Negative lod scores in a Danish sample. *Clinical Genetics, 32*, 118–119.

49. Rabin et al., op. cit. Smith et al., op. cit.

50. Froster, U., Schulte-Körne, G., Hebebrand, J., & Remschmidt, H. (1993). Cosegregation of balanced translocation (1;2) with retarded speech and dyslexia. *Lancet, 342*, 178–179.

51. Cardon et al., op. cit.

52. Grigorenko, E. L., Wood, F. B., Meyer, M. S., Hart, L. A., Speed, W. C., Shuster, A., & Pauls, D. L. (1997). Susceptibility loci for distinct components of developmental dyslexia on chromosomes 6 and 15. *American Journal of Human Genetics, 60*, 27–39.

53. Hansen, O., Nerup, J., & Holbek, B. (1986). A common specific origin of specific dyslexia and insulin-dependent diabetes mellitus? *Heretidas, 105*, 165–167. Hugdahl, K., Synnevag, B., & Saltz, P. (1990). Immune and autoimmune diseases in dyslexic children. *Neuropsychologia, 28*, 673–679. Lahita, R. G. (1988). Systemic lupus erythematosus: Learning disability in the male offspring of female patients and relations to laterality. *Psychoneuroendocrinology, 13*, 385–396.

54. Pennington, B. F., Smith, S. D., Kimberling, W. J., Green, P. A., & Haith, M. M. (1987). Left-handedness and immune disorders in familial dyslexics. *Archives of Neurology, 44*, 634–639.

55. Cardon et al., op. cit.

56. Grigorenko et al., op. cit.

57. Nelkin, D., & Lindee, M. S. (Contributor). (1996). *The DNA mystique: The gene as a cultural icon.* New York: W. H. Freeman.

Chapter Eight

1. This anecdote has been heard at linguists' parties (see Bialystock, E., & Hakuta, K. [1994]. *In other words.* New York: Basic Books) and psychologists' gatherings (M. Zuckerman, personal communication, Stockholm, June 1998).

2. Coleman, B. C. (Associated Press Medical Writer). (1998, February 10). Available: http://www.nando.net. Copyright © 1998 Nando.net. Copyright © 1998 The Associated Press.

3. Wise, B., & Olson, R. (1995). Computer-based phonological awareness and reading instruction. *Annals of Dyslexia, 45,* 99–122.

4. Orton Dyslexia Society. (1997). *Informed instruction for reading success: Foundations for teacher preparation.* Towson, MD.

5. Bell, J. A. (Ed.). (1995). *Promising practices and programs for improving student achievement.* Sacramento: California Department of Education.

6. Orton Dyslexia Society, op. cit.

7. Wise & Olson, op. cit.

8. Olson, R. K., Wise, B., Ring, J., & Johnson, M. (1997). Computer-based remedial training in phonemes awareness and phonological decoding: Effects on the post-training development of word recognition. *Scientific Studies of Reading 3,* 235–253..

9. Felton, R. H. (1998). The development of reading skills in poor readers: Educational implications. In C. Hulme & R. M. Joshi (Eds.), *Reading and spelling: Development and disorders* (pp. 219–233). Mahwah, NJ: Erlbaum.

10. Sternberg, R. J. (1997). *Successful intelligence.* New York: Plume.

11. Sternberg, R. J., Torff, B., & Grigorenko, E. L. (1998). Teaching for successful intelligence raises school achievement. *Phi Delta Kappan, 79,* 667–669. Sternberg, R. J., Torff, B., & Grigorenko, E. L. (1998). Teaching triarchically improves school achievement. *Journal of Educational Psychology, 90,* 374–384.

12. National Institute of Child Health and Human Development. (1997). *A synthesis of research on reading from the National Institute of Child Health and Human Development.* Bethesda, MD.

13. Adams, M. J. (1990). *Beginning to read: Thinking and learning about print.* Cambridge, MA: MIT Press. Gough, P., Ehri, L., & Treiman, R. (Eds.). (1992). *Reading acquisition.* Hillsdale, NJ: Erlbaum.

14. Brady, S., & Shankweiler, D. (Eds.). (1991). *Psychological processes in literacy: A tribute to Isabelle Y. Liberman.* Hillsdale, NJ: Erlbaum.

15. Blachman, B. (Ed.). (1997). *Foundations of reading acquisition and dyslexia: Implications for early intervention.* Hillsdale, NJ: Erlbaum.

16. Stanovich, K. E. (1994). Does dyslexia exist? *Journal of Child Psychology and Psychiatry, 35,* 579–595.

17. Samuels, S. J. (1999). Developing reading fluency in learning-disabled students. In R. J. Sternberg & L. Spear-Swerling (Eds.), *Perspectives*

on learning disabilities (pp.176–189). Boulder, CO: Westview. Sternberg, R. J., & Wagner, R. (1982). Automatization failure in learning disabilities. *Topics in Learning and Learning Disabilities, 2,* 1–11.

18. Adapted from *A synthesis of research on reading from the National Institute of Child Health and Human Development.* Center for the Future of Teaching and Learning. Available Internet: http://www.ksagroup.com/thecenter

19. Foorman, B. R., Francis, D. J., Novy, D. M., & Liberman, D. (1991). How letter-sound instruction mediates progress in first-grade reading and spelling. *Journal of Educational Psychology, 83,* 456–469. Foorman, B. R., Francis, D. J., Shaywitz, S. E., Shaywitz, B. A., & Fletcher, J. M. (1997). The case for early reading intervention. In B. A. Blachman (Ed.), *Foundations of reading acquisition and dyslexia* (pp. 243–264). Mahwah, NJ: Erlbaum. Torgesen, J. K., Wagner, R. K., Rashotte, C. A., Alexander, A., & Conway, T. (1997). Preventive and remedial interventions for children with severe reading disabilities. *Learning Disabilities: An Interdisciplinary Journal, 8,* 51–62.

20. Foorman, B. R., Francis, D. J., Novy, D. M., & Liberman, D. (1991). How letter-sound instruction mediates progress in first-grade reading and spelling. *Journal of Educational Psychology, 83,* 456–469.

21. Felton, op. cit. Fletcher, J. M., Shaywitz, S. E., Shankweiler, D. P., Katz, L., Liberman, I. Y., Fowler, A., Francis, D. J., Stuebing, K. K., & Shaywitz, B. A. (1994). Cognitive profiles of reading disability: Comparisons of discrepancy and low achievement definitions. *Journal of Educational Psychology, 85,* 1–18. Stanovich, K. E., & Siegel, L. S. (1994). The phenotypic performance profile of reading-disabled children: A regression-based test of the phonological-core variable-difference model. *Journal of Educational Psychology, 86,* 24–53.

22. Foorman, B. R., Francis, D. J., Shaywitz, S. E., Shaywitz, B. A., & Fletcher, J. M. (1997). The case for early reading intervention. In B. A. Blachman (Ed.), *Foundations of reading acquisition and dyslexia* (pp. 243–264). Mahwah, NJ: Erlbaum.

23. Case provided by Rebecca Felton.

24. Case provided by Rebecca Felton.

25. Blachman, B. (1997). *Foundations of reading acquisition and dyslexia: Implications for early intervention.* Mahwah, NJ: Erlbaum.

26. Nicholson, T. (1997). Closing the gap on reading failure: Social background, phonemic awareness, and learning to read. In B. A. Blachman (Ed.), *Foundations of reading acquisition and dyslexia* (pp. 381–408). Mahwah, NJ: Erlbaum.

27. Ibid.

28. Byrne, B., Fielding-Barnsley, R., Ashley, L., & Larsen, K. (1997). Assessing the child's and the environment's contribution to reading acquisition: What we know and what we don't know. In B. A. Blachman (Ed.), *Foundations of reading acquisition and dyslexia* (pp. 265–286). Mahwah, NJ: Erlbaum.

29. Castles, A., & Coltheart, M. (1993). Varieties of developmental dyslexia. *Cognition, 47,* 149–180.

30. Olson, R. K., Wise, B., Johnson, M. C., & Ring, J. (1997). The etiology and remediation of phonologically based word recognition and spelling disabilities: Are phonological deficits the "hole" story? In B. A. Blachman (Ed.), *Foundations of reading acquisition and dyslexia* (pp. 305–326). Mahwah, NJ: Erlbaum.

31. Ibid. Vellutino, F. R., Scanlon, D. M., & Sipay, E. R. (1997). Toward distinguishing between cognitive and experiential deficits as primary sources of difficulty in learning to read: The importance of early intervention in diagnosing specific reading disability. In B. A. Blachman (Ed.), *Foundations of reading acquisition and dyslexia* (pp. 347–380). Mahwah, NJ: Erlbaum. Vellutino, F. R., Scanlon, D. M., Sipay, E. R., Small, S. G., Pratt, A., Chen, R., & Denckla, M. B. (1996). Cognitive profiles of difficult to remediate and readily remediated poor readers: Early intervention as a vehicle for distinguishing between cognitive and experiential deficits as basic causes of specific reading disability. *Journal of Educational Psychology, 88,* 601–638.

32. Bell, op. cit.

33. Clay, M. M. (1985). *The early detection of reading difficulties* (3rd ed.). Auckland, New Zealand: Heinemann. Iverson, S., & Tunmer, W. (1993). Phonological processing skills and the reading recovery program. *Journal of Educational Psychology, 85,* 112–126. Orton Dyslexia Society. (1997). *Informed instruction for reading success: Foundations for teacher preparation.* Towson, MD. Pinnell, G. S. (1989). Reading recovery: Helping at risk children learn to read. *Elementary School Journal, 90,* 161–184. Vellutino, F. R., Scanlon, D. M., & Sipay, E. R. (1997). Toward distinguishing between cognitive and experiential deficits as primary sources of difficulty in learning to read: The importance of early intervention in diagnosing specific reading disability. In B. A. Blachman (Ed.), *Foundations of reading acquisition and dyslexia* (pp. 347–380). Mahwah, NJ: Erlbaum. Wasik, B. A., & Slavin, R. R. (1993). Preventing early reading failure with one-to-one tutoring: A review of five programs. *Reading Research Quarterly, 28,* 179–200.

Chapter Nine

1. United States District Court District of Massachusetts Civil Action No. 96-11426-PBS, Elizabeth Guckenberger, et al., Plaintiffs, v. Boston University, et al., Defendants (August 15, 1997). Findings of Fact, Conclusions of Law and Order of Judgment. Saris, U. S. D. J.

2. Ibid.

3. Florence County School District Four v. Shannon Carter, decision (November 9, 1993).

4. Special Education Due Process Appeals Review Panel Commonwealth of Pennsylvania in re the Educational Assignment of Matthew C., a student in the Special Education School District of Philadelphia, Opinion Number 748, before Appeals Panel Officers Salvia, Hartwig, and Gonick. Opinion by Hartwig.

5. Sternberg, R. J., & Lubart, T. I. (1995). *Defying the crowd: Cultivating creativity in a culture of conformity*. New York: Free Press.

Chapter Ten

1. Labaree, D. F. (1997). *How to succeed in school without really learning: The credentials race in American education*. New Haven: Yale University Press.

2. Gardner, H. (1983). *Frames of mind: The theory of multiple intelligences*. New York: Basic Books.

3. Herrnstein, R., & Murray, C. (1994). *The bell curve*. New York: Free Press.

4. Bronfenbrenner, U., McClelland, P., Wethington, E., Moen, P., & Ceci, S. J. (1996). *The state of Americans*. New York: Free Press.

5. Sternberg, R. J., Torff, B., & Grigorenko, E. L. (1998). Teaching triarchically improves school achievement. *Journal of Educational Psychology, 90*, 374–384.

Index

Abilities
  differentiation of, 3–6, 39–42
  environmental effects on,
    33–37
  interaction of nature and
    environment, 37–39
  natural origins of, 29–33
  See also Disabilities; Reading
Accomodations for learning
    disabilities
  at Boston University, 226–230,
    241–242
  as an entitlement, 88–89
  and the legal system,
    240–242
  limitations of, 6, 75–77, 87–88,
    241–242
  possibilities for, 89–90
  recommendations, 256–258
  teaching techniques, 77–83
  timing of tests, 83–87
  See also Educational
    intervention; Teaching
    reading
ACLD. *See* Association of
  Children with Learning
  Disabilities

ACT. *See* American College Test
ADHD. *See* Attention-deficit
  hyperactivity disorder
American College Test (ACT), 59,
  69, 83
American Psychiatric
  Association, 3
Association of Children with
  Learning Disabilities
  (ACLD), 22
Attention-deficit hyperactivity
  disorder (ADHD), x-xii, 12,
  225, 233–234
Autoimmune disorders, and
  reading disabilities, 125,
  185–186
Automatic word recognition,
  105–106

Biological factors. *See* Brain, the;
  Genetics; Heritability
Blachman, Benita, 217
Boston University, 225–235
Bouchard, Tom, 188
Brain, the
  activity of while reading,
    137–144

animals and research on,
151–152
biological knowledge of,
119–120
development of, 123–126
development of and reading
disabilities, 126–127, 153
difficulties in interpeting
research regarding, 144–145,
151
of individuals with reading
disorders, 145–148
mapping of, 121–123
models of and reading
disabilities, 148–151
structure of and reading
disabilities, 127–131
techniques for studying
functions of, 132–137
Broca, Paul, 26–27, 121–122
Butler, Samuel, 151

California, changes in teaching
reading, 219
California Achievement Test
(CAT), 83
Carter, Shannon, 235–238
CAT. See California Achievement
Test
Christensen, Carol, 28
Chromosomes, ix, 168–169
Closed systems, 14–19
Cognition and reading,
97–99
automatic word recognition,
105–106
controlled word recognition,
102–105
phonetic-cue word
recognition, 100–102

proficient adult reading,
117–118
strategic reading, 106–108
visual-cue word recognition,
99–100
Cognitive Assessment System,
40
Coles, Gerald, 28
Common sense. See Intelligence,
practical
Connecticut, variation in
identifying learning
disabilities, 63–64, 72
Controlled word recognition,
102–105
Council of State Governments,
237
Courts. See Litigation

Darwin, Charles, 151
Dax, Marc, 25–27
DeFries, J. C., 176
Deneberg, Victor, 125
Disabilities
diagnosis of. See Identification
of learning disabilities
foreign language, 78–81
learning. See Learning
disabilities
reading. See Dyslexia; Reading
disabilities
See also Abilities
Dyslexia
and autoimmune disorders,
125, 185–186
and the brain. See Brain, the
definition of, 195–196
and genetics. See Genetics
remediation of. See
Accomodations for learning

disabilities; Educational intervention
See also Reading disabilities

Educational intervention, 257–258
categories of, 199–200
examples of, 215–217
modifiable v. nonmodifiable factors, 196–198
principles, 8, 201–204
remediation of dyslexia, 196
reservations regarding, 217–219
significance of early exposure to reading, 198–199
timing of, 213–215
See also Accomodations for learning disabilities; Teaching reading
Education for All Handicapped Children Act (P.L. 101–476), 23–24
EEG. See Electroencephalograms
ELATE. See Expert Learning for All through Teacher Education
Electroencephalograms (EEG), 132–133
Environment
and early reading, 198–199
effects on intelligence, 33–37
extrinsic explanations of learning disabilities, 28
families, tendency for reading disabilities to run in, 161–162
and intelligence quotient, 18
nature, interaction with in intellectual development, 37–39

and sex-influenced transmission of reading disabilities, 173–174
v. genetic transmission of reading disabilities, 7–8, 178–181, 196–198
Everyday intelligence. See Intelligence, practical
Expert Learning for All through Teacher Education (ELATE), 109
early data on the program, 116–117
instructional materials, 109–116

Farrell, Steve, 197
Felton, Rebecca, 203
Fernald, Grace, 27
Finucci, J. M., 175
Flynn effect, 35–36
FMRI. See Functional magnetic resonance imaging
Foreign-language disability, 78–81
Fulker, David, 184
Functional magnetic resonance imaging (FMRI), 135–136, 147–148

Galaburda, Albert, 129, 149
Gall, Franz Josef, 26–27
Gardner, Howard, 41, 44–47, 250
Garret, Amy, 144, 147
Gating mechanism, tests as, 15–16, 70–71
Genetics
basic concepts of, 164–169
children, probability of inheriting reading disabilities, 160–164

families, reading disabilities in, 158–160
fictional family, reading disabilities in, 155–158
genetic transmission of reading abilities, 176–178, 181–182
genetic transmission of reading disabilities, 169–170, 175–176
and heritability, 32–33
reading disabilities, genetic transmission v. environment, 7–8, 178–181, 196–198
search for the reading gene, 182–188
sex-influenced transmission of reading disabilities, 170–174
See also Heritability; Nature
Genotype, defined, 30
Graduation Record Examination (GRE), 15
GRE. See Graduate Record Examination
Grigorenko, Elena, xii
Guckenberger, Elizabeth, 231–233, 235

Hallgren, Bertil, 158, 169–170
Harvard University, admissions criteria, 16–17
Hay, David, 181
Heath, Shirley, 50
Heritability, 30, 32–33
and environmental effects on intelligence, 33–36
of intelligence quotient, 18
See also Genetics; Nature
Hermann, Knud, 163

Herodotus, 120–121
Herrnstein, Richard, 17, 70
Hinshelwood, James, 27
Hippocrates, 221

Identification of learning disabilities
confounding of verbal and reading skills, 52–56
criteria for, 25
difference scores, unreliability of, 59–60
difference scores, variation in meaning of, 56–59
hypothetical example, 12–14
inadequacy of nonverbal intelligence quotient tests, 56
intelligence and intelligence quotient, 44–52
problems with conventional approaches, 43–44, 64
recommendations, 257
statistical regression of test scores, 60–63
variability of procedures, 63–64
variation over time, 35–36
Individuals with Disabilities Education Act of 1990 (P.L. 101–476), 23
Intelligence
Gardner's theory of multiple, 44–47
and intelligence quotient tests, 44–52
kinds of, 44–45
practical, 50–52, 246–248
and speed, 85–87
triarchic theory of, 203–204

Intelligence quotient (IQ),
31–32
and environment, 18
and environmental factors in
intelligence, 34–36
heritability of, 18
and intelligence, 44–52
problems with in identifying
learning disabilities. *See*
Identification of learning
disabilities
and socioeconomic success,
15–16
tests of, 5, 12, 39–40, 251
Iowa Tests of Basic Skills (ITBS),
83
IQ. *See* Intelligence Quotient
ITBS. *See* Iowa Tests of Basic Skills

James, William, 193
Johnson, George, 122
Justice, U.S. Department of, 237

Kenya, practical intelligence in,
48–49
Kirk, Samuel, 22
Klafter, Craig, 226–227

Labeling
differential effects of, 11–12
and the learning disability
lottery, ix, 3–5, 7, 10, 93,
243, 259
as political and ideological, 94.
See also Politics of learning
disabilities
reasons for, 8–10, 12, 71–73,
238
as self-fulfilling prophecy, 7.
See also Matthew effects

Law School Admission Test
(LSAT), 15, 231
Learning disabilities
accomodations for. *See*
Accomodations for learning
disabilities
as a labelling process. *See*
Labelling
definition of, 3, 5, 19–21
distinguished from attention-
deficit disorders, xi-xii
explanations for, extrinsic v.
intrinsic, 25–28
history of the concept, 21–25
identification of. *See*
Identification of learning
disabilities
lottery of, ix, 3–5, 7, 10, 93,
243, 259
number of children afflicted
with, 23
politics of. *See* Politics of
learning disabilities
recommendations regarding,
256–259
science of. *See* Science of
learning disabilities
See also Reading disabilities
Learning Disability Assocation of
America, 237, 262n13
Legal system. *See* Litigation
Litigation
Boston University case, court
ruling in the, 232–235
Boston University case, facts of
the, 225–232
case of Matthew C., 238–240
Florence County School
District v. Shannon Carter,
235–238

limitations in cases involving
  learning disabilities,
  234–235, 240–241
prevalence in U.S., 223–225,
  235
London, Jack, 211
Lottery of learning disabilities,
  ix, 3–5, 7, 10, 93, 243,
  259
LSAT. *See* Law School Admission
  Test
Lubs, Herbert, 145–146

Magnetic resonance imaging
  (MRI), 122, 128. *See also*
  Functional Magnetic
  Resonance Imaging
Marx, Karl, 195
MAT. *See* Metropolitan
  Achievement Tests
Matthew effects, 68–73. *See also*
  Socioeconomic status (SES)
MCAT. *See* Medical College
  Admission Test
McFadden, Dennis, 125
Medical College Admission Test
  (MCAT), 15
Mendel, Gregor, 165, 169
Mental age, 31
Mental retardation
  and genetics, 177–178
  heritability and treatability of,
  34
Metacognitive strategies, 106
Metropolitan Achievement Tests
  (MAT), 83
Morgan, W. P., 27
MRI. *See* Magnetic resonance
  imaging

Murray, Charles, 17, 70
National Alliance for the
  Mentally Ill, 237
National Association of
  Counties, 237
National Association of
  Protection and Advocacy
  Systems, 237
National Association of State
  Boards of Education, 237
National Center for Learning
  Disabilities Incorporated,
  262n13
National Governors' Association,
  237
National Head Injury
  Foundation, Inc., 237
National Institute of Child
  Health and Human
  Development (NICHD),
  194–195, 200, 204
National League of Cities, 237
National School Boards
  Association, 237
Nature
  and abilities, 29–33
  and differentiated abilities,
  39–42
  environment, interaction with
  in intellectual development,
  37–39
  See also Genetics; Heritability
Nelkin, Dorothy, 188
Neuroscience, 121–123
NICHD. *See* National Institute of
  Child Health and Human
  Development
North Carolina, language
  development in, 49–51

O'Connor, Sandra Day, 238
Olson, Richard, 202
Orton, Samuel, 27
Orton Dyslexia Society, 195, 200

Parents
    and the history of learning
        disabilities, 21–23
    reasons for labelling children,
        11–12, 19, 71–73
    significance of reading to/with
        children, 198–199
Pasanen, Edward, 125
Pauls, David, xii, 176
Pedigrees, and genetic research,
    165–166, 184
Pennington, Bruce, 176
PET. See Positron-emission
    tomography
Phenotype, defined, 30
Phenylketonuria, 34
Philadelphia school district, case
    of Matthew C., 238–240
Phonemic awareness, 100–101,
    204–207, 217
Phonetic-cue word recognition,
    100–102
Phonology-based intervention.
    See Educational intervention
Phrenology, 26–27
Politics of learning disabilities
    accomodations as an
        entitlement, 88–89
    labelling as ideological, 94
    legislation and social advocacy
        groups, 23–25
    politicization of the field, x–xi
    See also Matthew effects;
        Socioeconomic status

Positron-emission tomography
    (PET), 122, 133–134
Practical intelligence. See
    Intelligence, practical
Pugh, Kenneth, 143

Rakic, Pasko, 153
Raven Progressive Matrices, 35
Reading
    biological bases of. See Brain,
        the
    and cognition. See Cognition
        and reading
    confounding with verbal skills,
        52–56
    genetic bases of. See Genetics
    and success, 245–246
    teaching of. See Teaching
        reading
    tests of ability for, 64–68
Reading disabilities, 220–221
    genetic bases of. See Genetics
    identification of. See
        Identification of learning
        disabilities
    Matthew effects and
        socioeconomic status,
        68–73
    varieties of, 12–14
    See also Dyslexia; Learning
        disabilities
Ritalin, 187

Saris, Patti, 233
SAT. See Scholastic Assessment
    Test
Scholastic Assessment Test (SAT),
    15, 59, 69, 83, 248
Schoofs, Mark, 188

Schools
  abilities emphasized, 251
  crisis over teaching of reading,
    195
  dumbing down of textbooks,
    36–37
  grades and credentialing,
    247–248
  and legislative mandates,
    23–25
  limited resources of, 8–9, 240
  and Matthew effects, 68–70
  reasons for labelling, 9, 12,
    72–73
  special services. See
    Accomodation for learning
    disabilities
  See also Litigation; Teachers;
    Teaching reading
Science of learning disabilities
  biological factors. See Brain,
    the
  cognition. See Cognition and
    reading
  genetics. See Genetics
  reasons for popular ignorance
    of, 94–96
SES. See Socioeconomic status
Shaw, George Bernard, 253
Shaywitz, Bennett, 148
Shaywitz, Sally, 148
Skrtic, Thomas, 28
Social Darwinism, 71
Socioeconomic status (SES)
  and closed systems, 14–19
  differential effects of labelling,
    11–12
  and Matthew effects, 68–73

and preliteracy preparation,
    217–218
South Carolina, Florence County
    School District case, 235–238
Spear-Swerling, Louise, xi–xii
Special services. See
    Accomodations for learning
    disabilities
Stanford-Binet Intelligence Scale,
    40
Stanovich, Keith, 177
Statistical regression and test
    scores, 60–63
Sternberg, Robert, x–xii, 41, 46,
    84, 109, 203
Strategic reading, 106–108
Strauss, Alfred, 27
Strephosymbolia, 27
Success
  and closed social systems,
    14–19
  and intelligence quotient,
    15–16
  on tests vs. in life, 246–250
  and reading, 245–246
Supreme Court, U.S., Florence
    County School District v.
    Shannon Carter, 237–238
Systems, closed, 14–19

Teachers
  genetic studies, wariness of,
    187
  training, 9–10, 24, 200–201
Teaching reading, 219–221
  changes in California, 219
  effectiveness of instruction,
    200

emphasis on the most frequent sound-spelling relationships, 208–210
need for change in, 195
phonemic awareness, 204–207
recommendations for, 256–259
recommendations regarding curriculum, 259
reinforcing sound-spelling relationships using decodable text, 210–212
sounding out words, 210
sound-spelling correspondence, 207–208
stories, use of interesting and appropriate, 212–213
strategic reading and ELATE. *See* Expert Learning for All through Teacher Education
techniques, success of alternative, 253–256
techniques and learning disabilities, 77–83
triarchal approach, 203–204
whole-language approach, 27, 81–82, 99–100, 219
Wilson Reading System, 239
See also Educational intervention
Tests
American College Test (ACT), 59, 69, 83
California Achievement Test (CAT), 83
Cognitive Assessment System, 40
Iowa Tests of Basic Skills (ITBS), 83

Law School Admission Test (LSAT), 15, 231
limits of, 64–68, 246–250. *See also* Identification of learning disabilities
Medical College Admission Test (MCAT), 15
Metropolitan Achievement Tests (MAT), 83
Raven Progressive Matrices, 35
of reading ability, 64–68
recommendations regarding, 259
Scholastic Assessment Test (SAT), 15, 59, 69, 83, 248
stagnation of approach to, 250–253
standardized as gating mechanism, 15–16, 70–71
timing of, 83–87
and verbal skills, 52–56
Textbooks, dumbing down of, 36–36
Time, and intelligence, 83–87
Torgesen, Joseph, 94

U.S. Conference of Mayors, 237

Verbal skill, confounding with reading skill, 52–56
Visual-cue word recognition, 99–100

Wechsler Intelligence Scale for Children (WISC), 12, 39–40, 251
Wernicke, Carl, 26–27
Westling, Jon, 226–230

Whole-language teaching
practices, 27, 81–82, 99–100,
219
Wilson Reading System, 239
WISC. *See* Wechsler Intelligence
Scale for Children
Wise, Barbara, 202
Wood, Frank, xii, 144, 148–150

Word recognition
automatic, 105–106
controlled, 102–105
phonetic-cue, 100–102
visual-cue, 99–100

Yale University, admissions
criteria, 16